David Paterson

Zion's waymarks

Knowledge vs. mystery

David Paterson

Zion's waymarks
Knowledge vs. mystery

ISBN/EAN: 9783337221812

Printed in Europe, USA, Canada, Australia, Japan

Cover: Foto ©Andreas Hilbeck / pixelio.de

More available books at **www.hansebooks.com**

OR,

KNOWLEDGE vs. MYSTERY

BEING A DISCUSSION OF THE FOLLOWING QUESTIONS:

Is God a Triune Being? What Think ye of Christ? Is Man the Possessor of Inherent Immortality? Do Christians go to Heaven at Death? Are the Wicked Consigned to a Hell of Endless Torment? Shall Christ Sit on David's Throne, or does his Kingdom exist somewhere in the Skies? Are All Predestinated? Etc.

BY BISHOP D. D. PATERSON.

"BUY THE TRUTH AND SELL IT NOT; ALSO WISDOM, AND INSTRUCTION, AND UNDERSTANDING."—Prov. viii. 23.

GRAND RAPIDS, MICHIGAN:
W. W. HART, ARCADE BOOK AND JOB PRINTING HOUSE.
1883.

DEDICATION.

———

TO THOSE WHO ARE TEMPEST-TOST ON THE BILLOWS OF THE

OCEAN OF MYSTERY;

TO ALL SEEKERS AFTER AND LOVERS OF THE TRUTH;

AND TO FELLOW-PILGRIMS ON THE WAY THAT LEADS TO THE

"CITY WHICH HATH FOUNDATIONS, WHOSE BUILDER

AND MAKER IS GOD,"

THIS VOLUME IS RESPECTFULLY DEDICATED.

PREFACE.

Looking unto God to add his blessing, and with an eye single to his glory, we send forth this volume.

Infidelity like a flood is sweeping over the earth ; and the Bible is charged with defects and errors which properly belong to human traditions or to a corrupt theology.

The time has come when men " will not endure sound doctrine," when they ".turn away their ears from the truth," and are "turned unto fables."

Therefore we deem the following doctrinal dissertations opportune. It was decided at our Annual Conference in 1882 by the Publishing Committee, to have this work published at the earliest possible convenience.

And the many urgent requests we have had since then from friends and brethren on both sides of the Atlantic, really call for its publication. Consequently the undertaking is not premature.

We regard it also as a bounden duty we owe to
God, to let the light He has given us, shine
among our fellow-beings.

Whatever contention there may be in the work,
be it remembered it is a contention of principles
and not of beings. For in the spirit of meekness
and reverence, we merely give a reason of the
hope that is in us.

We thrust at no sect or party. The question
we endeavor by God's grace to solve is, "What is
truth?"

For truth alone satisfies. Truth alone edifies.
Truth alone sanctifies. Truth alone endures forever. Truth emanates from God, and like its
source, it is eternal.

There is, as it were, in these latter days, a vast
sieve in motion. The ideas of many minds are
being cast thereon, and the breezes of heaven are
separating the chaff from the wheat.

Or again : In the crucible of varied intellects
truth is being refined from the dross which has
surrounded it for centuries. As a result it falls,
yea, is being lavishly strewn, upon the common
pathway of mortals, in resplendent gems, reflect-
ing the brilliancy of heaven's own sunbeams.

The shades of evening are closing in upon a
mortal race. The day of salvation is ending.

The prophet Zechariah said, "At evening time
it shall be light." His words are virtually fulfilled. Light has arisen in the darkness. In the
present century alone the light that has flooded
the world is simply marvelous. However, it is

not all gold that glitters. Neither is it all truth that is put forth as such to-day. But it is ours to examine. The apostle enjoined, "Examine yourselves, whether ye be in the faith." The Bereans searched the scriptures to see whether the things they had heard were so, and they were approved for so doing. The Bible, Nature and Reason are given us as testing weights. The "wisdom" from above is the pivot upon which the balances hang. If we lack wisdom and ask of God in faith, the unfailing promise is, "it shall be given." Hence, there is no excuse for our walking in spiritual darkness.

Such thoughts as these led us to God, and to his Word. The result, in part, of our prayerful investigations, you will find in the following pages.

It is generally conceded that "light of truth" is essential to human happiness. But a "walking" in the light is essential to eternal life.

The beauty or glory of heaven's light is "HoLINESS UNTO THE LORD."

Here all true Christians can agree. Here is a standard around which all soldiers of the cross must rally, for without holiness none shall see the Lord.

But as the beauty of truth is holiness, so also, the beauty of holiness is truth.

Therefore, "He that speaketh truth sheweth forth righteousness." And the Lord "shall judge the world with righteousness, and the people with his *truth*." Hence, truth is the weapon of

heaven wielded on the earth for our righteousness, sanctification, and judgment. Like its concomitant, the " Spirit of truth," it convinces " the
world of sin, and of righteousness, and of judgment."

Christ prayed to the eternal Father, " Sanctify
them through thy truth ; *Thy Word is Truth,*"
and we with heart and voice respond, Amen !

D. D. P.

GRAND RAPIDS, MICHIGAN.

ZION'S WAYMARKS,

KNOWLEDGE VS. MYSTERY.

———•♦•———

CHAPTER I.

———

GOD, THE ETERNAL FATHER.

"I found an altar with this inscription, To THE UNKNOWN GOD. Whom therefore ye ignorantly worship, Him declare I unto you."—Acts xvii. 23.

The most mysterious of all the traditions, presented by modern theologians as truth, is their doctrine of the Godhead, which teaches that there are three Gods in one. The Bible tells us that there is but one God. The former is to human understanding a mystery. The latter can be comprehended by every rational mind. Jesus says, "This is life eternal that they might know·

Thee, the only true God, and Jesus Christ, whom Thou hast sent." (John xvii. 3.) Theology says, the doctrine of the Godhead cannot be comprehended by the finite mind, neither can the doctrine of Christ be understood only as an inexplicable mystery. According to the scriptures it is ours to know at least " in part," and to the true disciples of Jesus there is no such thing as inexplicable mystery, for to them it is given to understand the mysteries of God's kingdom.

To understand the doctrine of the great God is the foundation of all truth, and to know the doctrine of Jesus Christ is the basis of all true faith. Therefore it becomes us in order to our own eternal gain, to search the scriptures with an unbiased mind for an understanding of these great fundamental truths. Nor shall the honest seeker search in vain, for such will comply with the required conditions laid down in God's word in order to the reception of knowledge. Man is plainly told if he but do God's will he shall know of the doctrine. (John vii. 17.) By rendering obedience to God he has a promise given. him, (Acts ii. 38, 39) of the Spirit which shall " teach him all things." (John xiv. 26.) And thus with eyes anointed with the eye-salve from above, he shall seek, and he shall find.

But to return to the doctrine of the Godhead, and in order to illustrate the same, let us contrast " mystery " with " knowledge," or in other words, the traditions of men with the unadulterated Word of truth.

MYSTERY.	KNOWLEDGE.
"There are three persons in the Godhead, and these three are one, the same in substance, equal in power and glory."—*Church Catechism.*	"Hear, O Israel : The Lord our God is ONE LORD."–Deut. vi. 4. The same is repeated by Jesus himself, in Mark xii. 29–32 ; and reiterated by his apostles. Paul says, "To us there is but ONE GOD the Father, of whom are all things, and we by Him." (I. Cor. viii. 6, also v. 4.)
From the above men teach that there is God the Father, God the Son, and God the Holy Ghost.	The Bible teaches that there is "one God and Father of all, who is above all, and through all, and in you all." (Eph. iv. 6.) Again, "There is one God and one Mediator between God and men, the man Christ Jesus." (I. Tim. ii. 5.)
The foregoing also declares that these three Gods are *equal* in power and glory.	Jesus says, "My Father is greater than I." (John xiv. 28.) And in the form of prayer prescribed to his disciples, He ascribes to the Father the kingdom, the power and the glory.

While it is true that after Christ arose from the dead, the Father clothed Him with "all power," yet from the scriptures it is evident that that power was only given Him for the accomplishment of a certain purpose, or work. In speaking of the consummation of that work, Paul tells us in plain language, "Then cometh the end, when He (i. e. Christ) shall have delivered up the kingdom to God, even the Father ; when He shall have put down all rule, and all authority and

power." (I. Cor. xv. 24.)   And we are further
told, "Then shall the Son also himself be subject
unto Him (i. e. God) that put all things under
Him that God may be all in all." (28.)   And thus
we see that God is supreme, "The blessed and
only Potentate, the King of kings, and Lord of
lords."   For if Christ be equal to the Father, then
also is the lesser equal to the greater, and then
likewise is He that hath honor, power and glory
conferred on Him, equal to Him that hath conferred it, which is both absurd and contrary to
the scriptures.

As to the Holy Spirit being a separate person
in the Godhead the scriptures nowhere vouch for
such.   The Holy Spirit is but the immortal essence, as it were, of the Deity, the "living water," the quickening power of God.   (John vii.
37–39, and Rom. viii. 11.)   Such also is the me-
dium through which the mind of God is revealed
to man, (John xvi. 13; II. Peter i. 21) and
through which the children of God receive comfort (John xiv. 16–17) and enlightenment, etc.
But to return : There is, according to the scriptures, but the one God the Father, who is high
over all.   Jesus addresses Him as "Father, Lord
of heaven and earth."   Daniel calls Him "the
Most High," beside whom "all the inhabitants of
the earth are reputed as nothing : and He doeth
according to his will in the army of heaven and
among the inhabitants of the earth : and none
can stay his hand, or say unto Him, what doest
Thou ?" (iv. 34–35.)   And since the fear of God

is the beginning of wisdom, it follows that we must seek to understand the doctrine of the great Jehovah in order to approach Him with reverence and godly fear due unto his name. Then with Israel of old we shall be led to exclaim, "Who is like unto thee, O Lord, among the mighty ones, who is like unto thee, glorious in holiness, fearful in praises, doing wonders?" Or with the Psalmist, "Great is the Lord, and greatly to be praised in the city of our God, in the mountain of his holiness. For the Lord most high is terrible, He is a great king over all the earth." Or with Isaiah, "It is He that sitteth upon the circle of the earth, and the inhabitants thereof are as grasshoppers ; that stretcheth out the heavens as a curtain, and spreadeth them out as a tent to dwell in ; that bringeth princes to nothing ; He maketh the judges of the earth as vanity.   *   *   *   *   Hast thou not known ? hast thou not heard, that the everlasting God, the Lord, the Creator of the ends of the earth, fainteth not, neither is weary ? there is no searching of his understanding. He giveth power to the faint, and to them that have no might He increaseth strength." This great being, the " God of truth," the " King of Eternity," who dwellest in the light inaccessible, and who sittest on his throne in the excellent glory, is the source of all light and life, love and blessing, and truth and holiness. He holdeth the universe in his mighty grasp, and "the heavens declare his glory ; and the firmament showeth his handiwork." The

orbit of each heavenly body displays the eternity
of his being, having neither beginning nor end.
Like as the space above is boundless, so is God's
mercy towards them that fear Him. The beautiful order of the spangled heavens but bespeaks
the infinite wisdom of Him who commanded and
it was done. The brilliant rays of the sun but
tell us somewhat of the glory of the great I AM.
The mellow rays of reflected light from the earth's
satellite, is but a semblance of God's holy word,
which reflects to us the mind and will of the glorious Father, and the precious light of heaven.
In brief and in fact, God is to be seen in all his
works, both physical and spiritual. We behold
his majesty everywhere supreme. Especially
when we view his glorious plan of salvation for
poor fallen men, can we exclaim with the apostle,
" O the depth of the riches, both of the wisdom
and knowledge of God; how unsearchable are his
judgments, and his ways past finding out."

Yet this great God becomes, through Christ,
our Father. Jesus taught his disciples thus to
approach the eternal throne, " Our Father who
art in heaven, hallowed be thy name." What
simplicity, what confidence, and yet what sublime
reverence there is in these words ! *Simplicity*,
because we approach the great God as a child
does its parent. *Confidence*, because we not only
believe He exists, but also that He is the rewarder of them that diligently seek Him. *With reverence*, because He is the mighty One of Israel;
omnipotent is his arm, ubiquitous his eye, omnis-

cient his mind ; holiness, purity, truth and glory
are his garments ; in his one hand are power and
judgment ; in his other, long-suffering, mercy and
love. Jesus knows the Father, and consequently
taught his disciples of his majesty. He did not
say, "I am God, ask of me," but He told them to
ask the Father in his name. What a privilege
that we can call this great Being, even the lofty
One who inhabitest eternity, "our Father." Well
might the apostle John write, "Behold what
manner of love ! "

But the true doctrine is not enveloped in mystery. The light of heaven shines clearly around
it. Men's traditions and heathen myths have
shrouded it in the past, and they still hide its glory
from the eyes of many of God's people. But
thanks be to God, the Babel of men's traditions
is tottering. The veil is being rent. The eyes
of many are being opened. The standard of truth
is raised aloft in the name of Israel's God. Zion's
banner waves triumphantly upon the breeze of
heaven. On the one side is inscribed, "In the
cross of Christ I glory ; " on the other, "There is
one body, one Spirit, and one hope. One faith,
one baptism. ONE GOD and FATHER of all, who is
above all, and through all, and in you all." Praise
God the dark clouds of mystery are fast being dissipated by heaven's true and glorious light, and
the children of the Highest are being fed with the
pure and golden grain. The knowledge of God
increaseth as eternity approacheth. Theology
may attempt to divide his being, but it is in vain.

Infidelity may blaspheme, but its breath is but an idle blast hurled at the heavens in vain. God exists, and ere long the mighty trump shall summon all to his judgment bar.

> Then shall the people know, that high
>   O'er all is heaven's eternal King;
> And holy, holy is the Lord,
>   The seraphim above shall sing.

CHAPTER II.

CHRIST, THE ONLY BEGOTTEN OF THE FATHER.

"Whosoever transgresseth and abideth not in the doctrine of Christ, hath not God. He that abideth in the doctrine of Christ, hath both the Father and the Son."—II. John 9.

We have said, the doctrine of Jesus Christ is the basis of all true faith. The above text not only proves it to be such, but also makes a knowledge of the same, together with a continuance therein, as essential to salvation, for "this is life eternal that they might know Thee, the only true God," who according to the foregoing text cannot be known only by an abiding in the doctrine of Christ. Therefore it becomes every lover of truth to seek for the true understanding of a doctrine of such vital importance.

That Jesus Christ is "the only begotten of the Father," all who profess to believe in his name, concede. The time and manner of his being begotten are plainly revealed in scripture. (Luke i. 30–35.) But just here is where the true doctrine

2

of Christ is perverted. The large majority of professing Christians believe that Christ pre-existed, i. e. existed prior to his conception, as a separate being from the Father, which certainly is a mystery that grates harshly upon the reason with which God has endowed man, nor has such a dogma any foundation whatever in the scriptures. If the fundamental truth of Christianity be misconstrued, it must be evident to all that the superstructure cannot be sound. Hence has transpired the "falling away," as predicted by Paul. (II. Thes. ii. 3.)

If Christ existed as a perfect and an immortal being prior to conception, then the Son must be as old as his Father, which is impossible.

That which is immortal cannot die. This is a self-evident truth—an axiom.

Christ, according to the accepted theory and theology of to-day, being a corporeal entity, separate from and equal with the Father, must consequently have been immortal from all eternity. But according to the laws of nature, which are the laws of God, he must then have had to suffer death, or decomposition, or change, corporeally, in order to his being begotten in the womb of Mary; for seed sown is not quickened, or in other words, cannot spring into new life and being, except it first die or be subjected to change; and since that which is immortal is undying and unchangeable, therefore Christ could not have had a pre-existence apart from God and have been co-eternal with Him; else he could not have been begotten in the manner recorded in the scriptures. The former granted, he must have had an eternal existence before he was begotten at all, which is absurd in the extreme ; for no being can trace its origin as an individual entity beyond the time of its conception. Such can only be traced as a seed ungenerated in another form or body. Therefore, in this manner and in this manner alone, Christ pre-existed in the form, or body, or being of God the eternal Father.

Further, let it be granted that he had an eternal pre-existence as an individual entity apart from God. Then he could not have become "the *first-born* of every creature," as plainly taught in the scripture, and hence a dilemma or mystery arises.

But there is no authority in scripture for his pre-existence, consequently to the true disciple of Jesus there is no dilemma or mystery. (Luke viii. 10.) When knowledge steps in, mystery dissolves and vanishes. According to all the laws of God, as revealed to man either in the Bible or in nature, and according to reason, common sense and logic, the procreator must ever precede that which is begotten of him, and so with God and Christ. When Christ was begotten the germ of a new being sprang into existence. This every rational mind can comprehend. And after his birth we are told, "The child grew, and waxed strong in spirit, filled with wisdom : And the grace of God was upon him." (Luke ii. 40.) Again,

"And Jesus increased in wisdom and stature, and in favor with God and man." (Luke ii. 52.) And as the general traits of character of an earthly parent are apparent in his offspring, so we find the characteristics of a heavenly parent in the only begotten Son of God. Hence he may be said to have the mind of the Father. (John xii. 49, 50.) For "God, who at sundry times and in divers manners spake in time past unto the fathers by the prophets, hath in these last days spoken unto us by his Son." But we are told, "it became him, for whom are all things and by whom are all things, in bringing many sons unto glory, to make the Captain of their salvation perfect, through sufferings. For both He that sanctifieth and they who are sanctified are all one : for which cause He is not ashamed to call them brethren. Wherefore it behooved Him to be made like unto his brethren, that He might be a merciful and faithful high priest in things pertaining to God, to make reconciliation for the sins of the people." (Heb. ii. 10, 11, 17.) In these words the true Christ of scripture is made manifest, not as a perfect and an immortal being, but as one like unto his brethren, although "anointed with the oil of gladness above his fellows," being begotten of God, yet having to be made "perfect through sufferings." The mystery of Christ, if such we may call it, lies in his being begotten of the Holy Ghost. Man is conceived in sin and brought forth in iniquity. Christ was conceived in holiness and brought forth in purity, "who did no sin, neither was guile found in his mouth." To say such a conception is impossible, is to limit the creative power of God. The great Being who called worlds and systems of worlds into existence, sent forth the same word *(logos)* and it became flesh and blood in the form of his "beloved Son." By so doing, He violated none of his natural laws, but instead displayed his majesty, power and love.

Having the mind of the Father by inheritance, Jesus could, as it were, take eternity in his grasp. He says plainly, "I speak not of myself;" and again, "the Father who sent me gave me a commandment, what I should say and what I should speak." As already quoted, God spake unto the fathers by the prophets, but in these latter days unto us by his Son. As to the manner of communication we have it clearly given, viz: "Holy men of God spake as they were moved by the Holy Ghost." (II. Peter i. 21.) Therefore in like manner but in greater volume God spake to us by his Son, for "God gave not the Spirit by measure unto Him." "Who being the brightness of his Father's glory, and the express image of his person, and upholding all things by the word of his power, when He had through himself purged our sins, sat down on the right hand of the Majesty on high; being made so much better than the angels, as He hath by inheritance obtained a more excellent name than they." (Heb. i. 3, 4.) And we "see Jesus having been made for a little time inferior to the angels by the suffering of death, crowned with glory and honor." (ii. 9, *literal rendering.)* "Wherefore God hath also highly exalted Him, and given Him a name which is above every name ; that at the name of Jesus every knee should bow, of things in heaven, and things in earth, and things under the earth, and that every tongue should confess that Jesus Christ is Lord, to the glory of God the Father." (Phil. ii. 9–11.)

But while touching on the *Name*, it is claimed that Isaiah ix. 6, gives to Christ all the appellations of the Father, while others go even so far as to say that He is indeed the mighty God, the everlasting Father, than which nothing could be more absurd.

In our common version the text reads: "For unto us a child is born, unto us a Son is given; and the government shall be upon his shoulders; and his name shall be called Wonderful, Counselor, the mighty God, the everlasting Father, the Prince of Peace." Even this rendering does not say, He shall be nor that He is the "mighty God," etc., but "He shall be *called* the mighty God, the everlasting Father," etc. But the whole argument based upon this text, to prove the "born child" the "Son given," as the great Father himself, fades away when we give another translation from the Hebrew of the same text, which reads: "For a child is born unto us, a Son hath been given unto us, and the government is placed on his shoulders, and his name is Wonderful, Counselor of the mighty God, of the everlasting Father, the Prince of Peace." There is quite a difference between "the mighty God," and "Counselor of the mighty God." The Commentary of Rashi renders it, "And the Wonderful, Counselor, mighty God, the everlasting Father, hath called his name the Prince of Peace."

Aben Ezra applies all the words as epithets of an earthly prince, (Hezekiah) and renders it, "And people call Him Wonderful, Counselor, Mighty One of God, Perpetual Father, Prince of Peace."

By a careful comparison of the foregoing translations, it becomes evident that this text as a prop to the doctrine or dogma of a pre-existing Christ is entirely swept away. From none of the renderings can He be said to be "the mighty God." That He is the "mighty One of God," we freely admit, for all power is given unto Him in heaven and in earth. Nor do the above renderings detract from the glory of the great eternal Father.

In the Septuagint version we have as a literal rendering, "And his name shall be called a Messenger of great counsel;" and both of the appellations, "mighty God" and "everlasting Father" are wanting.

And thus the fundamental doctrine of popular theology—a pre-existing Christ—vanishes before the true light of God's Holy Word. For, "Hereby know ye the Spirit of God: every spirit that confesseth that Jesus Christ is come in the flesh is of God: and every spirit that confesseth not that Jesus Christ is come in the flesh is not

of God: and this is that spirit of antichrist,
whereof ye have heard that it should come." (I.
John iv. 2, 3.) Theology declares that it was the
Father himself, or at least one of the members of
a triune and eternal Godhead, who came in the
flesh. The scriptures tell us that Jesus the anointed one, the only begotten of the Father, came
in the flesh, and that the same Jesus shall appear
again the second time in the glory of the Father.
The contrast is clear, and cannot fail to strike the
honest-minded reader. The former is mist, the
latter is sunshine. The one is darkness, the other
true light. In the sunshine of the latter how
beautiful and how grand do the words of the ancient prophet appear: "Unto us a child is born,
unto us a Son is given." The very word *born*
implies the true doctrine. The prophet but foretold the event that in after years transpired as
recorded by the evangelist. How joyous the announcement, how glorious the scene that her-
alded the birth of the Saviour: "And there were
in the same country shepherds abiding in the
field, keeping watch over their flock by night.
And lo, the angel of the Lord came upon them,
and the glory of the Lord shone round about
them: and they were sore afraid. And the angel
said unto them, Fear not; for, behold, I bring
you good tidings of great joy, which shall be to all
people. For unto you is BORN this day in the city
of David a SAVIOUR, who is CHRIST THE LORD. . .
And suddenly there was with the angel a multitude of the heavenly host praising God, and say-

ing, Glory to God in the highest, and on earth peace, good will toward men." (Luke ii. 8-14.)

The word *born* implies a "bringing forth"—a coming into existence as a visible being; and as to the very time when Christ thus came into existence, the angel tells the shepherds clearly, "Unto you is born *this day* . . . a Saviour who is CHRIST the LORD." To say that Christ only changed the form of his being, is not only putting forth that which cannot be sustained by a "thus saith the Lord," but it is really admitting as true the mythical and nonsensical theories of Darwin. For if such a mighty change took place in the transformation of the Son of God, as popular theology teaches, then all things are possible, and there can be no fixed law. For according to the doctrine of Christ as popularly taught, Omniscience for a time becomes unconscious; Omnipotence, weak and helpless; Immutability is made subject to change; and that which is immortal becomes dying. Although it is written, "all things are possible with God," yet such can only be taken in a limited sense, for common sense teaches us that it is impossible for God to lie, and in like manner we say it is impossible for God to violate his own laws; and who dare say that He will make void that word which He has magnified above his name, (Ps. cxxxviii. 2) and which abides or endures forever; for Christ himself who spake the words given Him of the Father said: "Heaven and earth shall pass away, but my words shall not pass away." Therefore accord-

ing to the scriptures it is impossible for God to
do violation to his own sacred word. In like
manner also his laws are fixed and inviolable.
Therefore we conclude that all things are possible
with God only which harmonize with his divine
purposes, which are in accordance with his sacred
will, which accord with his unvarying word, and
which do not violate his immutable laws.

And therefore we claim that it is impossible for
Christ to have existed as a living, moving, acting
entity, visible to the angels and to God, and possessing all the attributes of the eternal Father,
prior to his actual birth; for such is an infringe-
ment of the law of procreation which God has established in nature, which law also is according
to the scriptures.

Those who have imbibed this popular doctrine
of a pre-existing Saviour, and who have lived up
to the best light they had as practical Christians
shall certainly at last receive according "as their
works shall be." But the *spirit* that teaches such
a dogma is nothing less than the spirit of antichrist, for it confesses not that Jesus, the anointed
one, came in the flesh; and when the final trump
shall sound it shall be manifest to every eye.
There will be a wonderful trimming of lamps
shortly. It will be well for those in that day who
have been taught of God. In this connection we
shall merely allude to that which is certainly one
of the more established of latter day delusions.
We refer to the visions of Mrs. E. G. White, of
Battle Creek, Mich. Alas for those who are

cleaving to her visions as though they were inspired of God, for the same spirit which through
her graphically describes the serpent that beguiled Eve, beholds also a pre-existing Christ
with the Father. (*The Great Controversy*, chap.
iii.) By subjecting this to the test.as given by
the apostle John (I. John iv. 1-3) it is self-con-
demned, and bears the unmistakable imprint of
the spirit of antichrist. We unhesitatingly denounce such as a mythical delusion or chimera
produced by the artful promptings of the same
serpent which beguiled Eve. Vain, subtle de-
ceiver, his days are numbered. His end shall
soon come. All the way through the day of salvation he has appeared as an angel of light don-
ning variform garbs in order that he might be
adapted to the manifold changes of the age, and
thus in these latter days he appears as above described among those who are looking for the Messiah soon to come. The foundation being false,
how shall the fabric stand the storm of the day
of wrath? The question is significant, and should
be weighed upon the balance of TRUTH by all whom
it may concern. However this, together with
kindred delusions, have reached the maximum of
their career.- Their decadence shall be swift.
The harvest is ripening fast. The reapers are
the angels. No chaff shall be garnered, only the
golden grain. Error shall fall with a mighty
crash. The Rock of Ages is the only sure foundation. That Rock is Christ, and we must know
Him in order to life eternal. To know Him is to

know the doctrine, and to know the doctrine is
to have both the Father and the Son.

In recapitulating, let us observe more closely
the announcement of the angels. The statement
as to who was born on the day specified contains no ambiguity. It is clear as the sunlight.
We have said the word *born* implies the true
doctrine. We inquire, who was born? The angel answers, " a Saviour who is CHRIST THE LORD."
By transposing we have, Christ the Lord, a
Saviour is born this day. And since we have
shown that the word *born* implies a coming into
existence as a visible entity or being, therefore
Christ the Lord came in like manner into existence at his birth. But this does not make Him
a mere man. He was begotten by the Spirit of
God, hence He is the only begotten Son of God.
The living Word, the quickening Spirit was made
flesh and dwelt among us. He partook of the
Father's bounties, and distributed to man's ne-
cessities. Consequently it is said, " He was rich,
yet for your sakes He became poor." He gave
of his heavenly wealth, and took up instead our
infirmities, our iniquities, and our transgressions.
He often denied himself of sweet communion with
the Father, that He might converse with the poor
and the needy. Possessing our nature, He knew
well our weaknesses. While praying the Father
for the poor outcasts of earth, He himself had
not whereon to lay his head. O, precious Redeemer, knowing thee we are taught to love thee.

As we follow Him in his peregrinations along

the meandering ·rugged path which so faithfully
He trod, by the shores of Galilee, around the
mountain base and o'er the burning sand, comforting his disciples, feeding or teaching the multitude, healing the sick, visiting the poor, or clam-
bering up the mountain side to spend the night
in prayer, we cannot fail to perceive that his origin was divine. " For the joy that was set before Him," (not left behind to take again) He
endured the cross and despised the shame. As
the conflict increased his love grew brighter. As
the mighty weight of our transgressions pressed
heavier and heavier upon his soul, the divine love
shone out all the more gloriously. Towards the
end of his earthly career we see Him on the side
of Mount Olivet in the garden of Gethsemane
prostrate in grief. 'Tis midnight, and alone He
prays; his sweat as drops of blood fall to the
ground. His agony is intense. A dark and
treacherous path lies before him. The hour of
decision has arrived. Calvary is near. He must
there yield himself a sacrifice for man. Jesus,
the anointed one, must die. The loving Father
sends an angel to strengthen Him. He leaves
the garden, falls into the hands of his betrayer
and is led to judgment. He is scourged, spit upon,
scorned, crowned with thorns, and finally is nailed
to the cross. The darkest scene the world ever
witnessed ensues, when Jesus the only begotten
of the Father yields to death. The finite mind
fails to comprehend the pangs, the sufferings of
the Lamb of God in those dark moments, when

he cried, "My God, my God, why hast thou forsaken me?" He dies, but does He really die?
The popular theory, dogma, or mystery, as you
may term it, says He did not die, but on the other hand that He was in Paradise or Heaven, while
his body lay in the tomb. This being granted,
the death of Christ is a mere illusion.

But we read, "Moreover, brethren, I declare
unto you the gospel which I preached unto you,
which also ye have received, and wherein ye
stand; by which also ye are saved if ye hold
fast. . . . For I delivered unto you first of
all that which I also received, how that CHRIST
DIED for our sins according to the scriptures; and
that HE was *buried*, and that HE *rose again the
third day* according to the scriptures." (I. Cor.
xv. 1-4.) From this quotation alone it is evident
that it was *Christ*—the being—that died, was
buried, and that rose again. After his resurrection, Jesus said to Mary, "Touch me not; for I
am *not yet* ascended to my Father." Theological
mystery tells us He was with the Father all the
time. Alas what darkness enshrouds the world!
According to such teachings the conception and
birth of Jesus, the Christ, was but a metamorpho-
sis, and his death a mere illusion. Avaunt Darwinism, avaunt spiritualism, for such teachings
are respectively tantamount to these obnoxious
and illusory theories of man, and are equally as
absurd. Christ died for our sins, is what the
scriptures teach, and any rational mind can accept the statement in its simplicity and take hold

of its truth. He was buried, but being begotten
of the Spirit of God, the immortal spark within
did not suffer his flesh to see corruption, and in
God's appointed time the mortal body of Jesus
was quickened and became immortal. He, (i. e.
the Christ,) rose victorious from the tomb, triumphant over death and the grave. Granting
the truth of the popularly accepted doctrine of
Christ, this, the most glorious theme of the Bible,
loses its savor, and becomes a mere phantom.
But understanding the true doctrine we behold
its glory, and exultantly exclaim with the apostle,
"Now is Christ risen from the dead and become
the first fruits of them that slept." It must be
apparent to all that unless Christ (not his mere
body but his being) had slept in actual death, he
could not have become the first fruits of them
that slept, for the word of God is not calculated
to mislead us, but is placed before us as a beacon
light, "And is profitable for doctrine, for reproof,
for correction, and for instruction in righteousness: that the man of God may be perfected."

Jesus not only rose from the dead but He rose
in the same body that suffered on the cross.
Even doubting Thomas was convinced of this.
(John xx. 24–28.) And in the same form, flesh of
our flesh and bone of our bone, immortalized, He
ascended to the Father's throne, as our great
High Priest and Mediator. "For there is one
God, and one Mediator between God and men,
the man Christ Jesus." (I. Tim. ii. 5.) For "this
man, after He had offered one sacrifice for sins

forever, sat down on the right hand of God; from henceforth expecting till his enemies be made his footstool." (Heb. x. 12, 13.) The men in white told the disciples of Galilee, "This *same* Jesus, who is taken up from you into heaven shall so come in like manner as ye have seen Him go into heaven." (Acts i. 11.) The same Jesus, it is not another—the same Lord that suffered, bled and died for our sins, that was buried and that rose again. Paul preached the same gospel, and tells us, "Christ was once offered to bear the sins of many; and unto them that look for Him shall He appear the second time without a *sin offering* unto salvation." (Heb. ix. 28.)

And now to sum up, it is essential to understand the doctrine of Christ, for according to the scriptures, "He that abideth not in the doctrine of Christ hath not God." If we take the word of God alone as our guide as aided by his Spirit we will find the doctrine simple and easy of comprehension. "The wayfaring men, though fools, shall not err therein." The popular doctrine, if such we may call it, is a confessed mystery, even to those who maintain it. According to the scriptures, to the true disciple of Jesus nothing should be held in mystery, for the Spirit which God bestows upon them will "lead them into all truth," and "teach them all things."

When we are told Christ was begotten and in due time born, we should take it as the terms respectively imply. And when we read that He died, was buried and rose again from the dead, we should believe it in preference to that tradition which endeavors to make believe that this only refers to his fleshly cage in which the being was embodied. By doing God's will we shall "know of the doctrine," and if we know not Jesus of Nazareth we cannot expect to know Him as the "same Jesus" when He descends from heaven in the glory of the Father. The same Jesus that bade the waves of Galilee be calm, cometh again to still forever the warring elements of a world of sin and iniquity.

> "Hark! a voice is heard above the troubled elements,
> A low, clear voice, which whispers, "Peace, be still."
> And all the winds have sunk to gentle breaths,
> And as on vexed Gennesaret of old
> When He rebuked the raging winds and waves,
> There is a mighty calm. The broken clouds
> Melt into colors like a dream. The Sun
> Of Righteousness with healing in his wings
> Has risen upon a world weary of night.
> Most glorious where emergent from the flood
> That from far Lebanon to Kadesh rolled
> Its waves of fire baptismal, Zion rose
> In perfect beauty."

CHAPTER III.

THE EXCELLENCIES OF CHRIST.

"What think ye of Christ?"—Matt. xxii. 42.

Theology has obscured Christ's glory as an individual being, in that it declares Him to be the very God incarnate; for if Christ be the very God, then the works He performed while on earth cease to be miraculous or wonderful. The great Creator did not require to come down from his throne in the excellent glory to display to man his power and wonderful works, in order to convince his creatures that He was God. The vast book of Nature is but a continuous, illimitable and marvelous demonstration both of his handiwork and of his omnipotence. But when we see Jesus as a prophet, raised up like unto his brethren, perform mighty works by the power of God, we marvel, and admire the man of Nazareth, and confess that He is the Messiah long promised. When we inquire, "What manner of man is this?" we are informed that He is the only begotten of the Father: even the voice from heaven replies, "This is my beloved Son in whom I am well pleased." And thus we perceive He was of noble birth and of heavenly origin. Begotten by the power of the Highest, the nature of that Being, "who only hath immortality," was planted as a germ in a mortal body. (Luke i. 35.) This gave to Christ power to lay down his life and to take it again, for after his decease the immortal spark, so to speak, only required the time appointed by heaven (three days) to kindle into flame and quicken the form of Jesus, and thus enable Him to triumph over death. (Rom. viii. 11.) But this was only according to the Father's commandment. (John x. 18.) Understanding the origin of his being, we do not marvel that the multitude were attracted by the man of Nazareth. The very expression of his countenance commanded admiration, for He was the brightness of his Father's glory, and the express image of his person.

As we behold the Lamb of God, we are at once struck with his marvelous wisdom, the excellencies of his character and the purity of his life, together with the hallowed example, which as rays divine by day, and heavenly dew drops by night, was strewed all along the pathway of his brief career. His mind was but a reflection of Jehovah's omniscience. His mien was majestic. He drew the multitude after Him. Heaven's glory rested upon his countenance. Gentle yet commanding, meek yet unbending, He feared no foe. The dev-

ils obeyed his voice. Hypocrisy He scathingly
rebuked. But to the weary and heavy-laden He
said, "Come unto me, and I will give you rest."
The sorrowing He comforted. The sick He
healed. He was the friend of sinners. Truly He
was the benefactor of his race. On the one hand
He was clothed with the power of heaven—even
the wind and the waves obeyed his voice. On
the other He held the banner of mercy, forbearance, compassion, and love divine. Clothed in
the garments of truth and salvation, Jesus of
Nazareth stood before the world as the Ambassador of the Most High, the one Mediator between
God and men, the King and Leader of Zion's
hosts. Of nature's noblemen He stands pre-emi-
nent. Of earth's heroes He is incomparably the
truest, the bravest and the noblest. He was despised by men who were jealous of his greatness,
and the very dignity of his person made the envious jeer at Him. What a noble representative
of Heaven!

"Wherefore, God also hath highly exalted Him,
and given Him a name which is above every
name: that at the name of Jesus every knee
should bow, of things in heaven, and things in
earth, and things under the earth; and that every
tongue should confess that Jesus Christ is Lord,
to the glory of God the Father." The impression
is too general that Jesus, the Christ, during his
first advent was a poor abused being, bound down
with the chain of human prejudices; and bowed
down because of the revilings and taunts of wicked

men. Instead "He moved the multitude at will," and his persecutors feared the people. He spake and acted as one having authority. Although He was meek and lowly in heart, yet He could command Satan, "Get thee behind me." And to the Scribes and Pharisees He sarcastically exclaimed, "Woe unto you, Scribes and Pharisees, hypocrites! for ye are like unto whited sepulchres, which indeed appear beautiful outward, but are within full of dead men's bones, and of all uncleanness. Even so ye also outwardly appear righteous unto men, but within ye are full of hypocrisy and iniquity."

Behold Him again in the temple scourging therefrom the money changers; and when asked, "By what authority doest thou these things?" He replied by asking significantly, "The baptism of John, whence was it? from heaven, or of men?" And they *dare* not reply. Then said Jesus, "Neither tell I you by what authority I do these things." Had they said John's baptism was from heaven, then Jesus having been baptized of John could have claimed the priesthood, and consequently authority to cleanse the temple. To deny this they feared the people, which proved on whose side the populace were. But we find dignity of bearing characterizes Jesus of Nazareth throughout his whole career. "For the joy that was set before Him He endured the cross *despising* the shame." The taunts, the insults and the jeers heaped upon Him He disdained to notice. He carried himself through all as becoming the

Prince of the kings of the earth. Even when led
before the mock tribunal, and when accused of
many things, and plied with derisive questions
He maintained the same dignity and answered
them nothing. He was the Man of Sorrows and
acquainted with grief, but it was because as the
just one He suffered for the unjust. He was the
despised and the rejected of men, only because
the world was not worthy of Him. Never in his
whole life was the nobility of his nature so vivid-
ly displayed, as when stretched upon the cross in
the midst of his crucifiers and revilers He cried,
"Father, forgive them, for they know not what
they do." As earth's grandest hero He lived, and
as earth's grandest hero He died. Monuments of
marble and of granite are erected to perpetuate
the memory of heroes who have climbed the pinnacle of fame through the blood of thousands or
ten of thousands of their fellows; but the Hero of
Calvary attained to glory by the offering of himself to save his fellows, by the shedding of his own
blood for the salvation of mankind. Soldiers, for
the love they hold for their country, their friends
or their homes, offer their lives in defence; but,
"God commendeth his love toward us in that
while we were yet sinners, (aliens or strangers)
Christ died for us." O, precious love of God!
O, precious Redeemer, thus to die a martyr for
our sake!

But through death He triumphed over death,
and became the Prince of life. Arising from the
tomb He assumes the majesty of heaven in the

announcement, "All power is given unto me in heaven and in earth." But He is the same Jesus, and his disciples know Him. He ascends to heaven, and the men of Galilee behold Him taken from them into glory. They gaze upwards in wonder. Angels comfort them with the words, "Ye men of Galilee, why stand ye gazing up into heaven? This same Jesus who is taken up from you into heaven shall so come in like manner as ye have seen Him go into heaven." A thought just here. The *same* Jesus is to come again in *like manner* as He ascended. He ascended as a hero, and as a conqueror, and He shall come as the Lion of the tribe of Judah, with the scepter of power in his hand. He ascended as the beauteous Lord; He shall descend as the " King in his beauty." He ascended in triumph over death; He shall come with the keys of death and the grave in his hand to call forth his sleeping saints. His ascension was visible; and " Behold He cometh with clouds; and every eye shall see Him, and they also who pierced Him; and all the kindreds of the earth shall wail because of Him." He ascended to reign with the Father in his throne in the heavens, which is the center of the universal kingdom of God; there He must reign "till He hath put all enemies under his feet. The last enemy that shall be destroyed is death." (I. Cor. xv. 25, 26.) But He comes again to take possession of the kingdoms of this world, (Rev. xi. 15) and to establish his own throne on Mount Zion forever, when those who have overcome shall sit with Him

in his throne, even as He also overcame and was
set with the Father in his throne. (Rev. iii. 21.)
"And the Lord shall be King over all the earth;
in that day shall there be one Lord, and his name
one." (Zech. xiv. 9.) "And we shall reign on the
earth." (Rev. v. 10.) He ascends as the "chief
among ten thousand;" He descends as the chief
of the universe, having a name above every other
name under God; for "when He saith, all things
are put under Him, it is manifest that He is excepted who did put all things under Him." (I.
Cor. xv. 27.) For the Father alone is supreme:
He reigns as "the blessed and only Potentate,
the King of kings and Lord of lords."

He ascended radiant with glory; He shall come
again in "the glory of his Father with his angels."
When the beloved disciple John saw this glory in
vision, he tells us, "His countenance was as the
sun shineth in his strength, and when I saw Him,
I fell at his feet as dead." Truly "an eternal
weight of glory" awaiteth the children of God,
when they shall be brought face to face with their
Immanuel and with the great I AM, the King
eternal.

We will briefly consider one more scene in this
connection, which beautifully portrays the glory
of the Son of God. (See Rev. v.) In the right
hand of God is seen a book written on two sides,
and sealed with seven seals. It is undoubtedly
the Book of Life. An angel proclaims with a loud
voice, "Who is worthy to open the book, and to
loose the seals thereof?" And no one is found

worthy to open it, neither to look thereon, until a voice was heard, saying, "Behold the Lion of the tribe of Judah, the Root of David, hath prevailed to open the book, and to loose the seven seals thereof." And then we have introduced to us the new song, saying, "Thou art worthy to take the book, and to open the seals thereof; for thou wast slain, and hast redeemed us to God by thy blood, out of every kindred, and tongue, and people, and nation; and hast made us unto our God kings and priests: and we shall reign on the earth. And I beheld, and I heard the voice of many angels round about the throne, and the living creatures, and the elders: and the number of them was ten thousand times ten thousand, and thousands of thousands; saying with a loud voice, "Worthy is the Lamb that was slain to receive power, and riches, and wisdom, and strength, and honor, and glory, and blessing."

And now, "What think ye of Christ?" Is He not a noble Leader? To be his disciple is the highest honor conferred on mortals. Still, many think to be a Christian implies a kind of semi-slavery, full of crosses and debasements. Such an idea is but a display of ignorance of the true knowledge of the Christ. To the follower of Jesus, crosses, so-called, become delights, and debasements are but the stepping-stones to that honor which is from above. Christ has well said, "He that loveth father or mother more than me is not worthy of me; and he that loveth son or daughter more than me is not worthy of me. And

he that taketh not his cross and followeth after
me, is not worthy of me." And when we consider
the excellencies of Christ and the glory of his being, we can well understand the force of his words:
"Whosoever shall be ashamed of me and of my
words, of him shall the Son of man be ashamed,
when he shall come in his own glory, and in his
Father's and of the holy angels."

What a marvel that such a being is not ashamed
to call us brethren; that through Him we can
become heirs of God and joint heirs with himself
to an inheritance incorruptible and undefiled.
"Behold what manner of love the Father hath
bestowed upon us, that we should be called the
sons of God: therefore the world knoweth us not
because it knew Him not." It is no wonder that
the early disciples prayed that they might be
counted worthy of death for Christ's sake. I praise
God for such a princely Leader as Jesus of Nazareth. With all other excellent qualities He was
holy. "In Him was no sin, neither was guile
found in his mouth." Knowing Him, we long to
see Him face to face. O, with what holy ecstasy
the multitude of the redeemed shall join in the
tribute of praise, Worthy art thou, O precious,
spotless, glorious Lamb of God!

And methinks I hear the golden harps touched
by immortal fingers mingling in the mellifluent
strains of the glad new song, in honor of Him
who once was slain, but liveth again, and sitteth
there upon the throne of his glory, as King of
Zion, the Messiah, our Immanuel, our Redeemer,

and our everlasting Friend. Even now shall we lift our voices in adoration of the Lamb.

To be his disciple is ennobling. When we walk in his footsteps we ascend the scale of humanity. If we keep our eyes on our Leader we must needs go on towards perfection. The moon is dark of itself, but when the sun shines thereon, it in turn sends a sweet pale light to the earth. So with the Christian. In himself he is dark; but when the Light of life shines into his heart he must needs reflect the light to those around him.

Christ is my all, and God my all in all. In sunshine, in storm, in peace or in tribulation, in trials or in distresses, I joyously and exultingly exclaim,

> "I'm not ashamed to own my Lord,
> Nor to defend his cause;
> Maintain the glory of his cross,
> And honor all his laws."

CHAPTER IV.

ONLY TWO THRONES.

"And there shall be no more curse: but the throne of God and of the Lamb shall be in it; and his servants shall serve Him."—Rev. xxii. 3.

We have not yet done with trinitarianism. Because the doctrine of a trinity is generally accepted is not proof of its soundness. The same mode of reasoning would prove Babylon of Revelation as a standard for the world: "For *all nations* have drunk of the wine of the wrath of her fornication." If the scriptures teach or set forth a triune God, if nature supports the dogma, and if reason and science accord therewith, then by these witnesses it must stand; but if it fail to find a single vestige of support from these, its fall is inevitable. Like the terms "immortal soul," "never-dying soul," etc., such appellations as "God in three persons," "Blessed Trinity," "Triune God," "Holy Trinity," are not once to be found in the whole Bible. Neither can such a dogma claim support from the word of God.

Theology says there are three persons in the Godhead, co-equal and co-eternal. If co-equal all must reign. If all reign there must be three thrones. God the Father reigns, and his throne is often mentioned in the scriptures. Christ, the Son, sits now with the Father in his throne, and has the promise, for himself, of the throne of his father David. (Luke i. 32, 33.) The same is implied in the text, "To him that overcometh will I grant to sit with me in my throne, even as I also overcame, and am set down with my Father in his throne." (Rev. iii. 21.) But nowhere can you find the throne of the Holy Ghost mentioned. Granting for the sake of argument the personality of the Holy Ghost, we here find a discrepancy that cannot be accounted for. If there are three persons vested with equal power and glory, it follows that since one reigns in power all must reign in power. But we have shown that only two reign, with no account of the third.

Of the two that reign there is not an equality, according to the scriptures. Paul in speaking of Christ's coming says, "Then cometh the end, when He (Christ) shall have delivered up the kingdom to God, even the Father: when He shall have put down all rule and all authority and power." "He must reign, (in the Father's throne) till He hath put all enemies under his feet. The last enemy that shall be destroyed is death." "But when He saith all things are put under Him, it is manifest that He is excepted, (i. e. God) who did put all things under Him. And when all things are subdued unto Him, then shall the Son also himself be *subject unto Him* that put all things under Him, that God may be all in all." It is thus the apostle continues in his first epistle to the Corinthians. (xv. 24–28.) Here we find that the "power" given to Christ from the Father has to be given up at the expiration of a certain period, that God the Father may be all in all, as blessed and only Potentate, as the one Supreme Being of the universe. And we are further explicitly told, "then shall the Son also himself be subject unto Him." But if God be supreme, and Christ be subject unto Him, how can they be equal? Then also can the lesser be equal unto the greater, which is absurd. Hence, since Christ has said, "My Father is greater than I," (John xiv. 28) and since the scriptures clearly and indubitably maintain the Father's supremacy, we therefore accept the words of Him who said, "Heaven and earth shall pass away, but my words shall not pass away," in preference to a theological dogma which now quivers as an aspen leaf before the breath of heaven's eternal truth, and whose ultimate fall is inevitable.

Again we read, "There is one God, and one Mediator between God and men, the man Christ Jesus." Now it is evident, that the office of mediator implies the supremacy of God the Father. A mediator is not of one, but stands between two parties, and pleads with the one in behalf of the other. How absurd to say that Christ mediates with Himself in our behalf. If He be co-equal

with the Father, there can be no need of mediation. God is not mocked. God is omnipotent;
his power will not admit of limitation. If Christ
be the very God, He is omnipotent. If He be omnipotent, his mediatorship is a mere farce. Hence
a dilemma arises. "But," objects one, "does not
He himself say, 'All power is given unto me in
heaven and in earth?'" True, but the very
words "*given me*" imply the supremacy of God,
and included in that power was undoubtedly the
power to mediate. Jesus, addressing the Father
in another instance, says: "All mine are thine,
and thine are mine; and I am glorified in them."
(John xvii. 10.) But again He acknowledges the
Father's supremacy in the words, "*I am glorified
in them.*" The glory evidently was conferred by
God; Christ was the recipient of that glory. And
in the twenty-second verse of the same chapter
He says, in reference to his disciples, "And the
glory which *thou gavest* me I have given them;
that they may be one, even as we are one: I in
them and thou in me, that they may be made perfect in one." Christ did not even claim to speak
of himself. He says: "I have not spoken of myself; but the Father which sent me, He gave me
a commandment, what I should say and what I
should speak; and I know that his commandment
is life everlasting: whatsoever I speak therefore,
even as the Father said unto me, so I speak."
(John xii. 49, 50.) In regard to his life He says:
"I have power to lay it down, and I have power to
take it again." But notice, He claims not this

power of himself, for He continues: "This commandment have I received of my Father." (John x. 18.)

In all things the pre-eminence of the Father is acknowledged by Christ, by the apostles, and by the prophets. If therefore we endeavor to bestow upon Christ what God has not bestowed upon Him, we are not only assuming a position higher than God, but we are detracting from his glory which He will not give to another. It is also adding to the word, (Rev. xxii. 18) which if done wittingly is but wresting it to our own destruction.

As with Christ's mediatorship, so also with his priesthood. We at once lose the beauty and the glory of Christ being our great High Priest if He be co-equal in power and glory with God. "For it is evident that our Lord sprang out of Judah; of which tribe Moses spake nothing concerning priesthood. And it is yet far more evident; for that after the similitude of Melchisedec there ariseth another priest, who is made (or *become so*, i. e. a priest) not after the law of a carnal commandment, but after the power of an endless life." (Heb. vii. 14-16.) For Christ being begotten by the power of the Highest had the germ of eternal life, or the life principle of God, planted within his being. And as this life was hid in God, and as an immortal spark came forth from God, and was made flesh and dwelt in the flesh, therefore as in its source it was eternal, so Christ was made a priest after the power of an endless life— the only begotten Son of God. So far as this principle of life is concerned—the principle of which He was brought into being, and which emanated from God—Christ may be said to have neither beginning of days nor end of life. But as to his corporeity as a separate entity from the Father, we cannot date beyond the time of his conception, and then only as a germ of being can we understand Him. In this sense we also understand his words, " Before Abraham was, I am."

"*Before Abraham was.*" Abraham still sleeps with the Fathers. He is not yet, and shall not be the possessor of *aionian* or eternal life until Christ, who is our life, shall appear. Then shall we also appear with Him in glory.

"*I am.*" That is, " I exist. The power of *aionian* or eternal life is within me." Thus Christ might have spoken: "It not only dwells within me, but I have power to lay it down and power to take it again. This body shall not see corruption as did father Abraham's. On the third day after my decease I shall arise." And arise He did on that glorious First-day morn, and now listen once more to his voice. It sounds from heaven: "I am He that liveth and was dead; and, behold, I am alive for evermore, Amen; and have the keys of *hades* and of death." " Before Abraham was,"— before any of the Fathers lived, behold I am, I exist, raised by the power of an endless life, as the first-born from the dead, as the first-fruits of them that slept: but " marvel not at this; for the hour is coming, in the which all that are in the graves shall hear his voice, and shall come forth; they that have done good, unto the resurrection of life; and they that have done evil unto the resurrection of condemnation." Then those who sleep in Christ shall come forth, and Abraham together with all the faithful shall be made partakers of the divine nature, and shall eternally live. But in the present "our life is hid with Christ *in God*," which again implies the supremacy of God.

For a period all power is given unto Christ in order that things in heaven, and things in earth, and things under the earth, i. e. in the grave, may be made one. When this work is completed, then the kingdoms of this world shall become the kingdoms of our Lord and of his Christ. Christ then shall receive the promised throne of his father David, and shall reign on Mount Zion and in Jerusalem, and before his ancients gloriously. The Father shall then assume once more his universal sway. The groans and travailings of earth shall then forever cease. The tossing billows and fitful seas of time shall settle into the stillness of heaven's peace. As blessed and only Potentate the mighty God shall reign. As King of earth the Lamb shall sit upon his beauteous throne, and the angels shall be seen ascending and descending from throne to throne. Then shall be heard "as it were the voice of a great multitude, and as the voice of mighty thunderings, saying, Alleluia; for the Lord God omnipotent reigneth." Mark well, the sound is not, Alleluia to the Father, and to the Son, and to the Holy Ghost.

Then also shall be heard voices saying, "We

give thee thanks, O Lord God Almighty, who art
and wast, and art to come; because thou hast
taken to thee thy GREAT POWER, and hast reigned."
Until Christ has completed his mission, the Father
holds back as it were his "great power" or full
sway; his long-suffering arm is stretched out to
save. But when He assumes all power once more,
his wrath is come and the judgment is set, and the
rewards shall be given, and his saints shall praise
Him henceforth evermore.

As to the Holy Ghost being the third person of
the Godhead, or even a person at all, there is no
scripture to sustain it. That it is the power by
which we can hold communication with heaven—
the living waters—the quickening power—the
scriptures clearly maintain. It is the life principle of the world to come—the life of Christ—a
radiating influence that emanates from Him, for
as Paul says, "The Lord is that Spirit." We
drink of it, and it is said to flow from us. (John
vii. 37-39.) On the day of Pentecost it came as
the rushing of a mighty wind, and all were filled
with it.

The idea of praying to the Holy Ghost is utterly unscriptural. Why people cling to such ideas
as truth is passing strange to us. However, we
have shown that there are but two thrones and
only two personages to occupy them. To God
the eternal Father we shall ascribe all glory; and
shall serve the Lord Christ by the aid of the divine Spirit, until we meet Him on Zion. There
we shall adore Him.

CHAPTER V.

DR. JOSEPH COOK ON THE TRINITY REVIEWED.

That doctors differ is an indisputable adage. But truth, like the God from whom it emanates, is invariable. There is what we call a "poetical license;" it would seem there is a theological license as well. Ministers of the same denomination hold diverse views on even standard doctrines, and .yet maintain Christian unity. In brief the atmosphere of modern theology is largely composed of varied opinions, complicated theories, absurd dogmas, human traditions, fables, myths, and vain speculations. When a member of fair intelligence doubts any of the accepted standards, and upon due and honest investigation conscientiously makes known his difficulties, he is at once declared to be upon the shoals and rocks, but there is seldom any attempt made to show him wherein the danger lies. If he demands examination, one class says: "We can only examine you by the *Confession of Faith*." "You had better read Mr. Joseph Cook's Monday Lectures," says another. The Bible, too frequently, is left to one side. If the dissenter submits not to their particular mode of procedure, he is cast overboard and branded as an heretic.

Praise God, where his Spirit is there is liberty. The Bereans were commended for searching the scriptures in the days when the church was pure both in her teachings and her practices. Much more will God commend those who with an honest purpose search the scriptures in these latter days to test the dogmas of a doubtful theology. Let the shackles of prelacy be broken, and let the slaves to a false theology be set free. The days of Babylon the Great are numbered. Her fall is nigh at hand.

As we have hitherto said, the dogma of a triune God is the MYSTERY which forms the foundation of Babylon's structure.

Dr. Joseph Cook's (Boston) Monday Lectures lie before me. These are claimed to be a standard authority on this dogma of the trinity. Some consider him as the star defender of the so-called faith; but we cannot harmonize faith with mystery. He says (p. 69):

"What is the definition of the trinity? 1. The Father, the Son, and the Holy Ghost are one God. 2. Each has a peculiarity incommunicable to the others. 3. Neither is God without the others. 4. Each, with the others, is God. That I suppose to be the standard definition."

Then follows an attempt to show that, "In God are not three wills, three consciences, three intellects, three sets of affections;" that "He is one substance; and in that one substance are three subsistences. But the subsistences are not individualities." Some may and do call this style of reasoning "learned." We deem it rather subtle. On page 72 he throws out the word "persons," as applying to the trinity, altogether; and adopts the word "subsistences." He says:

"Everybody of authority tells us, if you care for scholarly statement, that three *persons* never meant, in the standard discussions of this truth, three *personalities*, for these would be three Gods. . . . All these scholars will tell you that it is no evasion of the difficulties of this theme for me to throw out of this discussion at once the word "persons," as misleading; for that word had originally no such meaning in the Latin tongue as the word person has in our own."

But it is written in the good old book called the Bible: "I will destroy the wisdom of the wise, and will bring to nothing the understanding of the prudent." As it was in the beginning, "The world by wisdom knew not God," so it is now; and so shall it be until the trump of the last day shall scatter the clouds of mythological darkness forever.

To return. Mr. Cook but vainly attempts to prove the triunity of the Divine nature, for in the definition given us he really proves the *disunity* of the several subsistences, e. g., "Each has a peculiarity *incommunicable* to the others." "Incommunicable," and yet one? The absurdity is evident.

Again: "Neither is God without the others."
Hence while Christ was held in death, the universe was without a God, which is also most absurd.   In brief, by this outrageous dogma, God
had to die in order to save his creature man. And
yet those who hold to such monstrous absurdities
tell you that God is omnipotent. Such teaching
is akin to blasphemy—God humbling himself to
save vain man! At this point permit us to quote
from another of their standard teachers, who says:

"We are disposed to go a step farther, and to
assert the necessity of the incarnation for the existence of religion among men. We are finite
and fallen beings; we cannot approach to God;
He must approach to us.   There is a remoteness
between Him and us which cannot be bridged
over by the human intellect. *God must humble
himself*, manifest his divine perfections under the
veil of human feelings, exhibit his love and sympathy and condescension towards us, reveal himself as a divine humanity, in order to become the
object of our worship." *

We pity the flocks who are thus fed, for such
food detracts from God's glory. The very idea
that God must humble himself in order to become
the object of our worship, would place vain man
on a pinnacle above his Maker. Such an idea
cannot be too strongly repudiated.

But let us again follow Mr. Cook. Since he
has disposed of the word persons, as applicable to
the trinity, and has adopted instead the word

---

* P. J. Gloag, D.D., in "Life and Work," (Glasgow) Magazine.

subsistences, let us hear how he explains himself by a parallel illustration:

1. "Sunlight, the rainbow, and the heat of sunlight, are one solar radiance. 2. Each has a peculiarity incommunicable to the others. 3. Neither is full solar radiance without the others. 4. Each with the others is such solar radiance. Father, Son, Holy Ghost—one God." (pp. 72, 73.)

This is the sum of his argument. But the illustration used is not a parallel. Hence instead of giving light to the argument it only renders it the more obscure.

| Sunlight, Rainbow, Heat, | One solar radiance. | Father, Son, Holy Ghost, | One God. |

It is evident that sunlight, rainbow, and heat are but emanations from a substance or body called the sun. They are not the sun itself. These merely form together one combined emanation, viz: solar radiance—only a radiance when done. Father, Son and Holy Ghost, three emanations or subsistences, which form together one combined subsistency called God. Whence the source? One solar radiance is but a compound emanation from a given body or substance called the sun. The one God, according to the figure, is but a compound of three subsistences, and in order to be parallel must necessarily proceed from some body, or substance, or source. If by parallel illustrations Mr. Cook means self-contradictions, then we can the better understand him. But his logic only makes mystery the more mysterious.

Where does it lead? Christ on Calvary, a mere subsistency and yet God—a mere rainbow—an emanation—in brief an illusion. Avaunt such darkness.

Or again, when I hear the cry, "My God, my God, why hast thou forsaken me!" tell me, is it the voice of the omnipotent Jehovah crying to himself? Begone such outrages against heaven's eternal truth. The Almighty will undoubtedly rebuke it in fiery indignation in the day of judgment.

If in God are three subsistences, and if in Him "are not three wills, three consciences, three intellects, three sets of affections;" or if "He is one substance, composed of three subsistences, and if these subsistences be not "individualities," where, we ask in the name of common sense, does the individual exist to be worshiped? Who has the conscience? Who has the intellect? Who possesses the affections? The altar erected by Mr. Cook most truly bears the inscription, "TO THE UNKNOWN AND UNKNOWABLE GOD."

But we are told by Paul, "The invisible things of Him from the creation of the world are clearly seen, being understood by the things that are made." Therefore, according to the scriptures, God has individual form; for man was created in the image of God, and he possesses individuality.

Christ was the "express image of his (the Father's) person," and Christ was an individual like unto his brethren. God has a will. "He doeth according to his will in the army of heaven,

and among the inhabitants of the earth; and none
can stay his hand, or say unto Him, What doest
thou?" Christ acknowledged this will, and exclaimed, "Lo, I come to do thy will, O God."
But Christ also had a will of his own, as his words
in the garden clearly show: "Not as I will, but
as thou wilt."

God also possessed one set of affections: "For
God so loved the world that He gave his only begotten Son, that whosoever believeth in Him
should not perish, but have everlasting life." But
Christ had another set of affections, which are
demonstrated in that He freely offered himself
for us. To use his own words: "Greater love
hath no man than this, that a man lay down his
life for his friends." That God has an intellect
of his own is manifest in all the works of his creation. But it is also manifest that Christ, too,
has an intellect, for his office alone calls for it.
He could not otherwise act as Mediator between
God and men, else common sense and the force of
language must needs be dethroned. We also
read, "And Jesus increased in wisdom."

As to the Holy Ghost, the scriptures clearly
demonstrate that as light proceeds from the sun,
so the Spirit emanates from God as a heavenly
radiance, but not as an entity or being. As the
sun is the grand central light of a system, and the
center of attraction as well, so God the Father,
the Almighty, the great I AM, is the source of all
light and truth and life. He is also the center of
attraction. "No man," says Christ, "can come

unto me except the Father who hath sent me draw him." As the moon reflects the light of the sun to the earth, so Christ reflected the Father's glory to men. As the rays of light from sun or moon reveal to us their form, and also the beauties of God's book of Nature, unfolding to our vision the wondrous designs of the creation, so the Spirit as the golden rays from God as the Sun of Righteousness, or as the silvery rays from Christ the Lamb reveals to us the marvelous beauties of his word. The Spirit also leads us to know God and Christ." "And this is life eternal, that they might know thee, THE ONLY TRUE GOD, (not a mere subsistency dependent upon other subsistences) and Jesus Christ whom thou has sent." And, "Hereby know we that we dwell in Him, and He in us, because He hath given us of his Spirit." And with Paul once more we say, "To us there is but ONE GOD, the Father, of whom are all things and we in Him; and ONE LORD JESUS CHRIST, by whom are all things, and we by Him."

"And it is the Spirit (says John) that beareth witness, because the Spirit is truth." But there is a difference between the Spirit acting upon us directly from the Father, and acting upon us through the Son, similar to the difference of light and heat acting upon the earth from sun or moon. We could not behold the full blaze of the Father's glory as mortals and live. Although we are "not of the night nor of the darkness," yet we walk in the night still. The sun has not yet arisen. The shadows of night still cover the heavens. How-

ever, "the day is at hand." But "God hath sent
the Spirit of his Son into our hearts," and like
the pale moonbeams of heaven, the sweet and hallowed radiance of Christ falls on our pathway,
which as a "shining light, shineth more and more
unto the perfect day." When Christ comes in
glory, then shall we see eye to eye, face to face,
and know even as we are now known of Him.

We have shown that in Mr. Cook's attempts to
prove the *triunity* of his three subsistences, he
really has proven their disunity, for since each
subsistency possesses a peculiarity incommunicable with the others, and since without union there
can be no real unity, therefore this trinity means
a disunited compound of incommunicable pecu-
liarities. We have also shown the two sides of
his parallel illustration as leading in opposite di-
rections; hence not parallel. We have further
shown from scripture and from reason that God
and Christ have separate and individual forms of
being; and that each has a set of affections, a will,
and an intellect, in contradistinction to Mr.
Cook's assertion of non-individuality, and that
"in God are not three wills," etc., only three subsistences, not persons; in one substance, not in
one person.

We will now pass on to his second lecture on
this subject, entitled "*The Trinity a Practical
Truth.*" He endeavors to show:

1. "That the doctrine of the Trinity has always
been held by orthodoxy for its practical value.
2. That it was the doctrine of the trinity which

excluded from power in human cultured beliefs the thought of God as fate. And that the scholarship of the Roman Empire shook off its belief in the fatalism of Paganism by learning the doctrine of the trinity."

We admit that the "falling away" predicted by Paul (II. Thess. ii. 3) began at a very early period; and also that at a very early date Babylon the Great arose, and that the first stamp on her forehead was MYSTERY. That all nations were to drink of her abominable wine is a Biblical fact. If this dogma of the *trinity* has always been held by *orthodoxy*, then this latter term must accordingly imply heterodoxy. What saith the scripture? Mr. Cook may produce a mighty array of names, yea and even the names of learned men, but the testimony of God is true. "Yea, let God be true, but every man a liar."

But Mr. Cook fails to prove that his definition of "triunity" was even known to these ancients; and we in the spirit and meekness of Christ challenge him to prove that it was a belief in *three subsistences in one substance* that caused the scholarship of Rome to cast off Paganism. We affirm that this philosophy of Mr. C. was unknown to the ancients.

That corrupt doctrine soon crept into the early church is evident from historic records; but that the grace and power of God were to a like extent withdrawn is also evident. That to-day there are multitudes "having a form of godliness but denying the power thereof," is still further evident. That these multitudes cleave to mythical traditions, and mystical solutions of mystery, in preference to simple truth, is apparent.

The apostle truly prophesied of the present time when he said: "The time will come when they will not endure sound doctrine; but after their own lusts (desires) shall they heap to themselves teachers, having itching ears: (we prefer "tickling the ear;" see Diag. ver.) and they shall turn away their ears from the truth, and shall be turned unto fables. (II. Tim. iv. 3, 4.) All this but proves that the truth is not always with the masses. The race is not always to the swift, nor the battle to the strong. "Strait is the gate and narrow is the way that leads to life, and few there be that find it." "Fear not, little flock, for it is your Father's good pleasure to give you the kingdom." In Mr. Cook's next definition he further tells us (p. 110):

(3.) "It is such that each subsistence is of the same dignity as the others."

In a former chapter we have proven this to be unscriptural in the matter of the two thrones. There is the throne of God, and there is the throne of the Lamb, but no third throne is ever mentioned in the scriptures. We further proved by the scriptures, that between Father and Son there was a distinction of honor, power and precedence, and that they were not equal. But just how subsistences who are not individualities or persons can sit on a throne at all, we would kindly ask Mr. C. to explain.

(4.) It is such that each subsistence is of the same substance with the others."

But, Mr. Cook, God is immortal. He only hath immortality. Therefore Christ being of the same substance was immortal. He therefore could not die, for that which is immortal is undying. Paul says, "Christ *died* for our sins, according to the scriptures." Was Paul wrong? Christ died and rose again the third day, was the gospel Paul preached. "But," it is objected, "it was only the body died, not the Christ himself." Accordingly Christ did not die. But if Christ—*Christos*, the anointed—implies the person or being of Christ, then that being died according to the teaching of Paul and the true sense of language. If the mere body, or so-called tenement of clay, died, then Paul calls that body, Christ. Therefore it matters not in what sense you may view it, Christ died.

We suppose death, according to Mr. Cook, was the peculiarity in Christ incommunicable to the other two subsistences, and according to popular theology that peculiarity had to do only with the body. We claim however that death was real in the case of Christ. That if unreal our salvation is in like manner fabulous. "Sin when it is finished brings forth death." Therefore, since Christ was wounded for our transgressions and bruised for our iniquities, in order to complete the work of atonement and salvation, He must needs die for our sins according to the scriptures; for since death is the end of sin, in order to triumph over it, Christ must needs follow on to that end.

Further, in order to become the first-fruits of them that *slept*, Christ must needs pass into the sleep of death. That Christ did die the scriptures clearly maintain. That He was held in the chains of death until the third day is also evident. And with the apostle we exclaim, "But now is Christ risen from the dead, and become the first-fruits of them that slept." But God died not, neither can He die; He only hath immortality. Therefore until Christ rose from the dead He was not the same in substance with God the Father. He rose to the power of an endless life, but He possessed it not in fulness until He rose. Christ was born of a woman, and was like unto his brethren. Who would say God had a similar origin? That Christ was born of a woman proves his mortality. That He was begotten by the power of the Highest proves the divinity of his origin, but it does not prove Him to be that original Being by whom He was begotten, nor yet a subsistency without which that Being could not be God. If Christ had been the same in substance with God the Father, He had no need to pass through the dark portals of death in order to attain to an immortal or a deathless state. Mr. Cook's next paragraph is as follows:

"It is such that the chief office of one subsistence is best expressed by the words Creator and Father; of a second subsistence, by the words Redeemer and Son; and of a third, by the words Sanctifier and Comforter."

We have already shown that according to Mr. C.'s parallel illustration each subsistency in his triunity was but an emanation from some unnamed source; and now according to the foregoing the words "Creator," "Father," "Redeemer," "Son," etc., are but *mere expressions* of those emanations, or more correctly, of the chief offices of those emanations or subsistences. On the following page (111) Mr. C., in defining the difference between a mystery and a contradiction, says:

"A self-contradiction is the inconsistency of a proposition with itself, or with its own implications. Now, if there is in the Trinity a self-contradiction, we must throw its propositions overboard, in the name of learning and of clear thought."

Since therefore we have shown inconsistences and self-contradictions both in the trinity and in Mr. C.'s propositions and definitions relating to the trinity, according to his own rule the whole of his subtle reasonings must be thrown overboard "in the name of learning and of clear thought." But we prefer to review just a little farther. The remaining proposition of the definition under consideration is as follows:

(6.) "It is such that each subsistence with the others is God. Beyond these six traits it is neither necessary nor possible to define the subsistences."

Therefore Christ with the Holy Ghost and the Father is God, and *vice versa;* and therefore the Father can be the Son, or the Son can become the Father, or the Holy Ghost can be either

Father or Son. After such a mix up as this there is little wonder that even Mr. C., as he flounders in the mire of mythology and fabulous traditions, exclaims that "beyond these . . . it is neither *necessary nor possible to define the subsistences.*"

But further, since according to this definition each subsistency with the other can be God, and since this in turn implies that the Father can be the Son, the Son the Father, and the Holy Ghost either of the two, therefore it is but an equivalent to the expression," God the Father, God the Son, and God the Holy Ghost." Nor can we see that there is any point gained in adopting the word "subsistency" for that of "person." A person is really a subsistency, and a subsistency literally implies anything that subsists.

The words *Father* and *Creator* as applied to one of the subsistences implies a being who can create or procreate. The word *Son* as applied to a second subsistency, implies a being who has been brought into an existence according to God's laws of procreation. And *Sanctifier* really conveys the idea of one who makes holy.

Thus when viewed in all their bearings, Mr. C.'s subsistences can be conceived as nothing less than beings or persons. Otherwise his definition of the Godhead is but an attempt to demonstrate that which is not demonstrable, having no semblance to anything in the heavens above or in the earth beneath.

Christ is our teacher. He is incomparably the greatest teacher that ever stood upon our earth.

His wisdom was from above. When only a mere boy He confounded the doctors of the law. Does Mr. C. acknowledge his teaching? If so, then He never breathed a word about a trinity of three subsistences. The voice from heaven said, "This is my beloved Son in whom I am well pleased, hear ye Him." When asked concerning the commandments, Jesus answered, "The first of all the commandments is, Hear, O, Israel: The Lord, our God, is one Lord; and thou shalt love the Lord, thy God, with all thy heart, and with all thy soul, and with all thy mind, and with all thy strength; this is the first commandment. And the second is like, namely this, thou shalt love thy neighbor as thyself. There is none other commandment greater than these. And the scribe said unto Him, well Master, thou hast said the truth; for there is *one God;* and there is none other but He." (Mark xii. 29-32.)

We are further told, "When Jesus saw that He answered *discreetly*, He said unto him, thou art not far from the kingdom of God." Again, Christ says, "This is life eternal, that they might know thee, the only true God, and JESUS CHRIST, whom thou hast sent."

There are no three subsistences mentioned here. Instead there is the one and only true God, and Jesus Christ mentioned—two glorious personages—the former of whom is above all and in all, the "blessed and only Potentate, the King of kings, and Lord of lords." The latter is glorious, yet subservient, as his own words imply,

"My Father is greater than I." "Lo, I come (in the volume of the book it is written of me) to do *thy will*, O God." Now He is exalted as the one *Mediator* between God and men. The fact of his acting as Mediator proves his subordination. As to his ultimate subjection to the rule of the great and eternal Jehovah, it is clearly stated in I. Cor. xv. 28. Such a text as, "He that hath seen me, has seen the Father," is brought forward as an objection. But this is easily understood, when we consider that He was the *express image* of his Father's person. Man may have gods many, existing in persons, subsistences, or in any other manner, as may be suggested by the imagination. But again we repeat the Apostle's terse definition," To us there is but one God, the Father, of whom are all things, and we in Him; and one Lord, Jesus Christ, by whom are all things, and we by Him."

And as for Mr. C.'s rainbow illustration, if viewed in one light, it is parallel with his definition of three subsistences. When the sun breaks forth and the dark clouds are dissipated, the rainbow vanishes. In like manner, when the Sun of Righteousness sends forth his effulgent rays of truth divine, the clouds and mists of error and of human tradition flee away, and the rainbow of three subsistences disappears. At the base of this latter rainbow there is just as little likelihood of finding the vessel of God's sparkling truth, as there is of finding the fabulous pot of gold at the base of the natural rainbow.

It may be claimed that much learning and men of astute minds maintain the dogma of a triunity, but Jesus said, "I thank thee, O Father, Lord of heaven and earth, because thou hast hid these things from the wise and prudent, and hast revealed them unto babes. Even so Father: for so it seemed good in thy sight." And Paul quotes: "For it is written, I will destroy the wisdom of the wise, and will bring to nothing the understanding of the prudent."

And now, to the one eternal Father be glory, honor, power and dominion forever. And to his only begotten Son, our Lord and Saviour, Jesus Christ, be praise and adoration throughout the endless ages. Amen.

CHAPTER VI.

HOW DOCTORS DIFFER—ANOTHER REVIEW.

We mentioned in a former chapter that doctors differ on this doctrine of the trinity. As has already been quoted, Mr. Cook says:

"Everybody of authority tells us, if you care for scholarly statement, that three *persons* never meant, in the standard discussions of this truth, three *personalities*, for these would be three gods. . . . All these scholars will tell you that it is no evasion of the difficulties of this theme for me to throw out of this discussion at once the word 'persons,' as misleading; for that word had originally no such meaning in the Latin tongue as the word person has in our own."

And instead he adopts the word subsistences. We have already shown this evasion to be invalid as a support to his argument. We will now quote from *Life and Work*, (magazine) bearing date March, 1881. The first article is entitled "The Holy Trinity." The author is Mr. J. Macleod, B. A., minister, Govan, near Glasgow, Scotland. We have previously shown this appellation, "The

Holy Trinity," to be unscriptural. The great teacher, Jesus of Nazareth, never once uses it nor authorizes its use: Mr. Macleod thus begins:

"The doctrine of the Holy Trinity is a deep mystery. But in what sense? Not as being contrary to, albeit immeasurably above, reason."

Before quoting further, let me here note that this is just what we have been by the grace of God demonstrating, viz: that the dogma of the trinity as taught by modern theologians is a profound MYSTERRY, neither taught in the Bible nor by the analogies of nature. It is found however on the prow, or figure-head, of Babylon's monster ship of modern times. (Rev. xvii. 5.)

"*Immeasurably above reason.*" Yes, and above God, as we will herewith show. Reason is one of the best gifts with which God has endowed his creature man. Christ reasoned with the doctors of the law. He possessed superior reasoning powers, for as He increased in stature He increased in wisdom also. His disciples must also have possessed bright reasoning faculties, for Jesus told them, "It is given unto you to know the mysteries of the kingdom of heaven." Paul used his reason, and he appealed to the reason of his followers. "I speak as to wise men," he exclaims; "judge ye what I say." The Bereans were approved for searching the scriptures, and using their reasoning or discerning powers. We thank God for the reasoning faculties He has given to man, and also for the liberty of using the same in order to a growth in knowledge.

It is ours to know in part. Let it be granted
that the doctrine of God and of Christ was once a
mystery; but now by the Spirit of God the vail
has been rent so that we can know in part. This
the scriptures clearly maintain. But that which
is known or revealed, even in *part*, is no longer a
mystery; for revelation or knowledge in part implies that something previously unrevealed or unknown has been brought within the grasp of
reason, knowledge being the result; and therefore
since we can obtain a knowledge in part of both
God and Christ from the scriptures, corroborated
by nature and by reason, and testified to by the
Spirit, therefore the doctrine can no longer be
claimed to be a mystery, but a revelation; not
above reason, but known in part by reason, by the
analogy of nature, and by the plain teaching of
the Holy Scriptures, through the aid of the Divine
Spirit which teaches "all things," and guides into
"all truth." But this so-called mystery dethrones
reason, which God has enthroned above the other
faculties of our mind, and hence it claims a position above God. And further it is placed above
God's word by many of its supporters, who immediately cry out "heresy" if you bring scripture
to bear against it. But God has magnified his
word above his name. (Ps. cxxxviii. 2.) Therefore those who would claim for any such dogma a
higher place than Holy Writ are only exalting
themselves above all that is called God.

Mr. M. tells us "the subject is to be approached
with awe." Yes, wherein it deals with the name

of Jehovah. But where it is the mere handling of a "Holy Trinity," as the one God of the Bible, there will be *awe;* yes, and we fear awe-stricken ones when the sands of such mythical traditions are swept away. (Rev. xviii. 10.) In the same paragraph he tells us "*This is life eternal to know God.*" He italicises and puts on the quotation marks. Now the unlearned or those unversed in scripture might take it for granted that this was a scriptural quotation. He speaks of this quotation as God revealing himself. Why not give it as it reads? Here is the sentence which follows it:

"Every sectarian error may be traced to defective conceptions of God, or misapprehensions of the verity of the Holy Trinity."

Are we to infer that a part of the scripture—the word of Christ himself—has been omitted lest there should be any "*misapprehension of the verity of the Holy Trinity?*" For instead of trinity we read as correctly quoted, "This is life eternal, that they might know thee, THE ONLY TRUE GOD, and JESUS CHRIST whom thou hast sent." (John xvii. 3.) There is certainly no "trinity" mentioned here. Instead, a knowledge of the two glorious personages would seem to be indispensable to life eternal. After attempting to prove the unity or oneness of God under his first head, under the second heading he conflicts with his theological brother, Mr. Cook, in regard to the tri-personality of God. We quote:

"It has been revealed that there is *Tri-Person-*

ality in Godhead. The mystery of the tri-personality of the Godhead is not greater than that
implied in any conception of an Infinite Being.
But it needs more guarded statement. The place
whereon we here stand is indeed holy ground.
When we speak of the Three Persons of the Godhead, the Father, the Son, and the Holy Ghost,
we have to guard against a twofold liability—on
the one hand, the liability to substitute for the
conception of *Three Persons, eternally subsisting as such,* that of *One Person known in three
modes of manifestation;* and, on the other hand,
the liability, while confessing the faith of the
Three Persons, not merely to distinguish, but
mentally to *divide,* the *One Substance of Godhead*
from the *Three Persons subsisting.* The Substance, or Being, of Godhead exists not, save in
the three Divine persons. All the properties of
Godhead are personal, and can only belong to persons. It is affirmed, then, (and affirmed because
most surely revealed) that there are to be adored
Three Living Ones—the Eternal Father, the
Eternal Son, and the Eternal Holy Ghost, in each
of whom subsists *the one Substance or Being of
Godhead,* and each of whom is distinctly the One
God—'*distinctly,* for each is not the other, and
yet *indivisibly,* because each is the same one
God: and the Substance of the Godhead cannot
be divided.'"

What does Mr. Cook say to such a definition
as this? When compared with his there is a
direct contradiction of terms. How can they be
in the *unity* of one faith? One acknowledges and
prays to subsistences; the other, to persons. The
former declares that the word *persons,* used as
relating to the Trinity, is "misleading." The

latter affirms most positively that "The Substance, or Being, of Godhead *exists not save in the three Divine persons.*" Thus doctors differ, and unless both give ear to the voice of the Spirit, (Rev. iii. 18) we must leave them to their differences. If the blind will lead the blind they must inevitably sink together in the mire of error, no matter how great their knowledge of letters may be.

That there is not a "tri-personality in Godhead," according to the scriptures, we have already shown in previous chapters. The word Godhead only occurs three times in the scriptures, Acts xvii. 29; Rom. i. 20; Col. ii. 9. But the Greek word from which "Godhead" is derived, occurs five several times, being twice used in II. Pet. i. 3, 4. Here it is rendered Divine.. In the former quotations authorities differ as to the rendering. Some translators render the Greek words severally used, "Deity" instead of Godhead. (See Emphatic Diaglott, ver. of N. T.) Neither the Greek nor the English words imply plurality of idea. Take for example Col. ii. 9. "For in Him, (i. e. Christ) dwelleth all the fulness of the Godhead, (*theotetos*) bodily." The word *bodily*, as here used, means "corporeally," and not "wholly," or "completely," as might be inferred. (See Greenfield's N. T. Lexicon.)

But a body is not complete without the head. God is that Head. While the fulness of his glory dwells in Christ bodily, i. e. as relating to Christ and his church, which is in turn his, (Christ's) body, yet the fulness of God is not seen until we see Him as Head, i. e. over all; "One God and Father of all, who is *above* all, and through all, and in you all." (Eph. iv. 6.) In like manner we can be in the "fulness of Christ" bodily, but that fulness shall not be seen until Christ, as Head, shall reign over all. (12, 13.) That the church or body of Christ shall attain to the "fulness of Christ," does not imply that the church shall constitute the Christ himself, nor yet that any member thereof shall be on equal footing with Him. No more does Christ possessing the "fulness of the Godhead bodily," i. e. corporeally, imply that He shall be the very God himself, nor yet as regards power and position, does it imply He shall be on an equality with Him. The scripture is clear on this point. "When all things shall be subdued unto Him, (i. e. Christ) then shall the Son also himself be *subject unto Him*, (i. e. God) that put all things under Him, that God may be all in all." (I. Cor. xv. 28.) As there is one glory of the sun and another of the moon, so is there one glory of the Father and another of the Son, according to the scriptures. But what does Mr. M. mean by this:

"It is affirmed, then, (and affirmed because most surely revealed) that there are to be adored *Three Living Ones*—the Eternal Father, the Eternal Son, and the Eternal Holy Ghost."

It is an easy matter to affirm. It is another thing to prove. But we are told, "*affirmed because most surely revealed."* Where revealed? Not in the Bible we affirm, and we challenge the world to disprove this affirmation. Is the Bible the standard of true faith? Then the Bible nowhere tells you of " Three Living Ones " to be adored, neither in the present nor yet in the great hereafter. The Eternal Father, Eternal Son, Eternal Holy Ghost as a three one God is purely an emanation from a corrupt theology, and is an addition to God's Word when applied thereto. When Stephen saw heaven opened he beheld the glory of God, and Jesus standing on the right hand of God.

"The revelation of Jesus Christ, which God gave unto Him," tells us that the multitude exclaimed, " Worthy is the Lamb that was slain *to receive* power, and riches, and wisdom, and strength, and honor, and glory, and blessing. And every creature which is in heaven, and on the earth, and under the earth, and such as are in the sea, and all that are in them heard I saying, Blessing, and honor, and glory, and power be unto HIM that sitteth upon the throne, (i. e. God) and unto the LAMB for ever and ever." (Rev. v. 12, 13.)

When the seventh angel sounds, the kingdoms of this world become the kingdom of our LORD, and of his CHRIST. (xi. 15.) The "Lord God Almighty," and the Lamb are the temple of the city of our God. (xxi. 22.) And the throne of GOD and of the LAMB shall be in it. (xxii. 3.) Therefore we find only two personages mentioned to be adored when we take God's word for it. The one is the Eternal Father, the other the only begotten of the Father, the Lamb slain, He that liveth and was dead, but is now alive for evermore *to receive honor, glory, etc.;* for what He has was given Him of the Father.

We deem it unnecessary to add more on this point. As it is written, "The wise shall understand." If man will not believe the testimony of Moses and the prophets, nor the testimony of Him who rose from the dead, and his holy apostles, nothing short of God's revelation in judgment will convince him. Then shall he know the God who "will judge the world in righteousness by THAT MAN WHOM HE HATH ORDAINED." (Acts xvii. 31.)

Mr. Macleod exclaims, in conclusion: "O the preciousness of the One Mediator between God and men, the man Christ Jesus!" But he fails to know the preciousness of this one Mediator, if he "abideth not in the doctrine of Christ." (II. John, 9.) How can he claim to abide in the doctrine of Christ when he says that Christ is the very God himself? Then as Mediator He must needs mediate to himself. If to a superior He mediates, then He must be inferior. The office of Mediator calls for such terms as these to exist. Christ's own words, "My Father is greater than I," prove that such terms do exist. (See also I. Cor. xv. 28.) Therefore according to the scriptures God the Father is greater than Christ the Son, and the exaltation of the Son is due to the Father. "Every spirit that confesseth not that *Jesus Christ* is come in the flesh is not of God." (I. John iv. 3.) The dogma of the trinity as defined by these theologians confesses that it was God, even the Father, who came in the flesh. Hence the spirit (if spirit at all) that leads them, according to the scriptures, cannot be of God. The conclusion is sad, but it is inevitable. The Father is no more the Son than the procreator is the being procreated. No son can be as old as his father, i. e., individually. "God only hath immortality." He is the one eternal God. Therefore the Son cannot be eternal, else He is not a Son in the true acceptation of the term. But He is called "the only begotten of the Father," which proves Him not only to be a Son, but also as begotten, even as others are begotten, only by divine process, according to God's unchangeable law of procreation. Mr. M. concludes:

"Lastly, while you search the word, pray for the illumination of the Holy Ghost."

Which, if heeded, and attended to in sincerity and truth, would lead even himself out of such darkness to the acknowledgment of the one God of the Bible and the one Mediator between God and men, the man Christ Jesus; and also to see that the Holy Spirit is not a person at all, but the "living water," the life-giving power of God, conferred on man to fit him for an immortal state. But instead, he continues:

"Thus shall we advance, step by step, in the knowledge of God the Father, God the Son, and

God the Holy Ghost, WHOM to know is LIFE EVER-
LASTING."

It is written in the Word: "If any man shall
add unto these things, (contained therein) God
shall add unto him the plagues that are written
in this book." (Rev. xxii. 18.) Now the forego-
going is an addition to anything taught in the
Word. Where do you find "God the Holy Ghost,"
outside of traditional theology? Echo answers,
"Where?" And yet we heard with our own ears,
while on the Atlantic recently, a leading professor,
(Dr. Noyes) pronounce as a benediction: "Now
may the grace of God the Father, God the Son,
and God the Holy Ghost be with you all," etc.
Now I regard that man with respect. He has a
tender loving heart, and means well, but the error
breathed in prayer I must and do reject. There
is no scriptural ground for such an utterance, as
we have clearly shown.

What more shall we say? We have shown the
dogma of the trinity to be unscriptural, and contrary to nature and to reason. We have also
shown the definitions of the same as given by
learned men to be illogical, unscriptural, and full
of self-contradictions. Mr. Macleod says:

"Unless we hold fast the faith of the Holy
Trinity, the record of Revelation becomes unin-
telligible."

We affirm that it is the belief in this dogma
that has blinded the eyes of millions so that they
cannot see for themselves, and they merely accept
what is taught them unquestionably, because

"our learned minister" says so. We despise not
education. It is a boon from heaven when properly applied. But with all their learning both
Mr. Cook and Mr. Macleod have failed to make
the trinity as a doctrine intelligible. Nor can
any mortal make it intelligible in the light of
God's word.

The grand key-note of the Bible is, "There is
but *one* God, the Father," and besides Him there
is none other. And there is but *one* Mediator
between God and men. When the Bible is viewed
in this light by the aid of the Spirit—or eyesalve
of heaven—the "wayfaring men, though fools,
shall not err therein." Then mystery dissolves,
myths vanish, and fables flee away; and instead,
that wisdom which is from above, which is gentle
and easy to be entreated, leads us onward in the
ever brightening path. "Her ways are ways of
pleasantness, and all her paths are peace." Mr.
M. further says:

"Except we hold fast the faith of the Holy
Trinity, our personal salvation is left without
basis or reality."

Therefore he claims a belief in this dogma as
the foundation of their faith. Just what we
have been endeavoring to show. Christ says,
"Hear, O Israel, the Lord our God, is ONE LORD."
Paul says, "Other foundation *can no man lay*
than that which is laid, *which is Jesus Christ.*"

Which, reader, do you prefer, Mr. M.'s foundation, or that of Christ and of Paul? The former
is darkness. The latter is light. The one is

6

error. The other is the unchangeable Word of God. O God, we pray, open the eyes of the blind.

Once more we shall ring the glorious old gospel bell hung up in the spiritual heavens by the hand of Paul. Let the earth keep silence and give ear, "Be silent, O all flesh before the Lord." His truth endureth to all generations." Hark, it gives a certain sound :

"TO US THERE IS BUT ONE GOD,
THE FATHER,
OF WHOM ARE ALL THINGS, AND WE IN HIM; AND
ONE LORD, JESUS CHRIST,
BY WHOM ARE ALL THINGS, AND WE BY HIM."

This is the true light that rejoiceth the heart and maketh wise the simple.

> And in this precious light of thine
>   Blest Father guide me still:
> O in the darkness let it shine,
>   That men may do thy will.
> Blest are they who on God rely,
>   Whose precious truth doth sanctify.

CHAPTER VII.

MAN'S ORIGIN.

" What is man?"—Job vii. 17.

The pertinent "whys" and "wherefores" of a child should not be despised. Mankind are by nature endowed with reason. The whys and wherefores of children are but the buddings of reason. As an instinctive or inherent power reason endéavors to trace everything to a source. Consequently it is quite natural for man to be interested in tracing the origin of his own being. " Know thyself" is an important adage, but it is in general too much neglected.

Assumptions as to the origin, nature and destiny of man are easily formed; but it is quite another thing to prove these assumptions. That new and speculative theories are ever and anon being launched forth upon the world's sea of thought is not always an evidence of intellectual advancement. Nor is it always a sign of their truthfulness because they are accepted by the masses. Everything of genuine worth should be sustained by incontrovertible evidences, and should accord with the Bible, science, nature and reason. The Bible gives an account of man's origin. It is rather meager, but we should remember that those early historians had not the educational advantages of this age. "The Lord God formed man of the dust of the ground," is a simple, yet self-evident truth, with which nature and science both agree. Ice is a solid. Bring it in contact with heat and it is soon dissolved to water. This latter state proves that out of water it was formed at first, whether we had been cognizant of the process of congelation or not. So with man, when he, as a solid, corporeal being, comes in contact with the blasting wind of death, he is soon resolved to dust. This latter state of man, but proves that out of dust he was formed at first. This accords with what is written, "For dust thou art, and unto dust shalt thou return." That man resolves again to dust is evident. While mortality lasts it is daily evinced. That mortals breathe to-day is *prima facie* evidence that they were endowed with this faculty when created. But this breath of life further demonstrates that mortals live and have a being. All of which goes but to prove the correctness of the Biblical statement. (Gen. ii. 7.)

As to the manner of Eve's creation, as recorded in Genesis, if we but consider the greatness or the omnipotence of the Creator, there is nothing so very wonderful in it after all. It coincides, although in a higher degree, with the analogies of nature. It must be admitted that man is lord of creation as pertaining to this orb. Man considers it but a common process to cut a scion from a tree or plant out of which to raise another tree or plant. The farmer of to-day deems it no uncommon thing to cut a potato in slices from which to raise whole potatoes. In like manner vinegar plants may be divided, and each continue in growth. " But," it is objected, " the animal kingdom cannot be thus acted on by man, hence the analogy fails to apply." It only fails, we reply, providing God and man, as the two actors, are equal; but if God be greater than man then the analogy may be sustained.

Man as a flesh and blood creature is not empowered by the Creator thus to act on flesh and blood creatures, even though they may be inferior to himself. Neither is there any necessity for such actions since the law of procreation fulfills the demand. But he is empowered thus to act upon the vegetable world as already shown.

God is, in an infinite degree, greater than man. This must be conceded by all. His nature is also spiritual. The power of life dwells within his being. He is immortal. Men are but as trees in his sight, who live and bloom for a season, and then die. This figure is Biblical. Hence it would be limiting the. creative and life-giving power of God to deny that He could take a scion from a human being, and by his word of command cause it to grow into another member of the same family.

Further, which would be the easier or more

rational of the two, for God to form the second
being from the dust, or from a scion of the being
already formed out of the dust? If we follow the
analogies of nature the latter is the more rational.
It was certainly in his power to do either. The
nurseryman cuts his scions from plants already
formed; he cannot take them from the dust. According to natural law, a scion must have the
principle of life within it in order to growth. God
is the author of natural law. Hence God only
fulfilled his own law in taking a scion, which had
the principle of life within it, from a being already
created, in order to the formation of the second.
"So God created man in his own image, in the
image of God created He him; male and female
created He them. And God blessed them, and
God said unto them, Be fruitful, and multiply,
and replenish the earth, and subdue it."

That "God created man in his own image"
strikes Darwin's theory of evolution with a
deadly blow. "*In his (i. e. God's) own image.*"
These are the words which draw the line between
direct creation and the process of evolution.
Christ, as the Son of God, must either be accepted or rejected. If rejected, the grand system
which has revolutionized and civilized the world
must also be cast away. This includes all that
makes life really happy, and hope for the future
sure, with all the grand triumphs of faith and
displays of heaven-born heroism. To give up
which, we must needs trample reason under foot;
cast away our senses; accept all things only as

apparent, and nothing as real; reject the mass of
evidence, and accept the minimum, and acknowledge the brightest minds of earth to be but darkness; and we must also denounce the only path
which leads from evil to good, from sin to holi-
·ness, from iniquity to virtue as a mere phantasm.
And the light which has shone upon earth's desert
drear for over 1800 years, which has cheered so
many lone hearts, which has sent gleams of comfort into so many saddened homes; which has
raised the suffering ones above the dark billows
of affliction, and which has lit up the heavens
over the sea of death to so many millions of our
race must be cast away as a false glimmer—as
ignus fatuus. If Christ be accepted as the Son
of.God and the Saviour of mankind, then He is the
" express image of his Father's person." This
granted, we are further told, He was "like unto
his brethren." But Christ bore the image of
God, at the same time He bore the image of
man, therefore, man must bear the image of God ;
all of which but goes to prove the statement
given in Genesis relating to man's creation.

But we hesitate not to assert that all the intelligences of heaven bear the same image.
Angels have appeared on earth, and have been
designated as "men" in " shining garments" or
" white apparel." Christ tells us that they who
obtain the resurrection from the dead, " are equal
unto the angels." This likeness or image of God
in man is what elevates him above the brute creation.

Much as has been said about the theory of evolution it cannot be sustained by real living evidences. As another has tersely said, "Darwin endeavors to make man a little higher than the tadpoles," but the scripture triumphantly exclaims, "Thou hast made him a little lower than the angels, and hast crowned him with glory and honor."

When I was a boy I did not like reading over the genealogical portions of the Bible, but let me go over these ten thousand times rather than wade through the Darwinian genealogy once. "Give him credit for his bright ideas," said a gentleman one day to me, while in Scotland. "Bright ideas!" What brightness, we ask, is there in a theory which degrades man and defames the Creator, and Darwin's theory does nothing less. But had he faith in his own theory, and what would such a faith lead to? After penning and compiling a large volume on the subject, he says, "I am aware that much remains doubtful, but I have endeavored to give a fair view of the whole case." (Descent of Man, p. 613.) And on page 619 he tells us that he would as soon be descended from a monkey or an old baboon as from one of the savages of our race.

"*Much remains doubtful!*" Yes, thank God for it, and that "*much*," wherein it applies to the theory of man's descent by evolution, simply means the whole. For two thousand years of time are surely sufficient in which to prove such a theory either false or true. In that time history fails to record any baboons turning into men, or *vice versa*. And where are the proofs in the present? This doubtful faith, if faith you may call it, leads but to the mire of vain speculation and uncertainty. The scriptures would term it science, or knowledge, falsely so-called.

Of this theory of evolution, Bishop Simpson in his Yale lecture says: " Does the scientist tell me of the boundlessness of space? I rejoice; for they tell me of the work of my Father's hand. I believe in the survival of the fittest; for the Christian will survive the wreck of matter and the crush of worlds. If the watchmaker could make a watch which would evolve other watches, each finer and better, admiration for his skill would be enhanced. If my Creator has worked upon the plan of evolution, what is to hinder my being overwhelmed by the wonders of the present age? Give Christianity as much time for the accomplishment of its work as the scientist demands for evolution! We will find the great work of Christianity accomplished before the infidel scientists can procure the proof of their claims."

The closing words of Darwin in the volume previously named, are as follows:

" We must, however, acknowledge, as it seems to me, that man with all his noble qualities, with sympathy which feels for the most debased, with benevolence which extends not only to other men but to the humblest living creature, with his god-like intellect which has penetrated into the movements and constitution of the solar system—with

all these exalted powers—man still bears in his
bodily frame the indelible stamp of his lowly
origin." (p. 619.)

But, on the other hand, do we not behold in
man's "noble qualities," in his heart-felt and
wide-spread "sympathy," in his extensive "benevolence," in his "god-like intellect," which has
even penetrated into the depths of the heavens
above—in "all these exalted powers"—do we not
behold even in these, Darwin's own expressions,
the stamp of a divine creation in man—the image
of his Creator—which so far transcends the Darwinian "stamp" that the latter can only be seen
through the illusive glasses of a false and danger-
ous theory, which not only withholds the glory
due to God, but defames Him in that it defames
his noblest work of creation? O, vain man, that
degradest thyself and defamest thy Creator, thou
shalt see thy folly when man, even thy fellow,
shall sit in judgment upon thy works. As Paul
says, "Do ye not know that the saints shall judge
the world." "Know you not that we shall judge
angels." Then shall Christ be glorified in his
saints, when God shall clothe his creature man
with immortality, and the sons of God shall shout
aloud for joy. Avaunt Darwinism with all thy
wily snares, with all thy doubts and fears, with
all thy vain speculations. For "man still bears
in his bodily frame," in his comprehensive mind,
in the noble qualities of his soul, the indelible
stamp of his Creator. Welcome precious Truth,
thou comest with heavenly freshness and renewed

power home into my soul. Like the dove sent
forth from the ark, my mind has flown over the
flood of Darwinian ideas, but it could find no
resting spot thereon. Death, darkness and destruction are beneath the subtle currents of this
science falsely so-called. Welcome Ark window,
thou precious light of heaven. Welcome resting
place above the tide of destruction. And to thy
name Omnipotent Creator we would ascribe
honor, power, praise, and glory. Thou didst
make man in thine own image. He fell, but redemption through thy beloved Son restores that
image again. Who dare say thine image is beheld in the grimaces of a baboon! But man
filled with thy sweet Spirit divine, looketh
upward to the heavens, and his countenance all-
beaming with joy unspeakable and full of glory
reflecteth thy image still. Blest be thy name, O
God! When ushered in that auspicious morn,
even first creation's dawn, the morning stars together sang. And for thy mighty works of creation—even for thy creature man—praise waiteth
for Thee, O God in Zion still. Eternity alone
will utter all Thy praise. Then shall thine image
all perfected in us shine for aye.

But again, the Adamic creation is objected
to because that science has discovered unmistakable traces of a pre-Adamic race. Science
and scripture should agree. We claim that they
do agree. For when we examine the scriptures
aright we find that allusion is evidently made to
a pre-Adamic race in the words, "Be fruitful,

and multiply, and *replenish* the earth." (Gen. i. 28.) The same is repeated in the ninth chapter, first verse.

" *Replenish*." The word implies "to fill again after having been emptied," "to stock anew," and is derived from the latin *re*, again, *plenus*, full. "Multiply and replenish the earth" are inseparable terms, and since they apply to man at the Adamic creation, they also imply that the earth had been at some time prior to that creation plenished with mankind, else the term *replenish* would not have been used.

For edification the reader can compare other words beginning with the same prefix, such as redemption, resurrection and regeneration. To replenish your house with furniture implies that it has been filled with the same class of material before. In order to the redemption of the body there must necessarily have been a body to redeem. The doctrine of the resurrection evidently teaches the raising again of bodies which once stood upon the earth. So with regeneration, it points us forward to a time of second birth or a second generating of beings once before generated.

So the command to *replenish* the earth clearly implies that it had been peopled at some time previous thereto. And consequently science and the Bible agree upon this point. But a thought just here. This command to multiply and replenish the earth does not apply to the present time, although it is used by many as a cloak for licentiousness and as an authority for polygamy.

Such are but wresting the word of God to their own destruction; for the earth has been replenished, and in many parts to-day it is over-peopled. In numerous districts an excessive population cry out for daily bread.

But to return. The Bible doctrine of man's origin has been shown to harmonize with science, nature and reason. Therefore we not only accept its truth, but thank God therefor. Contrasted with the Darwinian theory the former is comforting light, the latter is misleading and repugnant darkness. The one glorifies God and exalts his creature man. The other defames the Creator and degrades his creature man. Accepting the former we can behold the glory of the grand scheme of redemption. Accepting the latter the grandest light that has ever fallen upon the path of mortals—the Christian's beacon light and polar star—dissipates as a mirage. But the beacon of Christianity still sheds its heavenly light on this dark world; and Christ as the polar star of the system still shines resplendent in the spiritual heavens, and the Bible theory of man's origin instead of being obliterated by the conflicts with science so-called, rises transcendent over every speculative theory of man. Our view as to man's estate is epitomized in the following stanza:

> Out of dust at first created,
>   Here, as mortal, lives and dies;
> Out of dust regenerated,
>   When through Christ the dead arise.

CHAPTER VIII.

MAN'S NATURE.

Man is either mortal or immortal by nature. The evidences of his mortality are manifold. Who has not seen a funeral cortege? Who has not lost a friend? Death everywhere wields his dreaded sword upon this earth as yet. Immortal means undying. It is the nature of God. God only hath immortality. Theology claims for man a dual nature—a body, and an immortal soul. When the body dies, this soul, it is claimed, as a living, conscious, acting entity, flees upwards to heaven. "Away up somewhere among the stars," is a phrase well known to theological writers. There they say the immortal saints, or rather the souls of the saints, dwell. Than this there can be no myth more foundationless. It is a mere chimera. God's word nowhere vouches for such. The reward of the saints is glory, honor and immortality. Such is not bestowed until the seventh angel sounds his trump. (Rev. xi. 15-18.)

But is man really a dual being? The Bible evidently teaches to the contrary. Nature gives us no parallel illustration of it. Reason opposes it. And science declares, "that no two bodies can occupy the same portion of space at the same time." Where then does this immortal soul exist? Does it abide in the mind of man? Some claim that it is the soul which thinks. The Psalmist says concerning man, "His breath goeth forth, he returneth to his earth; in that very day his thoughts perish." (cxlvi. 4.) "For in death there is no remembrance of thee; in the grave who shall give thee thanks?" (vi. 5.) "The dead praise not the Lord, neither any that go down into silence." (cxv. 17.)

Science has discovered, while experimenting upon a man's skull which had been fractured, his life in the meantime having been sustained for a period of several months, that while the fractured portion pressed upon the brain total unconsciousness was the result. The operators succeeded, however, after a time, in raising the fractured part, thus relieving the brain, and immediately thought commenced just where it had left off when the accident occurred. Where, we inquire, was the immortal soul during this period of silence? Or is it possible to silence an immortal entity by a slight mortal mishap, such as we have related? A certain doctor with whom we were conversing upon this subject objected to the foregoing example of soul silence, by saying, "But life in this instance was still within the body." To which we replied, "If while life was in the body the soul can be silenced by such injuries to the mortal frame, we can only infer that deeper silence would be the result were life to be totally extinguished."

It is required of man to give a reason of the hope that is within him, and if his hope be that his soul shall flee to heaven at death, he ought surely to be able to locate that soul in the present mortal state. It is an easy matter to repeat the words of the catechism:

"The souls of believers are at their death made perfect in holiness, and do immediately pass into glory; and their bodies, being still united to Christ, do rest in their graves till the resurrection."

But it is quite another thing to prove the assertions made. Even the learned Dr. Boyd, of Scotland, in writing on this paragraph says:

"The statement is clear and authoritative; but it goes into no details. No more does Holy Scripture. We need not pretend but that we should like to know a great deal more than we do. But, for whatever reason (and one can think of more than one weighty reason) the Christian revelation maintains a solemn reserve. This is a vital characteristic of it. If there were a chapter in the New Testament which gave us particulars of the present state and life of those who have gone before us, you know how that chapter would be read and re-read. But it is not there."—*St. Stephen's Parish Magazine.*

If the statement of the catechism be "clear and authoritative," why does not this learned man show wherein it is maintained by the scripture? Instead he admits that upon this point "the Christian revelation maintains a solemn reserve."

This is, at-least, an honest admission. But honest hearts demand more. A dogma of such pretentious magnitude should be sustained by truth. Even were the dogma true, such admissions only tend to weaken its force. But the writer makes no attempt to destroy its verity by his admission, for he afterward continues in his endeavors to sustain it, but fails to give his readers a single "weighty reason" in its support.

"We are to honor all (men) because all are immortal," is a statement we quote from a Boston paper. Then the writer of the article makes the assertion, "The Bible teaches it." We simply deny the assertion. Let us examine. Man says, "All are immortal." The Bible says, "God only hath immortality." (I. Tim. vi. 16.) Hence a contradiction. But if all are immortal there can be no more death, for that which is immortal cannot die. Therefore, the very fact that death prevails proves the assertion false. According to the word of Jesus, only those who shall be "accounted worthy to obtain that world, and the resurrection from the dead," shall be equal unto the angels, and shall die no more. (Luke xx. 35, 36.) To attempt an evasion of the point by stating that the body only dies, is mere quibbling. When we say a man dies, we mean the man— the thinking, acting, conscious being.

7

If man be mortal he must seek for immortality.
If he be already immortal then he is really as a
god. Let man however divest himself of the delusive ideas that have been inculcated in his
mind from early youth, and loose himself from
the chains or trammels of human traditions, and
he at once discovers he is but mortal. But on the
other hand let him drink of the wine of Babylon
and he will sing of his having

> "A never-dying soul to save,
> And fit it for the sky."

The idea of saving a never-dying soul is simply
absurd. If it be of God, and the Bible tells us,
"The gift of God is eternal life," then it is safe.
If it be of the devil, man cannot save him nor
anything that belongs to him.

As to the immortal life, man cannot obtain it
until the "book of life" is opened. This book is
not opened until the Judge is seated on the "great
white throne." Then the dead, small and great,
stand before God and are judged according to
their works. (Rev. xx. 11, 12.) In the present
our "life is hid with Christ in God. When
Christ, who is our life, shall appear, then (and
not till then) shall ye also appear with Him in
glory." (Col. iii. 3, 4.) "For since by man came
death, by man came also the resurrection of
the dead. For as in Adam, (i. e. those who continue in the Adamic, or fleshly, or sinful state,
see Rom. viii. 13) all die, even so in Christ, (i. e.
those who have put on Christ, or have been
grafted into Him) shall all be made alive. But

every man in his own order; Christ the first-
fruits; afterwards they that are Christ's at his
coming." (I. Cor. xv. 21-23.) Now those that
lay claim to immortality prior to that "coming"
must either concede that they are in error outright, or that they are tossed on the horns of a
three-fold dilemma, viz: That the resurrection is
already past; that the second advent of our Lord
is over; or that the devil told the truth in the
beginning when he said to man, "Thou shalt not
surely die." But such generally get past it by
cleaving to the mystery, or rather absurdity, that
man has been in the possession of immortality
from the creation.

The Bible tells us that we but seek for immortality here. (Rom. ii. 7.) And that Jesus
brought "life and immortality to light through
the gospel." Hence springs up mystery. However, as Paul says, "Let God be true but every
man a liar." According to the scriptures, man
is mortal. When God says he shall die, he dies;
and death means death, not life. Here, man is
but a probationer for immortality. If he serves
God faithfully he receives the earnest of the life
to come, in this the day of probation. This is
the seed of the body celestial, (I. Cor. xv. 38) or
in other words, that which shall quicken our mortal body at the appearing of Christ. "The last
enemy that shall be destroyed is death." (I. Cor.
xv. 26.) But death is not swallowed up in victory until "this corruptible shall have put on
incorruption, and this mortal shall have put on

immortality. (ver. 54.) According to the scriptures this does not take place at death, but "at the last trump; for the trumpet shall sound, and the dead shall be raised incorruptible, and we shall be changed." (ver. 52.) This doctrine is plain. A child may understand it.

According to the dogma of the immortality of the soul, death is no enemy at all, but the best friend mankind has, and thus it teaches the very opposite of the word of truth. Yonder is a poor bird, just caught and caged. See how it beats its bosom against the cruel wires. Would it not be a dear friend to the poor captive who would open the cage and set the prisoner free? So with man if this immortal soul doctrine be true. This mortal body is but the tenement or cage. The soul is the bird. Death as a *friend* comes along and opens the door and the bird escapes to fields of everlasting bliss. Such a tradition may be considered inspiring, and may form a theme for the poet, but when done it is but imaginary. To this dogma may be attributed the delusions of modern spiritualism, for it is the source from whence this latter day monstrosity springs.

A friend of the writer once said, "Take away my immortal soul and you can take my hope, my Bible, my all." Now, no one wanted to take away her "immortal soul." It was our desire to undeceive her, and to convince her that according to the scriptures she was but mortal. The trump of God alone will convince such. The Bible does not say, "God will bring all the immortal souls and reunite them to their respective bodies in that day;" but it does say, "Them who sleep in Jesus will God bring with Him."

Jesus does not say, "The hour is coming in the which all the immortal souls in heaven and in hell (place of torment) shall hear his voice and shall come forth to judgment." But He does say, "The hour is coming in the which all that are in the graves shall hear his voice and shall come forth; they that have done good unto the resurrection of life; and they that have done evil unto the resurrection of condemnation." (John v. 28, 29.) Again, quoting from the article previously mentioned, the writer truly says: "The good and the bad will stand before the bar of judgment." But this does not sustain his point. If the doctrine of the immortality of the soul be true, what need of a judgment bar? The souls of the saints have entered glory, and have been enjoying the felicity of heaven; while on the other hand the wicked have entered punishment and have been enduring the pangs of a hell of torment. Shall God call both before Him to send both back to the same places respectively? Such is indeed a monstrous doctrine, and we repeat, the Bible nowhere teaches it. Immortality is not once mentioned in the Old Testament scriptures. The following are the only passages in the whole Bible where the term is used:

"To them who by patient continuance in well-doing, seek for glory and honor and immortality, eternal life." (Rom. ii. 7.)

"Our Saviour Jesus Christ, who hath abolished
death, and hath brought life and immortality to
light through the gospel." (II. Tim. i. 10.)

"Behold, I show you a mystery. We shall not
all sleep, but we shall all be changed in a moment,
in the twinkling of an eye, at the last trump; for
the trumpet shall sound, and the dead shall be
raised incorruptible, and we shall be changed.
For this corruptible must put on incorruption,
and this mortal must put on immortality. So
when this corruptible shall have put on incorruption, and this mortal shall have put on immortality, then shall be brought to pass the saying that
is written, Death is swallowed up in victory."
(I. Cor. xv. 51-54.)

"Now unto the King eternal, immortal, invisible, the only wise God, be honor and glory forever and ever. Amen." (I. Tim. i. 17.)

"The blessed and only Potentate, the King of
kings, and Lord of lords; who only hath immortality." (I. Tim. vi. 15, 16.)

Now, in all these scriptures there is not one
word said about an immortal soul. And instead
of the rendering of Paul being, "The immortal
soul shall at death immediately pass into glory,
and at the sounding of the trump shall return
and be united to its body," we find that at the
last trump the dead are to be raised, and the significant statement is used, "this *mortal* must put
on immortality." And further, "when this *mortal* shall have put on immortality, then (and not
till then) shall be brought to pass the saying that
is written, Death is swallowed up in victory."
Out of Christ there is no promise of immortality,

according to the scriptures. In and through Christ immortality, or eternal life, is promised to the faithful at his second appearing. "The righteous shall then "go into life eternal." Christ says, "I am the resurrection and the life." The keys of death and of the grave are in his hand. But there is no promise of life in its fulness, until the dead are raised. The "Book of Life" is opened at the time of judgment, as has already been shown.

Job says, "Man dieth and wasteth away: yea, man giveth up the ghost, and where is he? As the waters fail from the sea, and the flood decayeth and drieth up: so man lieth down and riseth not: till the heavens be no more they shall not awake, nor be raised out of their sleep." (xiv. 10-12.) The Psalmist says, "As for me, . . . I shall be satisfied, when I awake, with thy likeness." And thus we might go on through the prophets, but we withhold their testimonies for the doctrine of the resurrection, which will be considered farther on. Since, therefore, the terms "never dying soul," "immortal soul," etc., are not to be found in the Bible, and since the scriptures do not sustain the dogma which claims for man a dual being, one fleshly and corrupt, the other spiritual and incorrupt, the latter capable of a separate existence, while the former molders into dust; in the light of that same word—the unchangeable word of God—we must reject the dogma as error. But this dogma is not merely an error, it is a serious one; for it mars

the beauty of God's word, destroys the doctrine
of the resurrection, which was virtually the hope
of the ancient fathers, and does away with the
necessity of a future judgment, and it perverts
and misleads its votaries. This latter clause is
the only serious crime with which it can be really
charged, for the word of God cannot be harmed
by mortals. Even though a mountain of traditions and myths be piled upon the good old Bible
the fire of the day of wrath will consume them
all, but the word of the Lord will endure forever.

On this dogma of inherent immortality Justin
Martyr puts forth a certain sound. He says, "If
you meet with some who are called Christians,
(referring to the Gnostics) who say that there is
no resurrection of the dead, but that at death
their souls are received up into heaven, do not
regard them as Christians."

Wm. Tyndale in his defence of Luther against
Moore says: "If the souls be in heaven, tell me
why they be not in as good case as the angels be?
And then what cause is there of the resurrection?" Dobney in his able work on *Future Punishment* says: "Reason cannot prove man to be
immortal. We may devoutly enter the temple
of nature, we may reverently tread her emerald
floor, and gaze on her blue 'star-pictured ceiling,'
but to our anxious inquiry, though proposed with
heart-breaking intensity, the oracle is dumb, or
like those of Delphi and Dodona it mutters only
an ambiguous reply, that leaves us in utter

bewilderment. So, much the more valuable is a written revelation." (pp. 107-8.)

Professor Stuart says: "The *light of nature* can never scatter the darkness in question. This light has never yet sufficed to make the question clear to any portion of a benighted race—whether the soul of man is immortal? Cicero, incomparably the most able defender of the soul's immortality of which the heathen world can yet boast, very ingenuously confesses, that after all the arguments which he had adduced in order to confirm the doctrine in question, it so fell out that his mind was satisfied of it only when directly employed in contemplating the arguments adduced in its favor. At all other times he fell unconsciously into a state of doubt and darkness." —*Exegetical Essays.*

That man is but mortal is evinced in nature, and reason accords therewith. Science also sustains it. "To them who, by patient continuance in well-doing, seek for glory and honor and immortality," eternal life is promised in the scriptures. That man is mortal, also coincides with the glorious doctrines of the resurrection, the regeneration, or new birth, and the eternal judgment. Immortal-soulism, spiritism, ghostism, all spring from a fabulous or mythical source. Corporeity is characteristic of being. Spiritism was believed in the days of Christ. Even after Christ's resurrection the disciples were not emptied of its leaven. When they saw Christ "they were terrified and affrighted, and supposed that

they had seen a spirit." But Christ rebuked
their wrong thoughts in the words, "Behold my
hands and my feet, that it is I myself: handle me
and see; for a spirit hath not flesh and bones as
ye see me have." Hence after Christ triumphed
over mortality he was still a corporeal being. He
was the express image of his Father's *person*.
Angels also, as recorded in scripture, possessed
corporeity. When Christ returns our bodies are
to be "fashioned like unto his glorious body."
Therefore flesh and bone corporeity will still be
ours in the glorified state. This harmonizes with
the teaching of the Patriarch Job when he says,
"After I shall awake, though this body be destroyed, yet out of my flesh shall I see God."
(xix. 26, *marg. rendering*.) As to ghostism, the
worst ghost any one will see is his own shadow.
Mortality is still the nature of man. An immortal nature can only be obtained through Christ.
Eternal life is the gift of God. Therefore let us
submit to God and lay hold on eternal life. The
prize is of inestimable value. Who can comprehend an eternity of bliss. Till Christ comes mortality lasts, and death continues as man's enemy.
Then mortality shall be abolished, and death
destroyed.

> Death is a tyrant, that shall hold full sway
>   Until our blessed Lord shall come again
> To usher in the bright eternal day,
>   And snap in twain forever his cold chain.

CHAPTER IX.

THE RESURRECTION—ISRAEL'S HOPE.

"Why should it be thought a thing incredible with you, that God should raise the dead?"—Acts xxvi. 8.

The nature of man and the resurrection run together. The latter is really a connecting link between mortality and immortality. Than the resurrection no doctrine of scripture is more mystified by the teachings of modern and popular theology, and yet no truth pertaining to man's salvation is more clearly set forth in the word of God. It is the Christian's hope. For the hope of Israel Paul was bound with chains. (Acts xxviii. 20.) That for which he was called in question was for preaching "there shall be a resurrection of the dead, both of the just and unjust." (xxiv. 14, 15-21.) Therefore, that the dead should rise was Israel's hope. Make this doctrine void and all hope vanishes. For, "if there be no resurrection of the dead, then is Christ not risen, and if Christ be not risen then is our

preaching vain, and your faith is also vain. . .
Then they also who are fallen asleep in Christ are
perished." (I. Cor. xv.) Christ is the resurrection and the life. He burst the bars of death and
rose triumphant from the tomb, and now eternal
life is his. The keys of death and the grave are
in his hand. God has given Him this power.
The hour is coming when the dead shall hear his
voice and shall come forth, some to life and some
to condemnation.

The new creation really dawned when Christ
arose from Joseph's tomb. Paul triumphantly
exclaims, "Now is Christ risen from the dead
and become the first-fruits of them that slept."
This is the assurance of our hope. It is the evidence from heaven, and "the witness of God is
greater than the witness of men." But we have
said that the resurrection was Israel's hope.
Isaiah exclaims, "Thy dead men shall live, together with my dead body shall they arise. Awake
and sing, ye that dwell in the dust; for thy dew
is as the dew of herbs, and the earth shall cast
out the dead." (xxvi. 19.) Ezekiel prophesies,
"Thus saith the Lord God: Behold, O my people, I will open your graves, and cause you to
come up out of your graves, and bring you into
the land of Israel. And ye shall know that I am
the Lord when I have opened your graves, O my
people, and brought you up out of your graves,
and shall put my Spirit in you, and ye shall live,
and I shall place you in your own land; then shall
ye know that I the Lord have spoken it, and per-

formed it, saith the Lord." (xxxvii. 12-14.) Daniel says, "Many of them that sleep in the dust of the earth shall awake." The same glorious doctrine was also taught by Christ, and reiterated by his apostles. The promise Jesus made to his disciples was that they should "sit upon twelve thrones, judging the twelve tribes of Israel," but this was to be in the time of the regeneration. (Matt. xix. 28.) We are further told, "They who shall be accounted worthy to obtain that world and the resurrection from the dead . . . are the children of God, being the children of the resurrection." (Luke xx. 35, 36.) Such die no more.

Why should it be thought a thing incredible that God should raise the dead? That which makes it appear incredible, and even absurd, is the mythical traditions by which it is enveloped. When men proclaim that death is not death, that there is no such thing as death, as Bulwer asserts in his last poem, and if such be accepted, what shall we believe? If there is no death there can be none in the region of the dead, and if none are dead it is impossible for the "dead to rise." If the dead rise not, then Christ is not risen; and if Christ be not risen our faith is vain. This conclusion is legitimate. It is vain to attempt getting around it by endeavoring to prove that man is a two-fold or a triune being. Such is a mere phantasm, the product of minds intoxicated with the wine of a corrupt theology, or imbued with heathen mythology. When we speak of man we speak of him as a being; when we address him, we address a being, and not a piece of insensible clay; and when we say man dies, it simply means his being ceases to exist. If he has served God, his life is *hid* with Christ in God, until Christ, who is our life, shall appear. As the scriptures term it, he "falls asleep," to be awakened only by the sound of the last trumpet. Then shall this mortal put on immortality, but not till then.

But the apostle Paul uses the term, "whole spirit, and soul, and body." Yes, and he prays that the same may "be preserved blameless unto the coming of our Lord Jesus Christ." He did not pray that one part should enjoy felicity as a conscious entity while another part of the being was decomposing in the grave. Scientific men embalm the bodies of distinguished men in order to preserve them from corruption. If our beings are saturated with the Spirit of Christ and the life principle hid with Christ in God, in the fulness of time this corruptible shall put on incorruption. Our whole being is thus preserved—not the body only.

The body is but the frame—the soul is the seat of life as it relates to the present, or, as it relates to the future, it is the germ or seed of the life to come. The spirit is the principle of life which acts upon the being. The whole constitutes an entity or being. Take away one part and the rest fails to exist in itself. At death the spirit or life principle returns to God, and is by Him retained until the Life-giver comes at the consummation of all things mortal, temporal or transient. The being sinks into the sleep of death, and "them that sleep in Jesus will God bring with Him." This is the consolation of the hope of the gospel. Concerning them who are asleep we triumphantly exclaim:

"They shall sleep but not forever,
 There will be a glorious dawn ;
We shall meet to part, no never,
 On the resurrection morn."

Asleep. We call attention to this word which is very frequently used in scripture. According to popular theories it is merely the body that sleeps: of the being it is said, "not dead but gone before." Now, this is simply sheer nonsense. It is *them that sleep* whom God shall bring. If it mean the bodies merely, these shall come forth. As for the union of a resurrected body with a full-fledged being called a soul, the Bible speaks nothing of it. Such only exists in the traditions of men or among the fables of heathendom. But the scriptures are clear on the point. Why quibble with the truth of God? "Them who sleep" evidently means the beings asleep. "They who are fallen asleep in Christ," certainly implies beings sunk into the sleep of death in hope of future life through Christ. Christ is the *first-fruits* of them that *slept*. If the ancient people of God all went to heaven at death, then Christ is not the first-fruits; but the word of God is sure, and we shall prefer its teachings before all others. If any go to heaven, why has Christ said, "No

man hath ascended up to heaven?" (John iii.
13.) If any of our fellow-beings are there they
are in the presence of God, and we are explicitly
told, "No man hath seen God at any time." (i.
18.) It is vain to say this has reference only to
man's fleshly tabernacle. Such can never behold
anything, for void of being it becomes insensible.
These statements apply to man as a being in this
present mortal state. The time is coming, as
scripture clearly demonstrates, when this mortal
clothed in immortality, "shall see Him (God) as
He is," (I. John iii. 2) for the tabernacle of God
shall be with men, "and He will dwell with them
and they shall be his people." (Rev. xxi. 3.) But
this is after, not before, the resurrection.

Two men who professed to be servants of the
Lord Jesus Christ called recently at our residence.
They were so impregnated with this monstrous
dogma of inherent immortality that they claimed
eternal pre-existence. "You have read," said
they, "of the sons of God as recorded in the book
of Genesis. John tells us in his epistle, 'we are
the sons of God.' Now, sir," they continued, "we
claim to be the same beings that existed in the
beginning. In the fulness of time we took these
bodies, but our existence never ceases, etc."
"Alas, what superstition or delusion," you exclaim. Alas, what willful ignorance, say we, for
both were intelligent enough to comprehend right
and wrong. Deceivers going about to deceive,
wresting the scriptures to their own destruction.
"For of this sort are they who creep into houses

and lead captive silly women laden with sins, led away with divers lusts." (II. Tim. iii. 6.) We denounced their dogmas *in toto* as "damnable delusions," and they left. They claimed their authority from Utah.

But to return. *Resurrection* means literally a raising up to life or being a second time. It implies also that the same beings shall be brought forth again. To construe the meaning other than this the word itself will have to be reconstructed, and the prefix *re* taken away. In like manner the word *regeneration* as used by Christ implies a second springing up to life or being. This also accords with what we are taught. We read, " And *this corruptible* must put on incorruption, and *this mortal* must put on immortality." But men say " our immortal souls shall take on their respective bodies, or enter them," which is the very opposite of these scripture statements.

Again, the apostle exclaims, " Not for that we would be unclothed, but *clothed upon*, that mortality might be swallowed up of life." This harmonizes with the rest. The same apostle uses the expression in his letter to the church at Philippi: "If by any means I might attain unto the resurrection of the dead," clearly demonstrating that he looked forward to that event as the fruition of hope. In nature we see the same foreshadowed. The sun sinks on the western horizon only to appear again in the east after the lapse of a night. Paul says, "the night is far spent, the day is at hand." Once at creation's

8

dawn "the morning stars sang together, and all the sons of God shouted for joy." But a night of darkness and of sin fell upon the world. Yet morning comes again—the resurrection morn— when the Sun of Righteousness shall arise, and life shall be given to the saints now slumbering in the tomb. Weeping endures but for the night; joy comes in the morning. Then shall be a happy re-union, and parting shall be known no more forever. "All nature dies and lives again." Winter symbolizes death in that nature sleeps, as it were, for a season.

> "Yet soon reviving plants and flowers,
>   Anew shall deck the plain;
> The woods shall hear the voice of Spring,
>   And flourish green again."

And season after season rolling past but reminds us of the grand eternal Spring when those who are plants of our Heavenly Father's planting— trees of righteousness—shall spring up in immortal and eternal bloom. In the natural we cannot tell the difference from year to year of the blade of grass, the flower or the leaf. The likeness is exact to what faded in the autumn. So shall it be in the resurrection of the dead. The same beings shall arise who were laid away, but they shall don the garments unfading, and "shine forth as the sun in the kingdom of their Father" forever.

Christ is the LIFE. And the gift of God to man is eternal life through Jesus Christ our Lord. "Lay hold on eternal life" is the command of scripture. When we lay hold of Christ He becomes "our life." Jesus says: "This is the will of Him that sent me, that every one who seeth the Son, and believeth in (*eis*) Him, may have everlasting life, and *I will raise him up at the last day*." (John vi. 40.) This final statement, or promise, is frequently used in the chapter quoted. It is not ambiguous. "I will raise *him*," evidently implies the being to whom the life is promised. It is adding to the word of God to say this refers merely to the body. Had Christ referred to the body alone, undoubtedly He would have used other language. But He who spake as never man spake, used such language that the wayfaring man, though a fool, need not err therein. The time also of resurrection is clearly given, viz: "*at the last day*." To expect to be raised to heaven at death is looking for something which God has not promised to man. At the sounding of the mighty trump, multitudes shall awake in amazement and consternation to acknowledge the truth of God when human props shall no longer be able to support vain traditions. But according to popular theology it is only a part of the being (the soul) that goes to heaven at death; the body goes to corruption. This is contrary to the laws of nature. One element or part of any body cannot decay without affecting the whole. To claim that man individually implies two distinct entities or beings is treading on mythical ground, as has been shown. That multitudes of our fellow-beings believe such a dogma, or rather profess to believe it, is not evidence for the same. Multitudes believe in the doctrines of Mahomet, but that does not make their faith true. Were it true, then we should leap for very joy at the death of every child of God. Why weep, if the "departed" has entered joys unfading—crowned with heaven's honors? We once attended the funeral services of a respected neighbor. The deceased, according to custom, was carried into the church. Tears flowed freely. Where natural affection dwells we cannot refrain from tears. Sorrow and sighing shall not flee away until the Lord shall bring again Zion. But heartfelt tears are not mockery. God hears the sighs of his children. We were simply shocked as an expression like the following fell from the minister's lips:

"My dear friends, while we thus mingle our tears over the mortal remains of our much respected brother, in all probability his spirit, together with angelic companions, may be hovering over us, smiling upon the scene with a heavenly smile, and singing the glad new song."

What is this if it be not mockery? God has commanded us to weep with them that weep. It is an outrage against the order and wisdom of heaven to say that God would permit one part of a being to smile and enjoy boundless happiness, while friends wept over the corrupt remains of another part of the same being. If such teachings were true then the morning of joy comes at death, and consequently the night of weeping should end; and many even say that Christ himself comes at death to each individual saint. To accept such absurdities we must reject the plain teachings of the word of God. "Weeping may endure for a night, but joy cometh in the morning." The wicked may annoy, but the upright shall have dominion over them in the morning. Perplexity may in the present possess men's minds, but the watchman shall see eye to eye when the Lord shall bring again Zion.

"The redeemed of the Lord shall return, and come with singing unto Zion; and everlasting joy shall be upon their head; they shall obtain gladness and joy; and sorrow and mourning shall flee away." And "He (God) will swallow up death in victory; and the Lord God shall wipe away tears from off all faces."

The Revelator says: "And I saw a great white throne, and Him that sat on it. . . . And I saw the dead, small and great, stand before God; and the books were opened; and another book was opened which is the book of life; and the dead were judged out of those things which were written in the books, according to their works. And the sea gave up the dead which were in it; and death and the *grave* delivered up the dead which were in them; and they were judged every man according to their works." (Rev. xx. 11-13.) All must agree that this scene takes place at the consummation of the present order of things, and refers to the general resurrection and the judgment. This granted, two other vital points must also be accepted:

First. That at this particular period every man shall receive according to his works, whether it be good or bad, which truth destroys the dogma that man receives reward or punishment at death.

Second. It is at the judgment scene that the book of life is opened, which fact conflicts with the unscriptural idea that man receives this immortal life at death. Until the appearing of the Messiah our life is hid with Christ in God. When the book of life is opened immortality is bestowed upon those whose names are written therein.

This harmonizes with the one grand leading and fundamental truth of Christianity, viz: that out of Christ there is no promise of immortal life to man, which life is bestowed only upon those who are found worthy when He comes to judge the living and the dead. "But," objects one, "does not Christ's promise to the thief on the cross ensure man of entering into glory at death?" We reply, Christ never made a promise to conflict with his own word, and since his teachings invariably point to the resurrection as the time when life and reward is to be given, He could not give life to the thief before the time appointed. Consequently, we must seek for a correct understanding of this much controverted portion of scripture.

The thief was no stranger to the hope of the gospel as his words clearly indicate. He did not ask, " Lord, remember me when thou ascendest to thy Father's throne." The petition was,

" Lord, remember me *when thou comest into thy kingdom.*" Jesus answered, " Verily, I say unto thee, to-day shalt thou be with me in Paradise." (Luke xxiii. 42, 43.) Some quibble over the punctuation of the sentence and explain it as a future promise made in the time called " to-day." But, we inquire, did the Lord refer to a literal day of twenty-four hours, and are we to infer that the thief and He were alive and in Paradise within the limits of that day? Such is simply absurd. Christ, the anointed One of God, (not his body merely) died on that day according to the scriptures, and was held by the power of death until the third day thereafter. To claim that Christ *died* and yet did not die, is to destroy the meaning of language, and also to deny the statements of scripture. Then would death mean life, and *vice versa.* The inverse statement, "in the midst of death we are in life," would then be true. Christ died, we are told, and rose again the third day. The same being that died rose again and became the *first-fruits* of them that slept. If He, the Christ, had not been asleep in death, He could not have become the first-fruits of them that slept. But this is the gospel as preached by Paul. After his resurrection, the *same* Jesus said to Mary, " Touch me not, for I am *not yet* ascended to my Father." (John xx. 17.) This was three days after his crucifixion, and requires no explanation, for no Christian dare doubt the words of his Lord. It must, therefore, be evident to every candid mind that " to-day," when considered as

denoting the time when the said promise is to be
fulfilled, cannot refer to a literal day of twenty-
four hours; for according to the conditions of the
promise, unless we accept Paradise as a synonym
of *hades*, which is absurd, the scriptures clearly
prove its fulfillment in the given time an impossibility.   But if the answer to the thief's question
be a direct one, and we have no reason to dispute
it, then "to-day" can be justly regarded as ex-
tending over a period of time to be known as a
day of the Lord.   For "one day is with the Lord
as a thousand years, and a thousand years *as* one
day."   (II. Peter iii. 8.)   For example, we know
that "now is the day of salvation."   "To-day, if
ye will hear his voice, harden not your hearts."
The *day of salvation* has extended already over
eighteen hundred years of time, and its comple-
tion is not yet.   Christ's first advent may be truly
termed the morning of the day of salvation.   In
the evening of the same period we look for his
second appearing.   That which was lost in Adam
is to be restored in Christ.   When Christ comes
to his kingdom, Paradise shall be regained.   The
day of salvation shall not be complete until the
second Adam (Christ) with his bride (the church)
glorified are placed upon the sinless soil of Eden
regained; and according to the promise of Christ
the malefactor shall be there.   This is in harmony with the teachings of scripture throughout.
Many have offered up the same prayer as the
thief, "Lord, remember me when thou comest
into thy kingdom," and the faithful shall enter

into the everlasting rest in the glorious evening time of the day of salvation to be forever with the Lord. "At evening time it shall be light." To every weary pilgrim the words come sweetly, "To-day shalt thou be with me in Paradise," for "surely I come quickly;" and the heart responds, "Amen. Even so, come, Lord Jesus."

The testimony of scripture is plain that Jesus the Christ *died* and *rose* again from the dead. If Christ rose not, his death avails not, and the hope of the Christian is vain. But we preach Christ risen as a surety that the dead will also rise at God's appointed time. "If there be no resurrection of the dead, then is Christ not risen. And if Christ be not risen, then is our preaching vain, and your faith is also vain. Yea, and we are found false witnesses of God; because we have testified of God that He raised up Christ, whom He raised not up, if so be that the dead rise not. For if the dead rise not then, then is Christ not raised; and if Christ be not raised your faith is vain; ye are yet in your sins. Then they also who are fallen asleep in Christ are perished." (I. Cor. xv. 13-18.) It is evident from this quotation that the resurrection is flesh, bone and sinew of the Christian's hope; and those who claim that man possesses in the present inherent immortality, and that as a conscious being the soul goes to reward or punishment at death, do cast aside this blessed hope, for praise God the theories of men cannot destroy it. And to-day multitudes who have imbibed this and similar dogmas as truth are

tossed to and fro upon the dark and uncertain sea
of mythology. God help them. But granted
that man possesses inherent immortality, how
comes the statement, "If Christ be not raised
. . then they also who are fallen asleep in Christ
are *perished?*" The dead are here represented as
having "*fallen asleep,*" and not as being in a state
of conscious bliss. If man possesses inherent
immortality, he has possessed it from the beginning. If the soul is immortal, it is consequently
deathless and imperishable, neither could the
resurrection of Christ affect it. But popular theology teaches that thousands of the ancients were
around the throne of God in heaven long before
the advent of Christ. If there, they were beyond
the state of corruption—they could not perish,
but like unto the angels die no more. It is vain
even to attempt eluding this point by saying it
is but the earthly bodies that Paul refers to. If
man enters heaven as a conscious being and
enjoys the unspeakable bliss of which we have
been told without his mortal body, it matters not
what becomes of it. If it perish let it perish,
since he is incorruptible. But Paul's words are
clear. He tells us *they that are fallen asleep* are
perished. The pronoun *they* undoubtedly refers
to beings—beings that are asleep. There is no
way of escape for such theorists who by vain and
absurd dogmas endeavor to explain away the
blessed word of God. The order of God is not
hard of comprehension. The triumphant exclam-
ation of the gospel is, "Now is Christ risen from

the dead, and become the first-fruits of them that *slept.* For since by man came death, by man came also the resurrection of the dead." The order of heaven in regard to life immortal is clearly given in the words, " Christ the first-fruits, afterwards *they that are Christ's at his coming.* Then cometh the end." (I. Cor. xv.) "For the Lord himself shall descend from heaven with a shout, with the voice of the archangel and with the trump of God: and the *dead in Christ shall rise first:* then we who are alive and remain shall be caught up together with them in the clouds, to meet the Lord in the air, and so shall we ever be with the Lord. Wherefore comfort one another with these words." (I. Thess. iv. 16-18.)

In Paul's letter to the Philippians we read, "But I am in a strait betwixt the two, having the desire to depart and be with Christ, for it is very far better; yet to abide in the flesh is more needful for your sake; and having this confidence I know that I shall abide," etc. (i. 23-25, revised version.) Some render the word *analusai* "the returning," (Diaglott version) which makes the passage to read thus: "Having an earnest desire for the returning and being with Christ." Now, for our part, we cannot form a preference between the renderings; because, when Christ returns, one fact remains indisputable, viz: the saints shall depart upward to meet Him, and shall hence be ever with their Lord.

The desire for this glorious event burned in the bosom of Paul, but it did not imply that death should bring a fulfillment of this desire. In the same letter (iii. 11) he exclaims: "If by any means I may attain unto the resurrection from the dead." Paul did not look for the crown until the dead should wake from slumber. At the end of his course he triumphantly exclaimed, "I have fought the good fight; I have finished the course; I have kept the faith; henceforth (not at death) there is *laid up* for me the crown of righteousness, which the Lord, the righteous Judge, shall give to me at that day, (not before); and not only to me, but also to all them that have loved his appearing." (II. Tim. iv. 8, rev. version.)

And thus we have found it, that not only has the true Christian a desire to depart and to be with Christ begotten within him, and which is preferable to all else on earth, but there is also begotten within his bosom its inseparable concomitant, a love for the appearing of the Messiah. But, according to the scriptures, the crown shall not be bestowed nor the desire gratified until "*that day*" when Christ, the life-giver, shall descend from heaven. "Yet to abide in the flesh is more needful for your sake," and we might add for our sakes as well, for had Paul's desire been just then gratified, millions including ourselves would have been barred from salvation, for hope would have reached its consummation, and the Christian race its culminating point. Hence Paul's knowledge rises above the fervent desire of his heart, and he says, "I know that I shall abide." And although eighteen centuries have rolled into the past since then, he (Paul) still abides in the flesh—asleep in Jesus. "For whether we live therefore or die we are the Lord's." (Rom. xiv. 8.) And according to his own preaching, this mortal, which includes his being, shall not put on immortality until the last trump shall sound.

"But," objects one, "what of the statement, ' For me to live is Christ, and to die is *gain?*'" As the death of Christ was an eternal gain to all Christians, so the death of every martyr may be considered as gain, for "if we suffer with Him, we shall also reign with Him." And it is written, "whosoever shall lose his life shall preserve it." (Luke xvii. 33.) Paul evidently anticipated this when he answered the weeping group: "What mean ye to weep, and to break mine heart? for I am ready not only to be bound, but also to die at Jerusalem for the name of the Lord Jesus." To die as a martyr as did Paul was indeed infinite gain, but that gain was not to be his at death. The rewards are not to be given until the seventh angel shall sound, and at that time the kingdom of this world shall become the kingdom of our Lord and of his Christ. (Rev. xi. 15-18.) In the early days of Christianity many even prayed that they might be accounted worthy of death for Christ's sake; and many did pass through fiery trials and death; "others were tortured, not accepting deliverance, that they might obtain a better resurrection." And thus

Paul's death was gain, for it was the seal or surety of heaven of a better resurrection.

Others bring the parable of the rich man and Lazarus as an unanswerable proof against the doctrine of the resurrection, but as we discuss its merits in another chapter ("The Destiny of the Wicked") we omit noticing it here.

The resurrection is also sustained by the analogy of nature. When men cast seed upon the soil, they look for a yield therefrom, nor do they look in vain. Mankind being formed in the very image of God, are more precious than all other seeds, and when cast into the ground must they lie there forever? God forbid. "The earth shall cast out her dead," is what we read and it is most reasonable. To us it does seem passing strange for men to profess a belief in the Bible story of man's creation, and yet deny the resurrection. The resurrection was prefigured in that man was first formed out of the dust of the earth. The first creation was but a type of the second or new creation. The God who formed man out of the dust in the beginning, shall bring them forth out of the dust a second time. " For all that are in the graves shall hear his voice and shall come forth." This power He has given to his Son. Christ is " the resurrection and the life." If our life be now hid with Christ in God, when He who is our life shall appear, we shall live again. Those in Christ who are alive at that blessed time, shall be changed from mortal to immortality without passing through the ordeal of death. But the dead in Christ shall rise, and to every seed shall be given his own body. The eternal Spring shall then bring forth, and the roses of Sharon and the lilies of the valley shall spring up in everlasting bloom.

Of death and the resurrection we are told, " It is sown in corruption, it is raised in incorruption; it is sown in dishonor, it is raised in glory; it is sown in weakness, it is raised in power; it is sown a natural body, it is raised a spiritual body." Man may just as well reason, when the season comes, and the seed is sown, and the rain falls, and the sun thereafter shines, that no crop will spring up, as to say that in God's own season the sleeping saints will not arise from their long slumber. The same Being is God over all, and it is limiting the power of the Creator to say that He cannot or will not re-create or regenerate. But a new creation or regeneration is taught in his Word; therefore, if we take God's Word as our guide or rule of faith, we must accept the doctrine of the resurrection.

" It is raised a spiritual body." That is, a body that shall be sustained by spirit life. The blood is that which sustains the natural body. In the immortal state the spirit merely takes the place of the blood. Hence we are told, "flesh and blood cannot inherit the kingdom of God." But that flesh and spirit shall inherit the kingdom we have ample proof. The first-fruits of a harvest are like the grain which is afterward reaped. Christ is the first-fruits of God's harvest field.

He had flesh and bones after his resurrection, and our bodies are to be "fashioned like unto his glorious body," therefore we shall have flesh and bones. Those who are alive at the time of his coming shall merely be changed i. e. from blood to spirit nature. "But that which thou sowest, thou sowest not that body that shall be, but bare grain, it may chance of wheat or of some other grain. But God giveth it a body as it hath pleased Him, and to every seed his own body." When a seed is cast into the ground it is evident to all that the body of that seed dissolves or decays, while the germ of the new body is forming. And although the new formed body is an exact likeness of that which decayed, still it is a different body. So also is the resurrection of the dead. (See I. Cor. xv.) But is this incredible? We deem it not only according to the scriptures, but according to reason as well. A skillful chemist can perform marvels in restoring dissolved bodies to their former elementary or component parts, and people are amazed at their skill. Electricians of late have made the world at large wonder at their amazing feats in bringing into practical use this once latent element of nature. Science in its every department has scaled giddy heights, and things which only a few years ago were considered impossibilities, we now see accomplished with comparative ease.

So much for man. But while man boasts of his skill and achievements, what of man's Creator? Tell the simple Bible story of the resurrection, and multitudes shake their heads in doubt. Behold, O unbelieving one, the universe! See world on worlds, system after system, glory after glory, and who, we ask, did frame them all? Gaze into the space above, and canst thou measure its depths? See yonder star burst into a flame and disappear. Measure the power that holds a million worlds in their orbits and keeps their motion perfect. Whence the origin of all these, and whence their Originator? You answer, "God." Then tell me, wilt thou limit the power of the Almighty in regard to the re-creation and the regeneration of those beings made in his own image?

"All nature dies and lives again," is ofttimes repeated thoughtlessly, yet it is a truth which requires no demonstration, for nature herself evinces it. This granted, shall man the prince of creation, the being who bears the image of his Creator, die and not live again? We reply that outside of Bible evidence God has given man good reasons to hope for a life beyond the grave. Intelligence calls for it, and there is an inherent principle in the human family generally which foreshadows it. When we come to the Bible the evidence is overwhelming. But this evidence is not made certain to man until he obeys the precepts laid down in God's word. When these are instilled into the mind, and put into daily and hourly practice, we receive an evidence beyond ourselves, even the testimony of God's Spirit. This gives hope as an anchor of the soul both

9

sure and steadfast, and which reaches to that within the vail, even Christ. This attained, a faith which stands not in the wisdom of men but in the power of God becomes our heritage.

Blessed doctrine of the resurrection, that tells the weeping mourner to look ahead to that land where death shall be no more known; where sorrow and sighing shall forever flee away; where God shall wipe away all tears; where the loved forms of our sleeping friends we shall behold once more; where hand shall clasp hand no more to part; where.the wicked shall cease from troubling and where the weary shall be at rest. You have seen a mourning group—perhaps you have yourself been bereaved, for who has not lost a friend—and as you beheld the tears and heard the sighs of the bereaved ones, has not your mind involuntarily been carried forward into the land of immortality? Or it may be that you have been led to pray for that blessed kingdom to come, where the inhabitants shall be like unto angels, neither can they die any more. The writer has parents dear, a beloved sister, a darling child, and endearing friends all down in the lone valley; therefore we long for the time when death shall be destroyed and when the graves shall yield up their inhabitants, so that we may meet and clasp those dear ones in fond and everlasting embrace. Behold that flower, too pure, too lovely for a polluted world, snatched suddenly away from our bosom or our home; who can refrain from tears, and sighs, and longings to meet again where these

flowers restored shall eternally bloom? Why
that pang as recollection brings those faces beloved to mind? Why that involuntary. tear?
Why cannot mortal cast such into oblivion? Can
we have no comfort void of hope? These very
pangs, and sighs, and tears, and longings but pre-
sage the happy time of reunion. To believe other
than this is to reflect on God as being unjust and
imperfect, for we must see and understand God
in his works. A night of weeping only tells us
joy cometh in the morning, and there is balm in
Gilead for every wounded heart. Our Father is
ready to bestow "the oil of joy for mourning, the
garment of praise for the spirit of heaviness."
We in order to an inheritance incorruptible must
needs be tried. Tribulation only worketh for our
eternal good if we but hold on to God. A lifetime is but a brief space to prepare for eternity,
therefore the process of purifying must be rigid.
Paul says: "I reckon that the sufferings of this
present time are not worthy to be compared with
the glory which shall be revealed in us."

Finally, let the mourners in Zion rejoice. The
morn of resurrection is at hand. Jesus is soon
coming. O, happy morn, all hail! No more
hence shall funeral cortege be seen. But a multitude which no man can number shall shout the
triumph of a life which shall have no end. There
we shall

Sound our bright harps beyond death's dismal sea,
Singing, Jesus hath triumphed, his Zion is free.

CHAPTER X.

THE ATONEMENT.

Than the doctrine of the atonement no tenet of the scriptures has been more mystified by the teachings of modern theology; nor has the glory of any truth of God been more obscured by the mythical traditions of men. The reason is two-fold: first, by misconceptions as to the nature of Christ, the Redeemer; second, by misapprehensions as to the nature of that which called for atonement or redemption. Under the first head: If Christ be the very God, which the dogma of the trinity teaches in that it declares that there are three persons in the Godhead, co-equal and co-eternal, and that these three are one, then the atonement detracts from the glory of God instead of adding thereto, because, such granted, God ceases to be omnipotent, for if omnipotence admits of depreciation it can no longer be omnipotence. But the dignity and majesty of Him who is the King of kings and Lord of lords is also lowered if we accept the dogma that He came down from his lofty throne in heaven, and became man in order to save man. According to this He must also needs leave immortality behind, and become mortal so as to die for our sins, which is most absurd, for according to the scriptures, "corruption doth not inherit incorruption," and *vice versa*. And Paul's gospel tells us "Christ died for our sins," which was an impossibility if so be Christ possessed immortality. But farther, according to such theories, the Creator is made to suffer untold anguish, excruciating pain, and even an ignominious death at the hands of his creatures, which is the most absurd of all. Why even the heathen would not tolerate subjects thus to treat a king; and the laws of civilization would both condemn and severely punish such outrageous actions between man and his fellow.

Undoubtedly the *power* by which all things were created was in Christ, viz: the Word. (See John i.) But God the eternal and Holy One retained his position upon his throne in the excellent glory unchanged and invariable. He was the source from which the *Word* emanated. Electricity flows from a battery, the operator acts upon the instrument, and as a result a message passes along the wire. But the message or the current passing along the wire is neither the operator, the instrument, nor the battery, yet it bears a certain connection with each, and emanates from the battery as a source. So is it with the Word which is in Christ, and which was made flesh and dwelt among us, and by which all things were created. It is but the message of heaven to earth. The current which conveys it is the Spirit of God. The operator is God himself, and He also is the source. This is the Word that said through the *Elohim* in the beginning: "Let there be light," and there was light, etc. (Gen. i.)

But observe while the Word went forth in command in those early days, that *word* did not become a component part of anything created. And when we come down to the prophets we are only told concerning them, that those holy men of old spake as they were moved by the Holy Ghost. Now mark the difference. When we reach the only begotten of the Father, we are informed that the *Word* was made flesh, i. e., became a component part thereof. Christ was a plant of the Father's own planting. He was begotten by the power of the Holy Spirit. Adam was the first being of the first creation, consequently was created by the direct agency of heaven. Christ, the second Adam, the first-born of the new creation, was also created by the direct agency of heaven. (Luke i. 35.) But the last shall be first. The first Adam fell, but the last Adam triumphed over death. The first had only a measure of God's Spirit; but on the latter the Spirit was poured without measure. That which was defective in Adam was supplied in Christ. The latter was brought into close relationship with God. The angel said to Mary, "That holy thing which shall be born of thee

shall be called the Son of God," but this was not
the very God himself. After his birth we read of
Him: " And Jesus *increased* in wisdom and stature, and in favor with God and man." Admitting Christ to be God and apply this statement,
and how does it sound? That God was in Christ
is easily enough understood, for "God who at
sundry times and in divers manners spake in time
past unto the fathers by the prophets, hath in
these last days spoken unto us by his Son."
(Heb. i. 1, 2.) God dwelt in Christ by his Spirit,
even as Christ dwells in us. But Christ being
begotten of the Holy Spirit gives him the pre-eminence. The rays of the sun fall upon the earth
continually and penetrate the soil, but the sun
itself retains its place in the heavens. So with
the Spirit of God, it falls upon man and permeates his being, but God retains his seat in the
heavens. Christ, like the moon, reflected the
light of the Father to this dark world of ours, and
opened a way of escape for fallen man. With this
view of Jesus, the anointed, we can understand
more clearly his great mission—the atonement.
He came as a prophet like unto his brethren to
take up what was lost through Adam's transgression, and to redeem fallen man. The challenge
of the past ages for a man to stand in the gap
before God for the land (Ezek. xxii. 30) was not
filled. No one could be found among all the
human race who could perfectly obey the mandates of heaven until Christ came saying, "Lo I
come (in the volume of the book it is written of

me) to do thy will, O God." But let us consider what man lost by the fall.

When Adam was created he was placed on a platform of probation, so to speak. Life and peace and happiness lay ahead of him. The conditions were obedience. He disobeyed and consequently fell, and therefore the sentence of death passed not only on Adam, but upon all. Through this transgression sin entered into the world, and death by sin. We have been asked, "Why should God, who is all-wise, permit man, his own creature, to fall, and also allow sin to enter into the world?" Were we to ask in turn, Why do men put ore into the furnace? Why is gold put through the crucible? the replies to such questions would be apparent. But by application they also reply to the former. The qualities of any being or thing cannot be tested or proven until opposing forces are brought to bear upon it. The granite column is much admired when shaped and polished, but it came not thus from the quarry. It must needs pass through the hands of the artist. Neither are the opposites in nature appreciated until brought into contrast. If we knew nothing of darkness we could not appreciate the light. But for the clouds we could not appreciate fully the sunshine. In like manner, only for sickness, one of the consequences of sin, we could not fully value health. It is only when men perceive the evil effects of sin that they are brought to value true holiness. Then if by the opposing forces of temptation and sin, or if by the

furnaces of trial and afflictions, God the great
Moulder sees fit to perfect us for an eternal life
in an Eden restored, who shall murmur or even
question his designs?

> "God moves in a mysterious way
> His wonders to perform."

"For the mystery of iniquity doth already work:
only he who now letteth will let, until he (that
wicked) be taken out of the way." Therefore we
conclude that "all things work together for good
to them that love God," and that sin and its consequences are permitted in order to the perfection
of our beings. To whom much is forgiven the same
loveth much. Hence, "Where sin abounded,
grace did much more abound." Even death, the
final result of sin, is a most refining process, not
only on the object directly acted upon, but also
to those upon whom it reflects, for it is indisputable that death as a reflective power works a
great good. It softens the callous heart. It
begets compassion, kindness and love. It in-
spires hope. It leads the heart upward to
God, and when viewed aright it brings the more
refined parts of our being into action, such as
dependence on God, submission to his will, pa-
tience, experience, hope, obedience, faith, trust,
mercy, forbearance, long-suffering, love, etc.
And that all such qualities are improved and perfected by or through the sufferings to which
mortality is prone, experience clearly demonstrates. The link of the chain that was broken
by Adam was obedience; death was the penalty.

The broken link was taken up by Christ in that
He rendered ·perfect obedience to God. (John
xv. 10.) The penalty was also lifted in that
Christ rose again from the dead. The way to
life was opened henceforth. Nearly all are famil-
iar with the Tay bridge railroad disaster which
occurred a few years ago. The bridge was over
two miles in length, and spanned the Firth of
Tay, just opposite the town of Dundee, Scotland.
For symmetry and strength it was deemed a
marvel of architecture; but one night as the pas-
senger train was arriving from London it gave
way. The train had reached the center, and was
all enclosed in the cage-work of the main span.
The night was boisterous, the sea was rough, and
the wind came swooping down from the hills and
swept the portion of the bridge referred to, with
the train and all its passengers into the foaming
waters beneath. No one survived to relate the
sad event. The bridge still stands with the gap
in its centre. No train will pass over it again
until the gap is filled. The architect and builder
must needs repair it before it can be used. The
gap may truly be designated the gap of death.
In like manner it may be said that Adam was as
it were passing over the bridge of probation,
which was intended to lead both him and his pos-
terity to the shores of life. But the gushing
winds of temptation came down, and he and the
portion of the bridge called "obedience," were
swept into the Valley of Death. And thus it
stood a broken bridge over which no one could

pass till Christ came. He erected anew the span of obedience, and passed safely over to the shores of a never-ending life. And now we have liberty to enter into the holiest by a new and living way, being begotten again unto a living hope by the resurrection of Jesus Christ from the dead.

We have also remission of sins through his blood, i. e., He gave his life for us. We have read of an American, who was condemned innocently in a foreign land, and was saved by the ambassador of his country wrapping himself in his flag and standing between the one condemned, and death. But while we were as yet sinners, Christ wrapping himself in the folds of the banner of heaven's love stood between us and eternal death, even praying for his enemies, saying: " Father, forgive them, for they know not what they do."

But if, instead of death, eternal torment be the penalty of man's first transgression, as is generally taught, then Christ must needs endure eternally before it can be expiated, which is absurd. We are, however, thankful that such a penalty was never pronounced on man by God, and we will show in a future chapter how unscriptural is the assumption, that the wicked shall be eternally tormented.

We therefore conclude that by the atonement, that which stood against us and was contrary to us, is taken out of the way; that the platform of probation has been restored; and that by obedience to the commands of God through Christ and by his grace wherein we now stand, the way is clear for us to attain unto life eternal. But it is both unreasonable and absurd to say that Christ has done *all* for us. We are commanded to work out our own salvation with fear and with trembling. The popular hue and cry of " only believe, only believe, Christ has done it all," is grossly misleading and unscriptural. Indolent and vile sinners have free and full scope to join in singing,

> "Nothing either great or small,
> Nothing, sinner, no,
> Jesus did it, did it all
> Long, long ago."

But when they reach the lines of this same song,

> " Doing is a deadly thing,
> Doing ends in death,"

they utter nothing less than a base insinuation · against the grand central principle of Christianity, and endeavor to inculcate a principle which is detrimental to the cause of Christ, and diametrically opposed to the teachings of the Bible. The idea of heaping all of our petty errings and willful sins upon the back of Jesus of Nazareth is simply monstrous. Does the general of an army do all the fighting? Does the captain of a ship do all the work on board? It is a thousand fold more outrageous to expect the Captain of man's salvation to perform for the millions who lay claim to eternal life through his name, what they really can do for themselves. Such a thought savors of barbarity, and is unworthy of this enlightened age.

God will not do for man what man can do for himself. There is no such thing as indolent Christianity. The work of atonement never opened up a path of laziness. " To them who by patient continuance in *well-doing* seek for glory, and honor and immortality," is eternal life promised. To "run" the race, to "fight" the good fight of faith, to let light shine that others may see your good works and glorify your Father who is in heaven, to " do good" unto all, evidently implies action; and when the great day comes every one shall receive according to his works. Were mere faith sufficient, then the devils also believe and tremble. But it is written, "faith without works is *dead*, being alone." Only is it promised, " To him that overcometh will I grant to sit with me in my throne, even as I also overcame, and am set down with my Father in his throne." It is surely enough that through his great work of atonement Christ has opened for us a way of escape. Righteous deeds are of the golden threads out of which the garment of salvation is woven.

But according to typical scripture the work of atonement shall not be complete until Christ appears a second time, or in other words until He comes out of the holiest. In the former, or Mosaical dispensation, the high priest did not come out of the holiest until he had made atonement "for himself, and for his household, and for all the congregation of Israel." (Lev. xvi. 17.) Christ, as our great High Priest, has entered the

holiest as our advocate with the Father, and as
the propitiation for our sins. When He expired
on Calvary He exclaimed, "It is finished." His
work as head of the body, as the great sacrifice
for sin, was truly finished at that time, but that
there was something left behind of the afflictions
of Christ, the words of Paul clearly show. (Col.
i. 24.) Every member has his own battle to wage,
his own race to run, his own crown to secure.
God supplies the grace through Christ. The
Spirit as the anti-type of the scape-goat (Lev.
xvi. 21) is let loose in the wilderness to convince
the world of sin, of righteousness and of judgment,
and by its groanings unutterable it intercedes in
behalf of Israel after the Spirit. (Rom. viii. 26.)
Christ as the head from which the Spirit flows
bears the transgressions of his people. But we,
through the Spirit, must mortify the deeds of the
body in order to life eternal. According to the
day of types when any garment was sprinkled
with blood it had to be washed in the holy place.
(Lev. vi. 27.) And so when the blood of Christ
is applied to our garments they are cleansed in
the holy place, i. e., we have liberty through his
blood to enter into the holiest, and receive therefrom remission of our sins, in other words a garment cleansed by the blood of Christ. And thus
we see, that while the work of salvation still continues, while the Spirit is yet abroad in the wilderness, and while Christ still intercedes in the
holiest, the atonement is not as yet complete.
But after the seventh, or last, angel pours out his

vial there shall be heard "a great voice out of the temple of heaven, from the throne, saying, IT IS DONE." To sum up. The ministration of Christ ratified all that was good in the Mosaical dispensation, and left for us a perfect code of precepts, which, when obeyed, lead to liberty, holiness, life and love divine. Christ held up to a sinful and corrupt world a banner of purity, as the only guide to happiness here and hereafter. He opened up a way whereby men might become sons of God. He introduced his disciples to the Great Jehovah as "Our Father who art in heaven." He blended mankind together in a common unity and was not ashamed to call his humble followers brethren. By his triumph over sin and death, he placed the resurrection, immortality, and the inheritance of the saints as fixed stars up in the spiritual heavens. In brief, the glad tidings of atonement through Christ has for more than eighteen centuries hung over the turbid and boisterous billows of a wicked world as a beacon to guide the honest-hearted seeker after righteousness, the sin-tost wanderer, and the weary and heavy laden one to the fold of safety, to the fountain of cleansing, to the streams of peace and gladness, and to the blessed haven of everlasting rest.

CHAPTER XI.

THE ETERNAL JUDGMENT.

The doctrine of eternal judgment, as revealed in the scriptures is solemn, grand and sublime. The Judge is set upon the throne of his glory, and before Him is gathered all nations. (Matt. xxv. 31-46.) The seventh seal is opened, and for a space silence reigns in heaven. (Rev. viii. 1.) Multitudes are in the "valley of decision," and each one shall be weighed upon the balances of heaven's mercy—every one shall receive " according as his work shall be." "And the fire shall try every man's work of what sort it is." " For the great day of his wrath is come; and who shall be able to stand." At that time men shall with amazement behold the infinite and unbounded mercy of Jehovah, as those whose works fail to stand the test of the great day are saved "so as by fire." (I. Cor. iii. 15.)

But there are some so narrow-minded and unmerciful in their views as to exclude from the everlasting kingdom all except those who have seen and walked in the very fullness of the gospel light. Jesus says: "Heaven and earth shall pass away, but my word shall not pass away." By that word we shall at last be judged. (John xii. 48.) When that word condemns now, if such condemnation be not removed by repentance and the rendering of more perfect obedience, it shall most assuredly condemn doubly in that day when the secrets of all shall be disclosed. Christ tells us, "He that receiveth a prophet in the name of a prophet shall receive a prophet's reward; and he that receiveth a righteous man in the name of a righteous man shall receive a righteous man's reward. And whosoever shall give to drink unto one of these little ones a cup of cold water only in the name of a disciple, verily I say unto you, he shall in no wise lose his reward." (Matt. x. 41, 42.) "For the Son of man shall come in the glory of his Father with his angels; and then He shall reward every man according to his works." (xvi. 27.) For the King shall say to those who have been mercifully separated from the vast multitude and placed on the right hand, "Come ye blessed of my Father, inherit the kingdom prepared for you from the foundation of the world; for I was an hungered, and ye gave me meat; I was thirsty, and ye gave me drink; I was a stranger, and ye took me in; naked and ye clothed me; I was sick and ye visited me; I was in prison, and ye came unto me." Realizing that it is only by the interposition of heaven's mercy that a way of escape has been thus opened

10

up for them, they exclaim: "When saw we thee
an hungered, and fed thee," etc. And the King
shall answer and say unto them, "Verily I say
unto you, inasmuch as ye have done it unto one
of the least of these my brethren, ye have done it
unto me." (xxv. 34-40.)

God is merciful. The Spirit of Christ teaches
us to be merciful. On the cross He prayed for his
persecutors, saying, "Father forgive them, for
they know not what they do." Jesus never
offered up a meaningless prayer. "If any man
have not the Spirit of Christ, he is none of his."
It is written, "Blessed are the merciful for they
shall obtain mercy." But there is no mercy in the
dogma that teaches "we *alone* are righteous—we
alone are the people of God—to us *alone* has God
revealed his truth—stand back; we are more holy
than you." Such is selfish in the extreme, and
the Spirit of the humble Nazarene is the very
opposite of selfishness. In the days of yore when
there was apparent grounds for such an assertion,
Elijah exclaimed: "I, even I only am left," but
he was informed of the Lord that there were yet
seven thousand in Israel who had not bowed the
knee to Baal. It therefore matters not what
dogmas man may set forth, "the foundation of
God standeth sure, having this seal: The Lord
knoweth them that are his." And the trumpet
voice of the Judge sounds clearly: "Behold I
come quickly; and my reward is with me, to give
every man according as his work shall be."

But theological mystery envelops the doctrine

of eternal judgment in a cloud of absurdities. It teaches that when the body of man is laid down in the grave his immortal soul (a living conscious entity apart from the body) goes either to heaven and at once enjoys felicity, or to a hell of torment where it endures untold pangs of woe. When the living and the dead are judged, this soul and body, we are told, re-unite, and then this double being made one stands before the bar of judgment to receive its sentence according as its work shall be, only to return where it was before; the absurdity of which views we have shown in previous chapters. When Christ comes He brings his reward with Him. It is absurd to say that this coming is at each individual death, for " Behold He cometh with clouds, and *every eye* shall see Him, and they also who pierced Him; and all the kindreds of the earth shall wail because of Him." (Rev. i. 7.) And He "shall judge the quick (living) and the dead at his appearing and his kingdom." (II. Tim. iv. 1.) And since the infliction of punishments and the bestowing of rewards succeed judgment according to the scriptures, the mere fact that man inverts the tenor of the scriptures does not, neither can it, affect the order of God.

In order to understand the doctrine of eternal judgment in its true light, as revealed in the scriptures, we should know somewhat, at least, of the classes that are to be judged. There is a high calling of God in Jesus Christ which implies a walking in the way of holiness—an abiding in

Christ—and "He that saith he abideth in Him ought himself also so to walk, even as He walked." (I. John ii. 6.)   This class are sanctified through the truth and by the Holy Ghost.   They have been grafted into Christ and walk in Him, i. e., in his ways.   "There therefore is now *no condemnation* to them who are *in* Christ Jesus, who walk not after the flesh, but after the Spirit."   These are "accepted in the Beloved," having sought and found the reconciliation of God.   By the grace of God they overcome the world, the flesh and the devil.   And "To him that overcometh will I grant to sit with me in my throne, even as I also overcame, and am set down with my Father in his throne."   (Rev. iii. 21.)   These constitute the Bride of the Lamb—"a kind of first-fruits of God's creatures," (Jas. i. 18)—"a chosen generation, a royal priesthood, a holy nation," (or company or multitude of people, as *ethnos* can be truly rendered.)   (I. Pet. ii. 9.)

Where there is no condemnation there can be no need of judgment; hence we see this class at the sounding of the trump are caught up to meet Christ in the air, and so shall they ever be with the Lord.   (I. Thess. iv. 16, 17.)   "These are they who follow the Lamb whithersoever He goeth.   These were redeemed from among men, being the first-fruits unto God and to the Lamb." (Rev. xiv. 4.)   It is evident that a general harvest must needs follow the reaping of the first-fruits.   "Know you not that the saints shall judge the world."   "When the Son of man shall

come in his glory, and all the holy angels with
Him, then shall He sit upon the throne of his
glory; and before Him shall be gathered all nations." But according to the scriptures those
who overcome are to sit with Him *in his throne.*
If in his throne they are not amongst the vast
throng before it. If judges, they cannot be
amongst those who are to be judged. Since the
first-fruits have ascended to meet the Lord, they
consequently have been made immortal. "The
dead *in Christ* shall rise first." Observe the
phrase, "in Christ," that is, the members of his
holy body, or those who have been duly grafted
into the living vine. But the *harvest* is the *end*
of the world, and the reapers are the angels.
Then shall every one receive according as his
work shall be. Christ does not say, "Inasmuch
as ye have done it unto one of yourselves," but
"unto one of the least of *these* my brethren,"
undoubtedly pointing to those seated with Him
in his throne.

And thus we find that even a cup of cold water
given to one of these little ones, only in the name
of a disciple, shall not lose its reward. The prayers of all saints are offered with incense upon the
golden altar before the throne. (Rev. viii. 3.)
God is just, and every good thing will be remembered by Him. His mercy endureth forever.
There is a class called *holy*, and another called
righteous. On the other side we see also two
classes, viz: the unjust and the filthy. (Rev.
xxii. 11.) The holy are those that pass in with-

out condemnation—the blood of the Lamb having been set to their seal. The righteous are
those whose good deeds are brought into remembrance at the bar of judgment, and who are saved
by the mercy of God through the mediation of
Christ, as "brands plucked from the burning."

We are told, "If the *righteous scarcely be saved,*
where shall the ungodly and the sinner appear?"
showing clearly that the righteous are saved "so
as by fire." But the holy, or those who by holy
living and by the grace of God, are made to par-
take of the divine nature, and who "give diligence
to make their calling and election sure." Of
these we are told, "Ye shall never fall; for so an
entrance shall be ministered unto you abundantly
into the everlasting kingdom of our Lord and
Saviour Jesus Christ." (II. Peter i. 4-11.) "O
the depth of the riches both of the wisdom and
knowledge of God! how unsearchable are his
judgments, and his ways past finding out. For
who hath known the mind of the Lord, or who
hath been his counselor?"

But a few thoughts just here. The kingdom
must have subjects as well as rulers in order to
be complete or perfect; hence the necessity of
others being saved besides those who shall sit
with Christ in his throne as kings and priests to
God. A marriage would, in the type, be considered incomplete with only bridegroom and bride.
The friends of both are present at the feast. And
so shall it be at the marriage of the Lamb. In
the holy mountain "shall the Lord of hosts make

unto all his people a feast of fat things," and "blessed are they who are called unto the marriage supper of the Lamb."

God's kingdom shall be perfect, and as we behold his handiwork in the heavens overhead, we perceive that one star differeth from another star in glory; so also shall it be with the resurrection of the dead. All, therefore, shall not be as suns, nor as the planets, else there would be no lesser stars. Therefore, we are commanded to "do good unto all, but especially unto them who are of the household of faith," and when done as unto the Lord, and not as unto men, it is recorded in our favor in heaven. And thus you may insure a lot in the glorious inheritance, and also by the grace of God you may be a means of opening up a way of escape for others in the day of eternal judgment. As action speaks more loudly than words, and since by their fruits the children of God are to be known, therefore the principles involved in the precepts of Christ should be carried into effect. In this manner your light shall shine before men, and glory shall redound to God. Having done all, that we may stand and not be ashamed before Him when He appears should be our constant aim. "For we must all appear before the judgment seat of Christ." The judgment shall virtually begin when the Messiah appears. Those who are prepared shall, as we have already shown, enter in without condemnation. In a moment, in the twinkling of an eye they shall be changed from mortal to immortality.

All others must appear at the judgment bar of God, there to render an account of the deeds done in the body. Dear reader, "strive to enter in at the strait gate, for many shall seek to enter in and shall not be able." The night is far spent; the day of judgment is at hand.

Behold the Judge now seated in his throne,
All Nature quakes and utters her last groan,
The nations filled with awe before Him stand,
And separated are to either hand.
This is the final scene; there's no appeal
To higher court. 'Tis woe or weal.
Those on the right hand hear his tender voice,
"Come, blessed of my Father, and rejoice;
The land inherit; enter into rest;
Hence ever with your Lord, and ever blest.
Those on the left hand wail, and shuddering start—
O sentence dire, 'Ye cursed ones depart!'"

CHAPTER XII.

PREDESTINATION.

" For whom He did foreknow, He also did predestinate to be conformed to the image of his Son, that He might be the first-born among many brethren." (Rom. viii. 29.)

The doctrine of election, as it is generally called, has given rise to much dispute, which in turn has led to divisions terminating not unfrequently in many sinking either into infidelity outright, or into stoic indifference as to the religion of the Bible, which is not much to be preferred. Now permit me to say at the outset, that all such disputes arise simply for the want of a true understanding of the word of God relating to this doctrine. When doctrines or truths are shrouded in mystery, nothing but the unraveling finger of Heaven can make them so as to be understood. And thus we find it with the doctrine of election.

A knowledge of the doctrine of eternal judgment is really indispensable to a proper understanding of the doctrine of election. In our last chapter having considered the doctrine of eternal judgment, we will now proceed with the subject at issue.

1. *Who are the elect of God?* Wherever the term "elect" is applied in the scriptures it is used to denote members of a living church who have been duly grafted into Christ. Being "in Christ" their condemnation is removed. (Rom. viii. 1.) The characteristics of this class are clearly pointed out in the scriptures. They are members one of another. Heavenly love binds them together as one. Spiritual gifts are manifested in their assemblies. Signs follow them. (Mark xvi. 17, 18.) The *power* of the Holy Ghost is with them. They commune with their God, his Spirit bearing witness with theirs that they are his children, "heirs of God, and joint heirs with Christ; if so be that we *suffer* with Him, that we may be also glorified together." For every one of this class must be perfected as his Master. These are "a kind of first-fruits of his creatures," and constitute the body of Christ. The same class is depicted in Rev. xiv. 1-5.

That God foreknew his only begotten Son will be conceded by all who claim truth as theirs. As a day-star he was to arise and give hope to God's people of a coming day of glory. He was the first-fruits of them that slept. But those grafted into Him are to be the first-fruits of the great harvest of the earth, according to the scriptures. We have said God had this Son in view by foreknowledge or predestination, but the Son is but the HEAD of a *body*, which is the living church. Therefore according to reason as well as scripture, since God foreknew the *head* He also foreknew the *body* for that head, for God being perfect can never perform an imperfect work. It would be incomplete were the *head* predestinated without a *body* for it. But God has given the head a body according to his wisdom, and by his foreknowledge; and this body is his church—the church of the first-born. But this does not apply to the general mass of religionists. Out of them all the general harvest will be reaped. "Christ (is) as a son over his own house, whose house we are," *but only*, "if we hold fast the confidence and the rejoicing of the hope firm unto the end." But this house of Christ or bride, the Lamb's wife, does not constitute the possessors *in toto* of the everlasting kingdom. The Congress or Parliament of a nation does not constitute the nation. There are certain members elected to govern the nation and to form its laws. If, therefore, earthly nations must needs have an elected number to guide the ship of state, is it not much more the province of God to elect a certain portion of his people to a kingly priesthood, who shall reign upon the earth in its purified state? (Rev. v. 9, 10.) And the scriptures clearly teach that such a class exist. That an elect number exists does not shut off salvation from those outside of that number, if such will but acknowledge and obey God, and do good to others. The elect are the first-fruits unto God and the Lamb, as already

stated, but their symbolic number is one hundred
and forty and four thousand. Of the saved we
read of a great multitude which no man could
number. (Rev. vii. 9.) After the first-fruits
there must be a general harvest. The harvest is
the end of the world. "When the Son of man
shall come in his glory, and all the holy angels
with Him, then shall He sit upon the throne of his
glory, and before Him shall be gathered all
nations; and He shall separate them one from
another as a shepherd divideth his sheep from
the goats." But the first-fruits—the elect—are
in his throne with him, for the saints shall judge
the world. They have overcome by the blood
of the Lamb. At the coming of Christ they rise
to meet Him in the air. But all are not overcomers, all are not kings and priests, neither are
all to be rulers. He whose pound had gained ten
pounds was made ruler over ten cities, and he
whose pound had gained five was made ruler over
five cities. Each city must needs imply a number of inhabitants. Hence one individual, according to this parable, is made ruler over many.
Be it also observed the many must needs be
saved as well as the ruler. His position is more
distinguished, but to all is given an inheritance
incorruptible. According to Daniel the saints
(holy ones) "possess" the kingdom. (Dan. vii.
22.) But we are told: "The kingdom and dominion, and the greatness of the kingdom under
the whole heaven, shall be given to the *people* of
the saints of the Most High." (27.) Thus it

will be perceived there are "the saints," and
"the *people* of the saints." The living Church
are addressed as saints by the early apostles, and
also as the "elect, according to the foreknowledge of God."

The witness of God is given to the elect. They
do not need to stand in doubt. The Holy Spirit
is that witness. If we leave all and follow Christ,
obeying his commands, the gift is promised us.
(Acts ii. 38, 39.) But be not deceived, this witness is not a mere feeling, or a simple thought.
It is a living power, which produces undeniable
results. If joint-heirs with Christ they can con-
fidently exclaim: "Hereby *know* we that we
dwell in Him and He in us, because He hath
given us of his Spirit." They have also the
sweet assurance, "Beloved, *now* are we the sons
of God, and it doth not yet appear what we shall
be; but we know that when He shall appear, we
shall be like Him; for we shall see Him as He is."
But this exalted position is neither attained nor
retained without walking closely with God, as
evinced in the words immediately following:
"And every man that hath this hope in Him
purifieth himself, *even as He is pure.*" (I. John
iii. 2, 3.) Many attempt to claim the position of
sons without complying with the conditions.
Others say it is ours by simply believing, and
endeavor to rest upon the words so frequently
heard: "Jesus has done it all for me, and has
left nothing for me to do." This is tantamount
to crying, "Peace, peace, when there is no

peace," for the words of the foregoing text are
definite: "purifieth himself," cannot be misconstrued. The effort must be made by us; God
will supply the grace. To whom much is given
of them much shall be required. We must obey:
"If ye love me keep my commandments," and,
"He that saith I know Him and keepeth not his
commandments, is a liar and the truth is not in
him." If we would attain to the high calling of
God in Christ Jesus, we must fight the good
fight, and run the race set before us. We must
walk as He walked, and be perfected as He was
perfected, and love as He loved, in order to the
crown. "In the world ye shall have tribulation,"
is what Christ said, and not the praise of men;
but we have the comforting words: "Be of good
cheer, I have overcome the world." Again He
says: "Ye are not of the world even as I am
not of the world," but the blessed consolation is
given in the words: "If we suffer with Him we
shall also reign with Him." That there is a
crown for all, is a sad mistake. Kings without
nations, rulers without companies to be ruled
over, priests without congregations, is simply
absurd. "The *nations* of them that are saved
shall walk in the light of it; and the *kings* of the
earth do bring their glory and honor into it."
While as to immortality and joys unfading there
shall be equality in the glorified state, yet according to the scriptures, there shall also be degrees
of glory. For, as "one star differeth from
another star in glory, so also is the resurrection

of the dead." " And they that be teachers shall
shine as the brightness of the firmament; and
they that turn many to righteousness as the stars
for ever and ever." And, as already shown by
the words of Christ, one shall be made ruler over
ten cities and another over five. At another
time Jesus said to his disciples: "Verily I say
unto you, that ye who have followed me, in the
regeneration when the Son of man shall sit
in the throne of his glory, ye also shall sit upon
twelve thrones, judging the twelve tribes of
Israel." (Matt. xix. 28.) We deem this point
clearly established in the word, that one class are
elected of God, and shall reign as kings and
priests in the Paradise restored, while another
class vastly larger in numbers shall be saved at
the eternal judgment, when every man shall
receive according as his work shall be. At that
day the former class—the saints or perfected ones
—shall sit in judgment over the others. (See I.
Cor. vi. 2, 3. Daniel vii. 22. Ps. cxlix. 9.)

This is the high calling of God in Christ Jesus,
" according as He hath chosen us *in Him* before
the foundation of the world, that we should be
holy and without blame before Him in love, having predestinated us unto the adoption of children by Jesus Christ to himself, according to the
good pleasure of his will, to the praise of the glory
of his grace wherein He hath made us accepted
in the beloved." (Eph. i. 4-6.) It will be observed that this class are " *holy and without
blame.*" They are also *sealed* with the Holy

Spirit of promise, "which is the earnest of our inheritance until the redemption of the purchased possession unto the praise of his glory." (13, 14.) "That He might present it *with*—(it must be evident that it is *with* himself that he will present the first-fruits to God and not *to* himself, which rendering we deem imperfect)—himself a glorious church, not having spot or wrinkle, or any such thing, but that it should be holy and without blemish." (v. 27.) For this living church, the bride, the Lamb's wife, must needs be "conformed to the image of his Son," the glorious bridegroom, in order to sit with Him in his throne and reign with Him. In order to this high calling worldly position is not essential, neither is worldly wisdom required. As Paul clearly states in his letter to the church at Corinth: "For ye see your calling, brethren, how that not many wise men after the flesh, not many mighty, not many noble are called. But God hath chosen the foolish things of the world to confound the wise; and God hath chosen the weak things of the world to confound the things which are mighty; and base things of the world, and things which are despised hath God chosen, yea, and things which are not, to bring to naught things that are: that no flesh should glory in his presence." And thus we find it in the days of Christ's own sojourn here. He called not the lofty, neither the learned doctors of the law; but poor, illiterate, humble fishermen were called. It does not imply that no wise, or mighty, or noble men after the flesh are to be called. The words are, "*not many*," which implies some, for God is no respecter of persons. Where there is a humble heart willing to walk in the narrow way, and leave all for Christ, no matter what the position held in life, the calling is open for such.

But to return. The bride cannot possibly be constituted of the whole vast body of the redeemed. The figure would be incomplete. At a marriage there must needs be guests as well as bridegroom and bride. The friends of both must be there. True, the bride's position is the more enviable one. She shall be holy. She hath made herself ready. (Rev. xix. 7.) She is adorned with the garments of righteousness. "Free from condemnation" is written on her noble forehead. But at the marriage a feast is prepared for all the friends. "They that are not against us are for us." And those who have even given as much as a cup of cold water to a disciple, in the name of a disciple, shall not be forgotten at the feast. The bride is the "elect lady." (II. John 1.) She reclines on the bosom of her bridegroom's love. She leans upon the arm of her beloved. But the multitude of the saved shall pass through the door of infinite mercy. Inasmuch as they have done favor to any of the members of the bride, they have done it to Christ; and to them the blessed invitation shall be extended: "Come ye blessed of my Father, inherit the kingdom prepared for you." They shall inherit the land and dwell therein forever. "When the wicked are cut off thou shalt see it."

2. *Is there a crown for all?* We emphatically answer no. From what we have already written it will be seen that all cannot reign, else whom shall they reign over? There are inheritors to the land as well as heirs to the crown. It is absurd to claim that all shall sit with him in his throne. Since the saints are the "temple" of God, the congregation of spiritual Israel must be standing somewhere without. And when we view Solomon as a type of Christ in regard to his sitting in the throne of his father David, and his erecting of the temple, it must be remembered that he erected a house to himself as well as the temple. And in the anti-type, as we have already shown, Christ is as a son over his own house. But He also builds the spiritual temple of the Most High. And outside of both shall be the vast congregation of the redeemed, who shall be judged every one according as his work shall be. Many who here claim to be heirs to the crown of life may in that day hear the words from Christ, "sit down here." In the olden times young men were wont to run a race, and each carried a burning lamp in his hand. Only those who reached the winning post with their lamps burning received the prize. And so is it in the Christian race. Our lights must be kept burning all the way if we would have the crown of life. It was only at the end of a successful race that Paul

could exclaim, "Henceforth there is a crown laid up for me."

3. *We must strive for the crown of life.* Even earthly glory must be striven after. And it is vain to expect a crown of eternal glory without striving for it. " To him that overcometh" it is promised. Although there is the elect number, yet we have the command, " Hold that fast which thou hast that no man take thy crown," which shows the possibility of losing the position. An earthly Parliament or Congress must be composed of a certain number of members, and there is a general contest or election. Some lose, others win. So is it with those who strive for the crown of life. Paul says: "Know ye not that they which run in a race run all, but one receiveth the prize? So run that ye may obtain?" Hence we must work out our own salvation with fear and trembling. It is in God's grace we stand. Not of works lest any should boast, yet not without works, for faith without works is dead.

To sum up: We have shown that there is an elect body, according to the scriptures, who shall reign as kings and priests to God; also that there is a vast number who shall be saved as by fire, passing through the door of eternal judgment. To say the elect alone shall be saved is simply doing away with the necessity of a judgment. If all were elect a judgment would have no reason in it, it would be merely a formal scene. But God is no mocker; and his scene of judgment will be the grandest event ever witnessed. There shall his mercy and his boundless love be extended to the multitudes of poor wayfarers, who have walked in the light they had, although imperfectly, yet with honest hearts before Him.

But upon the bride of Christ—the elect lady, or church of the First-born—bright glory shall rest. The members of this body shall reign as kings and priests unto God eternally.   They shall form, as it were, the King's body guard.   They are joint-heirs with Christ—ever with the Lord.

> O dazzling glory!   *One* with Christ their King;
>   They stand in presence of the great I AM,
> And with their harps of gold his praises sing,
>   And tributes pay unto their Lord the Lamb:
> Worthy art Thou, O blessed Lamb, they cry,
>   Thou hast redeemed us with thy precious blood,
> And made us kings and priests unto our God;
>   Their hallelujahs sound in earth and sky.
>   O what singing!
>   Music ringing,
>   Like thunder pealing,
>   Like waters rushing,
> It sweepeth over mountain, dell, and plain,
> Hark! Alleluia, God on high doth reign!

CHAPTER XIII.

THE SAINTS' INHERITANCE — THE PURCHASED POSSESSION OR PARADISE REDEEMED.

"Blessed are the meek for they shall inherit the earth."

When an inheritance is bequeathed to a man of this world there invariably follows a season of rejoicing. If it be not in the vicinity where he is located, he at once prepares for a journey. He cannot rest until he sets foot upon his new possessions. This is an ambition peculiar to human nature. The title deed is inquired into to see whether it be free from incumbrance. If satisfactory, friends are called in that they may congratulate him on his good fortune. Such an inheritance is but transient, and such rejoicings are fleeting. "The earth is the Lord's and the fullness thereof." Man in the present state has but a short lease of any portion that may fall to his lot. He must yield it up at last. It is therefore vain to boast of possessions which virtually belong to another. Rather let us exclaim with the apostle, "Here have we no continuing city, but we seek one to come." But God has promised his people an inheritance incorruptible, which fadeth not away, a kingdom which shall forever endure—a home where joys unspeakable and pleasures unfading shall be their portion. This inheritance is plainly revealed in his word. The wayfaring men though fools may learn of its glories; for, although it is written, "Eye hath not seen, nor ear heard, neither have entered into the heart of man, the things which God hath prepared for them that love Him;" yet "God hath revealed them unto us by his Spirit." (I. Cor. ii. 9, 10.)

The promise was first given to the patriarch Abraham: "And the Lord said unto Abram, lift up now thine eyes, and look from the place where thou art, northward, and southward, and eastward and westward; for all the land which thou seest, to thee will I give it, and to thy seed forever. And I will make thy seed as the dust of the earth; so that if a man can number the dust of the earth, then shall thy seed also be numbered. Arise, walk through the land, in the length of it and in the breadth of it; for I will give it unto thee." (Gen. xiii. 14-17.) Or again, "And I will give unto thee and to thy seed after thee, the land of thy sojournings (margin), all the land of Canaan, for an everlasting possession; and I will be their God." (xvii. 8.) Now let it be noticed that this promise is not couched in ambiguous language, as modern theories and creeds would lead people to understand. It is plain. The meaning of the language employed is evident.

As to the location of this inheritance, it is clearly defined: "All the land which thou seest," not among the stars overhead, but the veritable " land of Canaan," " to thee will I give it, and to thy seed forever." That Abraham did not receive a fulfillment of the promise in his day and generation is evident from the scriptures. We quote: " Abraham, when he was called to go out into a place which he should after receive for an inheritance, obeyed; and he went out not knowing whither he went. By faith he sojourned in the land of promise, as in a strange country, dwelling in tabernacles with Isaac and Jacob, the heirs with him of the same promise." (Heb. xi. 8, 9.) And in the thirteenth verse we are plainly told concerning the fathers, among whom Abraham is included: "These all died in faith, not having received the promises, but having received them afar off, and were persuaded of them, and embraced them, and confessed that they were strangers and pilgrims on the earth."

Paul tells us that by promise Abraham "should be the heir of the WORLD," conjointly with his "seed." (Rom. iv. 13.) For the promise was not made to Abraham only, but also to his SEED, which seed is Christ. (Gal. iii. 16.) Neither was the promise disannulled by the law: "For if the inheritance be of the law, it is no more of prom-

ise; but God gave it to Abraham by promise."
(17, 18.) "Therefore it is of faith that it might
be by grace; to the end the promise might be
sure to ALL the seed; not to that only which is of
the law, but to that also which is of the faith of
Abraham, who is the father of us all." (Rom.
iv. 16.) "And if ye be Christ's, then are ye
Abraham's seed, and heirs according to the promise." (Gal. iii. 29.) In this also we can perceive
how it is that the promised seed becomes so multitudinous. It implies all God's children, both
Jew and Gentile, as foreseen by the apostle John
through the Spirit: "I beheld, and lo, a great multitude which no man could number, of all nations,
and kindreds, and people, and tongues, stood
before the throne, and before the Lamb, clothed
with white robes, and palms in their hands."
(Rev. vii. 9.)

The land, or inheritance, as promised to Abraham, was the hope of the ancient Fathers. The
Psalmist of Israel expresses himself, "Those that
wait upon the Lord, they shall inherit THE EARTH."
"The Lord knoweth the days of the upright; and
their INHERITANCE shall be forever." "For such
as be blessed of him shall inherit THE EARTH."
"The righteous shall inherit THE LAND and dwell
therein forever." "Wait on the Lord, and keep
his way, and He shall exalt thee to inherit THE
LAND; when the wicked are cut off, thou shalt see
it." (Ps. xxxvii.) And as he gazed upon the
beauties of Palestine, no doubt anticipating the
time when the whole earth should be filled with

the glory of the Lord, (Num. xiv. 21) he exclaims: "Great is the Lord, and greatly to be praised in the city of our God, in the mountain of his holiness. Beautiful for situation, the joy of the whole earth, is MOUNT ZION, on the sides of the north, the city of the great King." (Ps. xlviii. 1, 2.) Solomon says, "The upright shall dwell in THE LAND, and the perfect shall remain in it." (Prov. ii. 21.) The words of the Lord as given through Isaiah are, "He that putteth his trust in Me shall possess THE LAND, and shall inherit my holy mountain." (lvii. 13.) "Violence shall no more be heard in thy LAND, wasting nor destruction within thy borders; but thou shalt call thy walls Salvation, and thy gates Praise. The sun shall be no more thy light by day; neither for brightness shall the moon give light unto thee: but the Lord shall be unto thee an everlasting light, and thy God thy glory. Thy people shall be all righteous; they shall inherit THE LAND forever, the branch of my planting, the work of my hands, that I may be glorified." (lx. 18–21.) "I have set watchmen upon thy walls, O Jerusalem, which shall never hold their peace day nor night; ye that are the Lord's remembrancers keep not silence, and give Him no rest till He establish, and till He make JERUSALEM a praise in the earth." (lxii. 6, 7.) "Therefore the redeemed of the Lord shall return, and come with singing unto ZION; and everlasting joy shall be upon their heads; they shall obtain gladness and joy; and sorrow and mourning shall flee away." (li.

11.) Through Ezekiel we have, "Thus saith the Lord God, Behold, O my people, I will open your graves, and cause you to come up out of your graves, and bring you into the LAND OF ISRAEL, and ye shall know that I am the Lord, when I have opened your graves, O my people, and brought you up out of your graves, and shall put my Spirit in you, and ye shall live, and I shall place you in your OWN LAND." (xxxvii. 12–14.) Daniel tells us of the same inheritance under the appellation of a kingdom. Amos prophecies, " Behold the days come, saith the Lord. And I will bring again the captivity of my people of Israel, and they shall build the waste cities, and inhabit them; and they shall plant vineyards, and drink the wine thereof; they shall also make gardens and eat the fruit of them. And I will plant them upon their LAND, and they shall no more be pulled up out of their LAND which I have given them, saith the Lord thy God." (ix. 13–15.)

The disciples of Jesus were inspired with the same hope when they were led to inquire, "Lord, wilt thou at this time restore again the kingdom to Israel?" (Acts i. 6.)

Jesus taught them this hope in the words, "Ye who have followed me, in the regeneration, when the Son of man shall sit in the throne of his glory, ye also shall sit upon twelve thrones, judging the twelve tribes of Israel." (Matt. xix. 28.) In another instance He told them, "Whither I go ye cannot come," referring to his ascension to heaven; but He reassured them with the words of sweet consolation, "I will come again, and receive you unto myself; that where I am, there ye may be also." "For the kingdom of heaven is as a man traveling into a far country, who called his own servants, and delivered unto them his goods. After a long time the Lord of those servants cometh, and reckoneth with them." (Matt. xxv. 14-19.) This evidently refers to the consummation of the same blessed hope. Jesus also taught his disciples to pray for the arrival of the glorious epoch in the words, "Thy kingdom come, thy will be done on THE EARTH as in heaven." Be it observed this is the first petition in the form of prayer dictated by our Lord, and this prayer remains unanswered, (i. e., literally) so long as sin holds sway upon the earth. The will of God shall not " be done on the earth as in heaven" until the perfect day is ushered in. " When this corruptible shall have put on incorruption, and this mortal shall have put on immortality, then shall be brought to pass the saying that is written, Death is swallowed up in victory," but not till then.

But according to the scriptures, the inheritance of the saints must needs be redeemed as well as the beings who are to possess its future glories. This formed a leading part of Christ's mission. The kingdom, or inheritance was prepared "from the foundation of the world." The earth as it stood in pristine bloom, fresh from the hands of the Creator, was evidently the kingdom, inheritance or home prepared for man, and hence

"from the foundation of the world." But when
Adam fell through disobedience, a curse was pronounced on the ground; as it is written, "Cursed
is the ground for thy sake; in sorrow shalt thou
eat of it all the days of thy life; thorns also and
thistles shall it bring forth to thee; and thou
shalt eat the herb of the field; in the sweat of thy
face shalt thou eat bread, till thou return unto
the ground; for out of it wast thou taken; for
dust thou art, and unto dust shalt thou return."
(Gen. iii. 17-19.) Eden's beauties were thus lost
in Adam, but through Christ they shall duly be
redeemed. The possession of a sinless earth was
lost through sin, therefore only through the blood
of a sinless Redeemer can it be redeemed or restored to its former state. Paul intimates this
truth in his letter to the church at Ephesus. He
says: "After that ye believed ye were sealed
with that holy Spirit of promise, which is the
earnest of our inheritance until the *redemption of
the purchased possession*, unto the praise of his
glory." (i. 13, 14.) But theology teaches that
the saints' inheritance is in heaven. If so, then
the curse needs not be removed from the earth.
If in heaven where God dwells in excellent
glory and holiness, then it never fell under a
curse, and consequently needeth not redemption.
Hence an alarming discrepancy at once becomes
apparent in this theory. For we are told by Paul
the seal of our hope is but the earnest (or surety)
from heaven until the "*redemption of the purchased possession*." However, when we lay aside

traditions of men and search the scriptures all becomes clear. For, amazing though it may appear, yet we affirm that the scriptures contain no promise whatever of an inheritance in heaven for man. "The heaven, even the heavens are the Lord's; but the earth hath he given to the children of men." Christ says: "Blessed are the meek; for they shall inherit the earth." The earth being the inheritance of God's children it follows that, since it fell under the curse because of sin, it must needs be redeemed from that curse, in order to its becoming a fit abode for saints.

And hence we perceive how that Christ crucified becomes to them that believe both the "power of God" and the "wisdom of God." He bore the weight of our transgressions upon that heart which was "exceeding sorrowful even unto death." He bore the curse upon his head; for the thorn was a product of the curse, and hence our inheritance was redeemed or purchased by the blood that trickled down beneath the thorny crown. When the day of redemption shall have fully come, every saint shall return to his possession—the purchased possession—and the jubilee of jubilees shall be proclaimed. But again let us look to Calvary. The hands of Christ were pierced, that in the land beyond, the hands of the redeemed might no more hang down in weariness from arduous toil. His feet shed blood that in Eden restored we might "run and not be weary," and "walk and not faint." "Therefore the redeemed of the Lord shall return, and come

with singing unto Zion; and everlasting joy shall
be upon their head; they shall obtain gladness
and joy; and sorrow and mourning shall flee
away." (Is. li. 11.) "For the Lord hath chosen
Zion, He hath desired it for his habitation."
(Ps. cxxxii. 13.) "Thine eyes shall see Jerusalem, a quiet habitation, a tabernacle that shall
not be taken down; not one of the stakes thereof
shall ever be removed, neither shall any of the
cords thereof be broken." (Is. xxxiii. 20.) "And
the Lord shall be king over all the earth; in that
day shall there be one Lord, and his name one."
For when the seventh angel sounds, great voices
in heaven shall be heard saying: "The kingdoms of *this world* are become the kingdom of
our Lord and of his Christ; and He shall reign
for ever and ever." (Rev. xi. 15.) "And the
kingdom and dominion, and the greatness of the
kingdom under the whole heaven shall be given
to the people of the saints of the Most High,
whose kingdom is an everlasting kingdom, and
all dominions shall serve and obey Him." (Dan.
vii. 27.) "And we shall reign on the earth."
(Rev. v. 10.) "And there shall be no more
curse; but the throne of God and of the Lamb
shall be in it; and his servants shall serve Him;
and they shall see his face; and his name shall be
in their foreheads. And there shall be no night
there; and they need no candle, neither light of
the sun; for the Lord God giveth them light;
and they shall reign for ever and ever." (Rev.
xxii. 3-5.) "The mountains and the hills (clad

with the multitude of the redeemed) shall break
forth before you into singing, and all the trees of
the field shall clap their hands," (for the saints
shall be called " trees of righteousness, the planting of the Lord.") " Instead of the thorn shall
come up the fir tree, and instead of the brier
shall come up the myrtle tree." (Is. lv. 12, 13.)
" And I heard a great voice out of heaven saying,
Behold, the tabernacle of God is *with men*, and
He will dwell with them, and they shall be his
people, and God himself shall be with them and
be their God. And God shall wipe away all tears
from their eyes; and there shall be no more
death, neither sorrow, nor crying, neither shall
there be any more pain; for the former things are
passed away." (Rev. xxi. 3, 4.) " Then the
moon shall be confounded, and the sun ashamed,
when the Lord of Hosts shall reign in Mount
Zion and in Jerusalem, and before his ancients
gloriously." (Is. xxiv. 23.) From these scriptures both the inheritance and its glory are
clearly defined.

As the veil of the temple rent and disclosed
the holy place at the crucifixion of Christ, so at
his second appearing shall the veil of the heavens rend and disclose the holiest place above;
and the Lord shall appear in his glory. Faith is
then lost in sight, and the King in his beauty we
shall behold. Instead of the thorny crown,
heaven's bight glory shall encircle his brow, and
the ransomed of the Lord shall strike their harps

of gold, and sing the glad new song in Paradise redeemed.

> The earth renewed, no sin dwells there,
>   From east to west, from south to north,
> All—all is beauteous, all is fair,
>   The righteous there shine forth:
>   In joy and peace, in love together,
>   No more to part, they live forever.

The inheritance, when promised to Father Abraham was set, as it were, in the spiritual heavens as the cheering " day star " of hope. Its soul-gladdening gleams fell upon the pathway of Isaac and of Jacob, heirs with Abraham of the same promise. (Gen. xxvi. 3-5; xxxv. 11, 12.) And so with all the seed of Abraham; for all the way through the Mosaical dispensation it shone effulgently upon the path of Zion's tempest-tost pilgrims. Israel desired and looked for an heavenly country—a sun-bright land. They relied upon the promises of God. Christ as the promised seed must needs come first. The curse could not be removed without a Redeemer. When He came light arose. He himself is the " Morning Star." Hope is made sure only through his triumph over death. The promises made unto Father Abraham are ratified through Christ. When we put on Christ, the " day star " arises in our hearts. For, " If ye be Christ's, then are ye Abraham's seed, and heirs according to the promise." " Unto them that look for Him shall He appear the second time without sin (or sin-offering) unto salvation." The purchased possession cannot be redeemed till the day of redemption come. Then shall that world be established wherein dwelleth righteousness; then shall the kingdom come for which the faithful have so long and so earnestly prayed; then shall the will of God be done on earth even as it is done in heaven; and the saints shall possess their inheritance forever—their sweet Eden home— and shall be forever with the Lord. Bright Paradise redeemed, all hail!

> " There is the home of the 'pure and the blest ;
> There shall the weary be ever at rest ;
> There shall life's trials and sorrows be o'er ;
> There shall the gathered ones part nevermore ;
> There shall the blest be from death ever free ;
> There their Redeemer in beauty they'll see ;
> Crowns of bright glory forever they'll wear ;
> O, to be with them !—we long to be there ! "

12

CHAPTER XIV.

THE ETERNAL KINGDOM.

One class of theologians tell us that we are to have a millennial reign of Christ, and base their theory on a literal acceptance of the twentieth chapter of Revelation. "Comparing spiritual things with spiritual," is the rule of scripture. If this rule be adopted, the so-called millennium must either dissolve and give place to comprehensible truth, or on the other hand it must be branded as an inexplicable mystery contrary to the plain teachings of Christ and the early apostles, and which also conflicts with scripture types. If we can prove from the scriptures that the theory of a thousand years peaceful reign of Christ on the earth before the ultimate establishment of the eternal kingdom is nothing less than a mystery, then the proper place to cast it is upon the forehead of Babylon the Great. (Rev. xvii. 5.) In order that we may be the more clearly understood, we will first define our position.

We affirm that the scriptures plainly teach that when the kingdom of God is established on the earth, its duration shall be eternal; that when it is thus established, mortality shall be swallowed up of life, and the time of probation ended; and that the judgment of all nations shall then be over, and consequently the rewards given to the righteous, and the wicked destroyed.

The establishment and duration of the kingdom. It is generally conceded by those who look for the second coming of the Messiah, that He is coming to establish his kingdom on this earth; but as to the nature of its establishment few agree. There are many channels of thought, but there is only one channel of *truth.* God has given us his word. It is like a golden casket enclosing many priceless gems. The Spirit of Truth is the key which opens the casket and brings the gems to view. (John xiv. 26, and xvi. 13.) This is where man, generally speaking, fails. He leans too much to his own understanding, and places his own interpretation on symbolic and prophetic scripture. If we interpret the symbolic aright, it must harmonize with the plain teachings of Jesus and his apostles. But when a given interpretation conflicts with the plainly revealed word, such confliction should be sufficient to convince the interpreter of his error. The book of Revelation contains much that is symbolic, still when it says "a thousand years," it is accepted by many in all its literalness. Yet when we compare scripture with scripture, we find it recorded, "that one day is with the Lord *as* a thousand years, and a thousand years *as* one day." (II. Pet. iii. 8.) Taking the term in its symbolic sense, we see that it refers to a period of time without exact limitation as to time. This period may be termed a season or day of the Lord. For example, the period transpiring from the first to the second advent of Christ is called the day of salvation. This day is now over eighteen hundred years in length. The exact length of the Lord's seasons as relating to the future, is not given in the word. Jesus told his disciples, "It is not for you to know the times or the seasons, which the Father hath put in his own power." (Acts i. 7.) Therefore according to this view the thousand years referred to must have been used in a symbolic sense. But by close investigation and comparing scripture with scripture, we find that the events of the period specified, all apply to the day of salvation, nor can they apply to anything else when we consider the events which immediately succeed. Let us here briefly consider, by way of comment, the twentieth chapter of Revelation.

Verse 1. *"And I saw an angel come down from heaven having the key of the bottomless pit and a great chain in his hand."* This can all apply to Christ during his first advent. He truly had the key of death and the grave, and a " great chain in his hand," viz: the Spirit power of God.

Verse 2. *"And he laid hold on the dragon, that old serpent, which is the devil, and Satan, and bound him a thousand years.*" The mission of Christ was to proclaim liberty to the captives, and to destroy the works of Satan. He says: "If I cast out devils by the Spirit of God, then the kingdom of God is come unto you. Or else how can one enter a strong man's house, and spoil his goods, except *he first bind the strong man?* and then he will spoil his house." (Matt. xii. 28, 29.) Christ's mission procured for us the protection of the Almighty. To the child of God, Satan is virtually bound. Hence the command, "Resist the devil and he will flee from you." His power is so limited that it is impossible for him to deceive the elect of God. The disciples returned rejoicing when they found that even the devils were subject unto them through Christ's name. (Luke x. 17.) The church of Christ is founded on a rock, " and the gates of hell shall not prevail against it." (Matt. xvi. 18.) To claim that Satan has sway, is to detract from the glory of the Son of God, who said after his resurrection, "*All* power is given unto me in heaven and in earth."

Verse 3. "*That he should deceive the nations no more till the thousand years should be fulfilled.*" While the word *ethne* is here rendered nations, it can as truly be rendered " companies," "band of comrades," " a body of men," etc. In chapter xxi. 24, we read, "and the *nations* of them who are saved shall walk in the light of it." Companies, instead of nations, is decidedly the more preferable rendering. And in both instances quoted it must be evident that the companies of the redeemed is that which is implied, for according to the scriptures, "evil men and seducers shall wax worse and worse, deceiving and being deceived."

Verse 4. *"And I saw the souls of them who were beheaded for the witness of Jesus . . and they lived and reigned with Christ a thousand years."* Here is the real basis of all millennialism. But, we inquire, who or what lives and reigns with Christ during this period? The scripture replies, "the souls (*psuchas*) of them." That "souls" is the antecedent of the pronoun *they* is evident. The *Emphatic Diaglott* renders the word *psuchas*, "persons" instead of "souls," but this rendering is evidently defective, for *psuchee*, from which *psuchas* is derived, really implies the life principle, and not the person. But the imperfection of this rendering is quite easily perceived by simply examining the construction of the sentence as a whole, "And *I saw* the persons of those who had been beheaded," etc. After the demonstrative *those*, the noun *persons* is evidently understood. Its harshness, therefore, becomes apparent by filling up the ellipsis: "And *I saw* the persons of those persons," etc. If the beings are really there, then the first part of the sentence is superfluous. But it does not so read. We are merely told that John saw the souls (lives or life principle) of the beheaded ones. That Christ now reigns at the right hand of the Father is an established fact. That the life of those referred to, as well as the life of all saints, "is hid with

Christ in God," (Col. iii. 3, 4) is a scriptural fact. Therefore since Christ reigns, the life reigns with Him, until He who is our life shall appear; then shall the persons to whom the life shall be given appear with Him in glory. At that time the overcomers shall reign with Christ in person forever.

Verse 5. The clause, "*But the rest of the dead lived not again until the thousand years were finished,*" is not found in the Vatican MS., and consequently is of disputed authority. However it neither adds to nor detracts from the strength of the argument. "*This is the first resurrection,*" connects in sense with verse fourth. According to what we have already given, the resurrection here referred to must be spiritual. This also is sustained by scripture. Jesus said: "Verily, I say unto you, the hour is coming and *now is* when the dead shall hear the voice of the Son of God; and they that hear shall live." Paul says: "Awake thou that sleepest, and arise from the dead, and Christ shall give thee light." For, as the same apostle writes: "God, who is rich in mercy, for his great love wherewith he loved us, even when we were dead in sins, hath quickened us together with Christ, . . . and hath raised us up together, and made us sit together in heavenly places, in Christ Jesus." Therefore, "If ye then be risen with Christ, seek those things which are above." These scriptures clearly imply a spiritual resurrection from a state of sin to a state of righteousness, and from darkness and death to light and life. But will this fill the requirements of the succeeding verse? Let us examine.

Verse 6. *"Blessed and holy is he that hath part in the first resurrection."* No one will question the fact that the true child of God is *blessed* in this dispensation; and as to being *holy*, Paul besought his brethren at Rome to present their bodies, a living sacrifice, *holy*, acceptable unto God, which was their reasonable service. Christ is the " resurrection and the life." He is also the "first-fruits of them that slept," or in other words the first-fruits of the resurrection. If we "put on Christ," we at once become members of his body, therefore have a part in Him who is the first born from the dead. His righteousness then applies to us, since through Him God is reconciled. We thus become *blessed* of the Father and *holy*, being "accepted in the Beloved." Of course, this class tread the narrow path. *"On such the second death hath no power."* If our life is hid with Christ in God, death hath no longer dominion over us. Those in Christ who even pass down the lone valley into the tomb, are only said to be asleep in Jesus, and "Them that sleep in Jesus will God bring with Him." And "There is therefore now no condemnation to them who are in Christ Jesus, who walk not after the flesh but after the Spirit." (Rom. viii. 1.) This class, at the sounding of the trump, are caught up to meet the Lord in the air, and then shall they ever be with the Lord. (I. Thess. iv. 16, 17.) Hence, on such the second death hath no power, for their names are written in the Lamb's book of life.

"*They shall be priests of God and of Christ.*" This does not necessarily imply futurity. John says: "Unto Him tl.at loved us, and washed us from our sins in his own blood, and *hath made* us kings and priests unto God and his Father; to Him be glory and dominion forever." (Rev. i. 5, 6.) Here we find the present perfect tense of the verb used. Peter designates the saints as "a holy priesthood," and as a "royal priesthood." Thus we find that this scripture applies to the present dispensation. As to the loosing of Satan, and his gathering of the multitudes to battle, it is simply absurd to say that such a scene will take place after Christ and his saints have been reigning a thousand years. Such a view is an outrage against the wisdom, the omnipotence and the truth of God. But on this point scripture again comes to our aid, and we find that just such a scene is to occur at the closing of the day of salvation. When the sixth angel pours out his vial, three unclean spirits go forth. "They are the spirits of devils working miracles." Their mission is to gather the masses "to the battle of that great day of God Almighty." (Rev. xvi. 12-14.) This coincides with Rev. xx. 8. That these three unclean spirits have gone forth is evident. This proves our position to be correct. One of these unclean spirits proceeds out of the mouth of the dragon, (the devil) and in the wonder workings of modern spiritualism he manifests himself. The

second proceeds out of the mouth of the beast,
(Babylon) and Knock, in Ireland, recently laid
claim to some of his miracles, where, it is said, a
vision was also seen of the virgin and two of the
early apostles by her side. The third emanates
from the mouth of the false prophet, and is none
other than the monstrous and filthy spirit of Mor-
monism. The influence exerted by these three
spirit principles over the masses of humanity at
the present time will not be fully known until the
trump of God shall sound. "Then shall that
wicked be revealed, whom the Lord shall consume
with the spirit of his mouth, and shall destroy
with the brightness of his coming, even him whose
coming is after the working of Satan, with all
power, and signs, and lying wonders." (II. Thess.
ii. 8, 9.) Here we have a most striking coinci-
dence with Rev. xx. 9. When the camp of the
saints is compassed about, fire comes down from
God out of heaven and devours them. As it is
written, "Our God is a consuming fire." And
"The Lord Jesus shall be revealed from heaven
with his mighty angels in flaming fire, yielding
vengeance on them that know not God, and that
obey not the gospel of our Lord Jesus Christ, who
shall be punished with everlasting destruction
from the presence of the Lord, and from the glory
of his power, when He shall come to be glorified
in his saints." And "every man's work shall be
made manifest; for the day shall declare it, because it shall be revealed by fire; and the fire
shall try every man's work of what sort it is."

Since, therefore, that "Wicked one" is to be *destroyed* with the brightness of the coming Messiah, and since those who know not nor obey God are to be punished with *everlasting destruction*, when Jesus comes to be glorified in his saints, how shall the wicked ones be preserved until a thousand years after that coming? Christ's coming to be glorified in his saints, and the punishment of the wicked with everlasting destruction evidently synchronize.

Reader, open your eyes and look about you. The way of truth you will find is well nigh encompassed about to-day. The devil is indeed abroad in the earth gathering his hosts, and the last great conflict is truly progressing. Skepticism of things sacred, and evil of every description fill the very air. A little longer and 'Jesus shall be revealed in flaming fire. Wrong and evil may apparently triumph now, but the righteous shall soon sound the note of victory eternal.

Verse 11. "*And I saw a great white throne, and Him that sat on it, from whose face the earth and the heaven fled away.*" If millenarians are correct in their views, is it not strange that this throne of judgment appears at the expiration of the thousand years, instead of at the commencement of that period? For scripture everywhere harmonizes with the view—nay teaches—that judgment precedes the reign of righteousness. The scene recorded from the 11th verse to the end of the chapter is strictly parallel with that described by our Lord himself in Matt. xxv. 31-

46. In fact, the inaugural scene of the kingdom
is judgment. The separation is no sooner made
than Jesus addresses the righteous, "Come ye
blessed of my Father, inherit the kingdom prepared for you from the foundation of the world."
Be it also observed that "before Him shall be
gathered *all* nations." Who then shall be left
until the end of a thousand years? The tenor of
scripture does not sustain the view of two judgment scenes.

Verse 12. *"And the books were opened, and
another book was opened which is the book of life."*
Stranger still, the book of life is not opened till
after the millennial reign is ended. Whence then
do the reigning ones derive their life which sustains them during this period? Such a mix up
as this is simply absurd. Order is God's most
sacred law, and by infinite wisdom He ruleth all
in all. When Christ comes the second time, He
comes as the sin-destroyer, and also as the life-
giver of the saints. Paul tells us that this life
shall be given at Christ's coming. (I. Cor. xv.
22, 23.) He also tells us how it shall be done.
"We shall not all sleep, but we shall all be
changed, in a moment, in the twinkling of an eye,
at the last trump: for the trumpet shall .sound,
and the dead shall be raised incorruptible, and we
shall be changed." (51, 52.) Death then is swallowed up in victory. (54.) Hence there can be
no more dying; consequently judgment must be
over.

The saints, i. e., those who form the great Christ
body, shall rise to meet the Lord. The invita-

tion shall be, "Come, my people, enter into thy chambers, and shut thy doors about thee: hide thyself, as it were, for a little moment until the indignation be overpast, for behold the Lord cometh out of his place to punish the inhabitants of the earth for their iniquity." "For," says the Psalmist, "in the time of trouble He shall hide me in his pavillion, in the secret of his tabernacle shall He hide me." As it was in the days of Noah, and as it was in the days of Lot, so shall it be in that great day. One thing is evident: in those days destruction came suddenly upon the wicked, and the righteous alone were saved. No thousand years then transpired before the judgment came.

Paul tells us that the Lord Jesus Christ "shall judge the quick (living) and the dead *at his appearing and his kingdom.*" (II. Tim. iv. 1.) From this it is evident that the appearing, the kingdom, and the judgment are to be cotemporaneous. No thousand years after Christ's appearing is mentioned. It must be admitted that Paul knew what he was talking about. Though the faith of the whole world should have error for its basis, truth abideth the same. A certain time must elapse from the appearing of the Messiah until the kingdom is established, still the scriptures sustain the view that the appearing, the judgment and final establishment of the kingdom shall follow each other in rapid and connected succession. The connection of the events is clearly given in Rev. xi. 15-18: "And the seventh angel sounded; and there were great voices in heaven, saying, The kingdoms of this world are become the kingdoms of our Lord, and of his Christ; and He shall reign forever and ever. . . . And the nations were angry, and thy wrath is come, and *the time* of the dead that they should be judged, and that thou shouldest give reward unto thy servants, the prophets, and them that fear thy name, small and great, and shouldest destroy them who corrupt the earth.''

It is evident that the sound of the seventh angel's trumpet denotes the appearing of Christ. As Paul tells us, "The Lord shall descend from heaven with a shout, with the voice of the archangel, and with the *trump* of God." At which sound the kingdoms of this world shall surrender in consternation. Or as Jesus himself says," Then shall all the tribes of the earth mourn, and they shall see the Son of man coming in the clouds of heaven. And He shall send his angels with a great sound of a *trumpet*, and they shall gather together his elect from the four winds, from the one end of heaven to the other." This point established, its concomitants must also be accepted; viz: angry nations, the day of wrath come, the time arrived for the judgment of the dead, and also for the bestowing of rewards upon God's servants and children, together with the destruction of the wicked. This is truly a parallel to the judgment scene as depicted in both Rev. xx. 11-15, and Matt. xxv. 31-46. And since the scriptures clearly prove that the same is connected with the appearing of Christ, the millennium as popularly taught must dissolve sooner or later; for if the truth be not now accepted, one thing is inevitable, it shall be enforced at the sounding of the last trump. We are told, "The saints shall judge the world." (I. Cor. vi. 2.) The Psalmist says, "To execute upon them (the nations) the judgment written: this honor have all the saints." And Daniel tells us that "judgment was given to the saints of the Most High;" and in connection therewith, he continues, "And the time came that the saints possessed the kingdom." (Dan. vii. 22.) Here we have another instance where judgment and the establishment of the kingdom go hand in hand. If we take the parables of Christ, they invariably teach the same thing. And it is certainly strange, granting there is to be a millennium, that the great Teacher himself said nothing about it when on earth; nor did Paul, although we are told he declared the whole counsel of God.

The tares and the good seed grow together till the harvest; then comes the separation. When the tares or children of the wicked one are cast into the furnace of fire, it is then and not till then, that the righteous shall " shine forth as the sun in the kingdom of their Father." (Matt. xiii. 40–43.) In the same chapter the kingdom of heaven is compared to a net, which is not drawn ashore until it is full, and the good is then separated from the bad. Or, as it is given in plain language, " So shall it be at the end of the world;

the angels shall come forth, and sever the wicked from among the just, and shall cast them into a furnace of fire; there shall be wailing and gnashing of teeth."

In the parable of the ten virgins, the wise are taken into the marriage and the unwise shut out at the coming of the Bridegroom. And when once the Master hath shut to the door, we are told those without shall hear the doleful sentence, "Depart from me all ye workers of iniquity." (Luke xiii. 25-28.) When the Lord comes a second time it is to reckon with his servants. We are also told, "it shall be revealed by fire." "For the day of the Lord shall come as a thief in the night; in the which the heavens shall pass away with a great noise, and the elements shall melt with fervent heat, the earth also and the works that are therein shall be burned up. . . Nevertheless we, according to his promise, look for new heavens and a new earth, wherein dwelleth righteousness." (II. Peter iii. 10-13.) Or as given by Malachi, "Behold the day cometh that shall burn as an oven; and all the proud, yea, and all that do wickedly shall be stubble; and the day that cometh shall burn them up, saith the Lord of hosts, that it shall leave them neither root nor branch."

Now millenarians must either concede that Christ shall reign a thousand years on an unpurified earth, or that the judgment takes place at the beginning of said reign, and consequently prior to the establishment of the everlasting kingdom.

To concede the former would be virtually acknowledging the error in which they stand, and to own the latter is to admit that the thousand years of Rev. xx. is but a symbol of a period prior to the coming of Christ to sit in judgment. It is clearly given that the fire of destruction precedes the new heavens and the new earth, and the same fire, according to Malachi, destroys all the proud and all that do wickedly. Therefore the purging fire and the punishment of the wicked precede the reign of righteousness, according to the scriptures. Hence the Psalmist enjoins, " Wait on the Lord, and keep his way, and He shall exalt thee to inherit the land; when the wicked are cut off, thou shalt see it." Therefore, the dogma that tells man he shall inherit the land, and reign in peace with Christ a thousand years before even the wicked are judged, to say nothing of their being " *cut off*," is evidently contrary to the scriptures.

" Behold I come quickly; and my reward is with me to give every man according as his work shall be." If some receive reward a thousand years before others, or if there is to be a millennium in which mortals are to have privileges which they cannot have now, then God is a respecter of persons. But God's word teaches no such absurdity. Christ comes as the rewarder of his saints, and as the avenger of evil. Every one shall receive according as his work shall be, and those worthy shall be made perfect at one and the same time. (See Heb. xi. 40.) When Christ comes,

13

the day of redemption shall be ushered in, the earth shall be redeemed from the curse, and the bloom of Eden shall be restored no more to be blighted with a liberated devil, neither at the end of a millennium nor at any other time forever. When the liberty comes it shall be "the glorious liberty of the children of God." No more will the camp of the saints be encompassed with the hosts of the adversary. When the heavens reveal the coming Messiah, the hosts of this world surrender unconditionally, even as the scripture tells us, "The kings of the earth, and the great men, and the rich men, and the chief captains, and the mighty men, and every bondman, and every freeman hid themselves in the dens and in the rocks of the mountains, and said to the mountains and rocks, Fall on us, and hide us from the face of Him that sitteth on the throne, and from the wrath of the Lamb; for the great day of his wrath is come, and who shall be able to stand?" (Rev. vi. 15-17.) The idea of Christ's kingdom being attacked by Satan is monstrously absurd. The head of the serpent shall be bruised before the joys of Eden shall be restored. And when Christ regains that which was lost in Adam, it shall be an eternal restitution.

But what of the antitype of the Sabbath? It is generally accepted that a thousand years is the symbol of a day of the Lord, and that at the end of six thousand years there shall be a Sabbath of rest which shall complete the seven thousand and thus fill out the week of days. There is, we

admit, an apparent ground for this belief, but it
is only apparent. The foundation would be real,
providing that the weeks were to continue, but
when the seventh angel stands with one foot on
sea and one on land, "time" shall be no more.
Time is but a term accommodated to the present
state of mortality. When this mortal shall have
put on immortality, the ages shall be eternal.
Let us examine. When God ended his work of
creation, He entered into rest the seventh day.
But be it observed that rest has remained unbroken ever since. His work of creation in the
finite state was completed. What then of the
regeneration or new creation? We are told,
"There remaineth, therefore, a rest (marg. keeping of a Sabbath) to the people of God." (Heb.
iv. 9.) But we are further told that, "He that is
entered into his rest, he also hath *ceased* from
his own works *as God did from his.*" (10.)
Therefore since God's rest from creation once
entered upon was abiding and eternal; so in like
manner shall the rest of his people, when entered
upon, be from everlasting to everlasting. In the
type there was no break at the end of a thousand
years, neither shall there be in the antitype. As
was the first creation, so shall be the new creation. We shall not have to wait a thousand years
after Christ comes for the perfect day. Types,
in scripture, are but the " shadows of good things
to come," " and not the very image of the things."
They are but transitory, and consequently kept
up by repetition. When the antitype is reached

transition ceases, or rather is swallowed up by that which is eternal. This is where many fail in obtaining the truth. They look for repetition in the spiritual as they find it in the natural, forgetting that when the spiritual is reached repetition must necessarily cease, as it is no longer required. We can only walk in the shadow until we arrive at the substance. And when Christ appears the second time every shadow shall have reached its culminating point. The rising of the Sun of Righteousness shall dispel all darkness, therefore shadows will be no more forever.

When the seventh angel sounds, those who sit before the throne of God exclaim, " We give thee thanks, O Lord God Almighty, who art, and wast, and art to come; because thou hast taken to thee thy great power, and hast reigned." (Rev. xi. 17.) Or again, "I heard, as it were, the voice of a great multitude, and as the voice of many waters, and as the voice of mighty thunderings, saying: Alleluia; for the Lord God Omnipotent reigneth." (xix. 6.)

At that time, and not before, the kingdom of God shall be established; and nothing hence shall mar its glory or interrupt its peace, according to the scriptures, "and the kingdom and dominion, and the greatness of the kingdom under the whole heavens, shall be given to the people of the saints of the Most High, whose kingdom is an everlasting kingdom, and all dominions shall serve and obey him." (Dan. vii. 27.) Zion shall then rejoice, and shall see no more sorrow. Even

now the·morn is breaking, and the still small
voice whispers the words of the ancient prophet
in our ears: "Break forth into joy, sing together,
ye waste places of Jerusalem; for the Lord hath
comforted his people, He hath redeemed Jerusalem. The Lord hath made bare his holy arm in
the eyes of all nations; and all the ends of the
earth shall see the salvation of our God."

And as the King in beauty they behold—
  The Chief 'mong thousands, and the lovely One—
They wave their palms, and strike their harps of gold
  In praise to Him who sitteth on heav'n's throne.
      Like rush of waters as they flow,
      Or voice of mighty thunderings now,
      Hark! "Alleluia, God doth reign!
      Alleluia, amen! amen!"
      And Zion shall no more be sad,
      Lift up thy voice, rejoice, be glad,
      The marriage of the Lamb has come,
      And ours for aye a sun-bright home,
      And sweetly now with one accord,
      We cry, "FOREVER WITH THE LORD."

CHAPTER XV.

_____

THE DESTINY OF THE WICKED — A DOGMA WHICH DEFAMES GOD'S CHARACTER REVIEWED.

"The wages of sin is _death;_ but the gift of God is _eternal life_ through Jesus Christ our Lord."—Rom. vi. 23.

If a charge be preferred falsely against an earthly parent, what son, worthy of the name, would not stand up in defense of his parent?

Infinitely more then should we who claim to be the "sons of God" stand up when the character of our holy Father in heaven is impeached. And no greater libel could be preferred against the character of the Almighty than the dogma which consigns the wicked—a large portion of the beings of his own creation—to a hell of endless torments. The Bible does not teach any such dogma; traditions of men do. And it is passing strange that so many men of intellect, men of talent, educated men, should hold, and teach, and profess to believe such a gross absurdity; for science, nature, and reason all revolt against it; and the only support it can claim from the Bible is the perversion and misinterpretation of scripture.

The following paragraph we quote from *Boston's Four-Fold State*. As a charge against the justice of God we deem it akin to blasphemy. It may be objected that Boston belongs to the old school. But the fact that modern theologians quote him as an authority and maintain the same dogma makes the objection void. He says:

"The torments in hell are manifold. Put the case that a man were, at one and the same time, under the violence of the gout, gravel, and whatsoever diseases and pains have ever met together in one body; the torment of such a one would be but light in comparison with the torments of the damned. For as in hell there is an absence of *all* that is *good* and desirable, so there is the *confluence of all evils* there; since all the effects of sin and of the curse take their place in it, after the last judgment. (Rev. xx. 14.) *And death and hell were cast into the lake of fire.* There they will find a *prison* they can never escape out of; *a lake of fire*, wherein they will be ever swimming and burning; *a pit*, where they will never find a bottom. The *worm* that *dieth not* shall feed on them, as on bodies which are interred; the fire that *is not quenched*, shall devour them, as dead bodies which are burned. Their eyes shall be kept in blackness of darkness, without the least comfortable gleam of light; their *ears* filled with the frightful yellings of the infernal crew. They shall *taste* nothing but the vinegar of God's wrath, *the dregs of the cup of his fury*. The stench of the burning lake of brimstone will be the *smell* there; and they shall feel extreme *pains* for evermore."

If "the worm that dieth not shall feed on them as on bodies which are interred," it necessarily follows that it must soon end, else the figure is sadly defective. It does not take worms long to strip the bones of bodies interred. Again: If "the fire that *is not quenched* shall devour them as dead bodies which are burned," it follows, in like manner, according to the figure used, that consummation must soon be reached; for "dead bodies which are burned" are resolved to ashes in a very brief space of time. However, this but proves the adage that "truth will out."

But those who want something of more recent date will find it in the following from Spurgeon:

"When thou diest thy soul will be tormented alone, that will be a hell for it, but at the Day of Judgment thy body will join thy soul, and then thou wilt have twin-hells, thy soul sweating drops of blood, and thy body suffused with agony. In fire, exactly like that which we have on earth, thy body will lie, asbestos-like, forever unconsumed, all thy veins roads for the feet of pain to travel on, every nerve a string on which the Devil shall forever play his diabolical tune of hell's unutterable lament."

Now, these men may have good hearts, and may have done much good by way of preaching righteousness. And they shall both receive according to their works in the day of judgment. But in regard to the above distorted, perverse, mythical, traditional, yea, diabolical dogma, we deem it nothing less than an outrageous defamation of the character of the all-wise, the just, the ever-merciful God—a calumny against Him whose *love* is infinite and boundless. The pictures, as drawn by these men, make the very blood curdle, as it were, in our veins.

God is either more or less merciful than man. To deny the former and accept the latter would be simply equivalent to a denial of his Godhead; for if man's mercy be in the ascendant, then man must be the God.

But if the dogma of an endless torment, as taught by modern theologians, be accepted as truth, then man is the more merciful, for the very idea of endless wailings, and gnashings of teeth, of unending pangs, and pains, and woes, is intensely repugnant to the finer feelings of our being. Nay, it is even horrifying. As a friend recently said, while conversing on this topic, "Let it be granted that for a serious crime an earthly judge imposes just such a punishment upon the condemned; so that the flames of torture should prey upon his flesh, if possible, for a lifetime of say fifty or sixty years. And let it also be granted that the inhabitants of the city could behold his anguish, hear his bitter wailings, and his hoarse pleadings for mercy. Who could endure it? Would not the whole city rebel instantly against such treatment?" Nay, we might add, would not the civilized world rise *en masse* and pronounce a righteous verdict against such cruelty?

And methinks the cruel monster who pronounced the harsh judgment would in some districts, at least, be lynched, and that without hesitation. Why if man sees an animal suffering intensely he does not hesitate to put an end to its existence.

Now, theology ascribes to the loving and long-suffering God dealings with his creatures infinitely more diabolical than the foregoing. Do you doubt it? Then listen: We are told that heaven, the place of celestial bliss, and hell, the pit of woe, are in sight of each other, even within speaking distance. The parable of the rich man and Lazarus, which abounds in Jewish metaphor, and which we will hereafter discuss, is claimed as authority for the same. *Heaven and hell within sight of each other?* Then all the attributes of heaven must needs lose their hallowed sweetness, when with indurated feelings the saints of glory can indifferently gaze upon such scenes of indescribable anguish. And *within speaking distance!* Then, instead of sweet harmony, alas, what a medley. For while the seraphims cry, "Holy, holy, holy is the Lord," and while the saints sing the glad new song, the "diabolical tune of hell's unutterable lament" must mingle discordantly in the strain. Hence, instead of unity there is anomaly, and just how "joys unfading," and woes unending can dwell so near each other and blend in harmony is to us a mystery inexplicable.

But further: Behold a son in heaven, while his mother is in woe. She looks up with a glance that would melt a heart of stone, and in anguish she wails and cries, "My son! my son! O my son! come and cool this parched tongue. I burn! I faint! O, come!" Tell me that God is love, and that he would permit such a scene as this in the midst of infinite bliss! Tell me that son, unless his heart be as adamant, unless he be as unfeeling as the devil himself, tell me that he can close his ears against the cry of her who gave him birth!

Or reverse the scene. The mother in bliss, and the son in woe. Be it remembered that according to the teachings of this fearful dogma of an endless torment, millions of such scenes are quite possible. The son with piteous screams fixes his gaze upon that once beloved parent. "O mother! dear mother! thou who didst give me birth! O bring me some relief!" The mother, unheeding, continues the strains of heaven's new song. In melting tones of grief he repeats: "O darling mother! where thy once loving heart! Once thou couldst weep over my slightest suffering! Once thou didst minister to my smallest griefs. Once thou didst plead to God to guide my youthful steps! O canst thou not plead again to Him in my behalf with that sweet voice immortal? O hast thou stopped thine ears? Has heaven's love stilled thy once tender heart? Where, where, thy God of love? Where now compassion? O Mercy, hast thou fled? Yet thou, dear mother, didst teach me once that "*His mercy endureth forever*," and that "He retaineth not his anger forever." Yea, thou didst read it out of the good Book. O didst thou tell me truth? O where the

tender feelings, the gentle care I once admired
in thee, my mother? Where now those traits of
character that made me feel thou wert God's
child? Gone, alas! for now thou laughest at my
calamity."

You may say I am exaggerating the picture.
But if the teachings of this monstrous dogma be
accepted, then pictures beyond the power of pen
to describe of this diabolical panorama will continue to unfold throughout the endless ages of
eternity. But thanks be unto God, "The wages
of sin is *death*," not endless life in torment.
Praise be unto his holy name, his mercy endures
forever! Life through Christ is the gift of God.
There is no promise of eternal life through the
devil. Even that wicked one "The Lord shall
consume with the spirit of his mouth, and shall
destroy with the brightness of his coming." (II.
Thess. ii. 8.) "And all the proud, yea, and all
that do wickedly shall be *stubble;* and the day
that cometh shall *burn them up*, saith the Lord
of Hosts, that it shall leave them neither *root nor
branch*." (Mal. iv. 1.) Now, what meaneth
"consume," "destroy," or stubble burned up so
that neither "root nor branch" is left? Certainly it does not mean eternal duration, else language fails in conveying ideas. It means destruction and nothing less; as also does the teaching
of Christ in the parable of the wheat and the
tares. He declares the parable to his disciples.
Its teaching is not ambiguous. He says:

"The field is the world; the good seed are the

children of the kingdom; but the tares *are* the children of the wicked one. The enemy that sowed them is the devil; the harvest is the end of the world; and the reapers are the angels. *As therefore the tares are gathered and burned in the fire, so shall it be in the end of the world.*" (Matt. xiii. 38-40.)

When tares are burned what is left? So shall it be with the children of the wicked one. Christ says so. Shall we reject his plain teachings? And the prophet Malachi long before the day of Christ said, "And ye shall tread down the wicked; for they shall be *ashes* under the soles of your feet in the day that I shall do this, saith the Lord of Hosts." (iv. 3.)

You will observe that the only text quoted by Boston in the extract we have given from his book is Rev. xx. 14. Instead of teaching eternal torment, it teaches the very opposite, viz: annihilation.

The text reads: "*And death and hell* (hades or the grave) *were cast into the lake of fire. This is the second death.*" It simply means that the heirs of death and of the grave are cast into the lake of fire for consummation. And we are explicitly told, "This is the *second death.*" The first death is the opposite of first life; beyond it there is hope of resurrection. There is no hope of life beyond the second death.

If death means dying and yet never to die, then the last enemy, Death, shall never be destroyed; for if second death means a conscious existence in torments eternally, then Death as a living, tormenting agency is man's enemy forever. But, bless God, it is recorded, "The last enemy that shall be destroyed (revised ver. *Abolished,*) is death." And we believe the record of Heaven.

We repeat, death is the opposite of life, else language fails to convey a true meaning. If it be claimed that the second death means "dying and yet never to die," on the same principle the second life would mean living and yet never to live, the absurdity of which must indeed be apparent to every thinking mind; for according to such logic the wicked alone would have *aionion* or eternal life. But eternal life is not promised to the wicked, and according to the scriptures it only comes to man through Christ. The statement is clear, "The gift of God is eternal life through Jesus Christ our Lord." It contains no ambiguity. If therefore the wicked are to live eternally it must needs come to them from God through Christ. This only leads us to mystical ground, for the scriptures teach no such absurdity. That death shall be destroyed is the unambiguous testimony of God's word. According to the teachings of modern theology, the second death means a lake of unquenchable, unconsuming fire, into which immortal beings are cast to be tormented eternally; than which nothing could be more absurd, or more bitterly cruel. Some, however, attempt to modify the dogma by denying the literalness of the fire, and accepting instead the idea that conscience is to be the burning, stinging agent of torment. They carefully elude a modifying of the torment itself, or the length of its duration. Take what view you may of it, it is a fearful measure of woe to mete out to any poor fallen creature.

It is void of all the characteristics which we admire in man's nature. It defames the glorious attributes of God, such as mercy, forbearance, long-suffering, compassion and divine love. It is contrary to the scriptures, although professedly taken therefrom. It is repugnant to the finer feelings of our being. Reason revolts against it, and we can find no analogy in Nature to harmonize therewith.

Let it be granted that man was created in the image of God. It must be admitted that only the intelligent part of his being reflects that image. No one dare assert that the brutal propensities of fallen mortals reflects the likeness of God. And yet the cruelties perpetrated against our race by such monsters as Nero and the train of blood-thirsty murderers that followed down to the barbarous Jeffries of England, or the notorious and heartless Claverhouse of Scotland, including the indescribable horrors of the Inquisition, all fade before the tortures as taught by this dogma of an endless torment. Compared therewith, all the horrors pertaining to mortality are but as invisible specks. The contrast is wide as eternal diameters; for the one is but momentary as compared with eternity.

Even to contemplate the picture of hell fire

eternal torments as depicted by men of learning, it makes the flesh cringe on our bones, and our inmost soul shudder. In order to the acceptance of such a libel against the justice of heaven, reason must needs degenerate or be enchained by the shackles of mythical tradition.

We deem the following one of the pearls of scripture, viz: "*For his* (God's) *mercy endureth forever.*" But view it in the light of the dogma under consideration, and it fades away as a meaningless or misleading utterance. However, heaven and earth shall pass away, but his word shall not pass away. Therefore, with the ancient prophet we exclaim: "Who is a God like unto thee, that pardoneth iniquity, and passeth by the transgression of the remnant of his heritage? *He retaineth not his anger forever, because He delighteth in mercy.*" (Mic. vii. 18.)

And the words of Nahum are a fitting rebuke to those who hold and teach that the wicked shall be consigned to a pit of endless woe:

"*What do ye imagine against the Lord? He will make an utter end: affliction shall not rise up the second time. For while they are folden together as thorns, and while they are drunken as drunkards, they shall be devoured as stubble fully dry.*" (i. 9, 10.)

The Psalmist tells us: "The wicked shall perish, and the enemies of the Lord shall be as the fat of lambs: *they shall consume: into smoke shall they consume away.*" (xxxvii. 20.) ' The transgressors shall be destroyed together: the end of the wicked shall be cut off." (38.) Isaiah says:

"The destruction of the transgressors and of the sinners shall be together, and they that forsake the Lord shall be consumed." (i. 28.) "The people shall be as the burnings of lime: as thorns cut up shall they be burned in the fire." And when the question is asked, "Who among us shall dwell with the devouring fire? Who among us shall dwell with everlasting burnings?" the reply is not that "the wicked shall," but *it is*, "He that walketh righteously, and speaketh uprightly; he that despiseth the gain of oppressions, that shaketh his hands from the holding of bribes, that stoppeth his ears from hearing of bloods, and shutteth his eyes from seeing evil. He shall dwell on high." (xxxiii. 12-16.)

Paul writes: "When the Lord Jesus shall be revealed from heaven with his mighty angels in flaming fire, yielding (marg.) vengeance on them that know not God, and that obey not the gospel of our Lord Jesus Christ: Who shall be punished with *everlasting destruction* from the presence of the Lord, and from the glory of his power." (II. Thess. i. 7-9.) These scriptures give forth a certain sound, and require no comment.

Let us now consider the parable of *Dives* and *Lazarus*. (Luke xvi. 19-31.) This is claimed as the Gibraltar of "eternal tormentism."

1. We must accept this portion of scripture, either as a parable, or as a narrative. If as a narrative, then it must be taken literally, and upon the absurdity of which view we have previously animadverted. If we view it as a parable, we

14

must consequently allow that the language used is figurative. If figurative, then the true meaning of the figures employed should be sought after. And here we find that the only true course, which is also the scriptural one, is to compare spiritual things with spiritual. The dogma of endless torments has not only to do with a majority of the human family while in the mortal state, but in regard to their destiny it penetrates into eternal depths. The basis of such an important dogma should therefore be most secure. Figurative language may be wrongly interpreted, and always does admit of varied and even adverse views. The parable of Dives and Lazarus abounds in Jewish figures, which may be misconstrued, therefore such a parable should not be accepted as the basis of any important doctrine, and more especially when the views based thereon are evidently contrary to the general tenor of the scriptures. Even the learned Dr. Smith who maintains the dogma of endless torment, says in regard to this parable:

"It is impossible to ground the proof of an important theological doctrine on a passage which confessedly abounds in Jewish metaphors." (Dict. of the Bible, vol. 1, p. 782.)

2. The figures used and the scenes portrayed evidently carry the mind forward to the day of judgment; consequently the parable is but a vision of the future, given to or brought before the minds of the pharisaical Jews as a lesson of warning to them, that they might avert the wrath of

God while opportunity was theirs. Let us examine: "*And it came to pass, that the beggar died, and was carried by the angels into Abraham's bosom.*"

"*The beggar died.*" Here is a simple statement which implies that life had ceased in the beggar. It certainly does not mean that he was just then beginning to live.

"*And was carried by the angels.*" It does not say *then* nor *immediately.* God's order of time must be considered and observed. There is no record in scripture to show that angels come at death to carry an immortal soul or spiritual entity, or being, separate and apart from the body, to some unseen abode in the skies. "Them that sleep in Jesus will God bring with Him." "The dead in Christ shall rise first." "As in Adam all die, so in Christ shall all be made alive. But every man in his own order: Christ the *first-fruits,* afterward *they that are Christ's at his coming.*" These are the scriptural statements, and like the tenor of scripture throughout they only give promise of life to men at Christ's appearing, i. e. when the seventh angel sounds his trump.

"*Carried by the angels.*" When? Christ himself replies: "And they shall see the Son of man coming in the clouds of heaven with power and great glory. And he shall *send his angels* (then, but not till then) with a trumpet and a great voice (marg.) and they shall gather together his elect from the four winds, from one end of heaven to the other." (Matt. xxiv. 30, 31.) Here then is a plain, literal statement, emanating from the very Source of truth which refers to this gathering in by the angels. By comparing spiritual things with spiritual, we are compelled to accept Christ's own rendering as to the time when the angels shall gather in the elect of God, at which time, undoubtedly, the beggar will be attended to.

"*Into Abraham's bosom.*" It was only by faith Abraham sojourned in the land of promise as in a strange country. He with the other Patriarchs, "All died in faith, not having received the promises, but having seen them afar off, and were persuaded of them, and embraced them, and confessed that they were strangers and pilgrims on the earth." (Heb. xi. 13.) "God having provided some better thing for us *that they without us should not be made perfect.*" (40.) In point of time, therefore, this synchronizes with what has already been given, viz: that not until He comes, whose right it is to reign, will the angels be sent to gather in the elect; neither can Abraham, being one of the elect, be an inheritor of the kingdom till then. Hence neither Abraham nor the beggar can possess the inheritance or everlasting home till God's time comes. The rewards shall be given after the seventh angel sounds, and not till then according to the scriptures. (Rev. xi. 18.) "*The rich man also died and was buried.*" This is a bare record of a fact which may be witnessed every day of our lives. "*And in hell* (hades or the grave) *he lifted up*

his eyes being in torments." We would reply to
this by again using Christ's words, " Marvel not
at this; for the hour is coming in the which *all*
that are in the graves shall hear his voice, and
shall come forth; they that have done good, unto
the resurrection of life; and they that have done
evil, unto the resurrection of damnation."
(John v. 28, 29.)   But to say that the rich man
or any other shall lift up his eyes from the grave
prior to the time of resurrection, is tantamount
to an addition to the word of God.   How can a
dead man lift up his eyes until he be awakened
by the last trump?   It is not only unscriptural
but absurd to assert it.   The rich man could no
more open his eyes in the grave until the final
trump than the beggar could be carried by the
angels to Abraham's bosom until the reapers of
earth's harvest come, which is at the end of the
world.   (Matt. xiii. 39.)

  " *And seeth Abraham afar off, and Lazarus in
his bosom.*"   This is in perfect harmony with
what has been given; and the order of the scriptures is most apparent.   "The dead in Christ
shall rise *first*," and together with them who are
alive and remain at that time shall be caught up
to meet the Lord in the air. (I. Thess. iv. 16,
17.)   Hence the rich man being among the
wicked is thereafter raised, and the first sight he
beholds is Lazarus up with Father Abraham. He
is in torments, for at that time "The Son of man
shall send forth his angels, and they shall gather
out of his kingdom all things that offend, and

them who do iniquity, and shall cast▲them into a furnace of fire; there shall be wailing and gnashing of teeth." (Matt. xiii. 41, 42.) Like many more when that day comes, he cries for mercy when forever too late. Christ, like his disciple Paul, preached of a judgment to come, and this parable is a striking figure of the final scene. This view, properly understood, explains the whole. The rich man is evidently the representative of that portion of the Jewish nation which rejected Christ. He calls Abraham "*father.*" And Abraham calls him "*son,*" which clearly proves it to be a parable referring to the Jewish nation. Lazarus is undoubtedly the type of that class of the Jews who received Christ. "He came unto his own, and his own received Him not. But as many as received Him, to them gave He power to become sons of God." (John i. 11, 12.) In this passage both *Dives* and Lazarus can be clearly seen.

When the rich man is awakened to a sense of his peril, he at once wants to send some one to his father's house. Abraham is represented as telling, or rather reminding him, that they have Moses and the prophets, "let them hear them." And he replies, "Nay, Father Abraham, but if one went unto them *from the dead* they will repent." "*From the dead,*" mark the words, not from this state of *life,* but from the dead. This, in itself, proves the parable to be but a picture of future judgment made, as it were, present, which rule is also quite in harmony with the general manner of setting forth scriptural truths. The reply of Abraham is significant. "If they will not hear Moses and the prophets, neither will they be persuaded, though one rose from the dead." And neither were they persuaded, when shortly thereafter Jesus Christ did rise from the dead. Upon this very point even the disciples themselves were slow of belief. And the last verse of the parable evidently refers to this glorious event. Christ thus addresses his disciples: " O fools and slow of heart to believe all that the prophets have spoken. Ought not Christ to suffer these things, and to enter into his glory? And beginning at Moses and all the prophets, he expounded unto them in all the scriptures the things concerning himself." (Luke xxiv. 25-27.)

3. This view of the parable harmonizes with every other passage of scripture referring to the end of all things, to Christ's coming, or to the judgment. The accepted popular view of it conflicts with every other portion of scripture which depicts the final scenes of time. The former view accords with reason. The latter view must be rejected by reason, not only as absurd, but also as a defamation of the character of a merciful, just and all-wise God. "Prove all things, hold fast that which is good," is the injunction of scripture. Therefore, having put this parable to the test of the word itself, and proving thereby the popularly accepted view not only to be erroneous, but seriously so, in that it affects the character, and mercy, and justice of the great

God, we cast the error away, and shall hold fast
the blessed truth, which is nourishment indeed;
and with meekness, and gratitude, receive the
engrafted word, which is able to save our souls.

"*And these shall go away into everlasting punishment, but the righteous into life eternal.*"
This is another of the texts which is claimed as ·
maintaining the dogma of endless torments.

1. *Everlasting punishment.* It is evident that
"everlasting punishment" and "everlasting destruction" are synonymous. Both are spiritual
terms which are applied to the wicked. That
destruction is punishment no one can dispute.
The modifying term "everlasting" indicates that
the punishment is final, and implies that beyond
judgment there is no hope of life or happiness.
"The wages of sin is death," and death is the
end of existence. Death in the present state is
the opposite of mortal life, and in like manner the
second death shall be the opposite of second life.
"The gift of God is eternal life through Jesus
Christ our Lord." Out of Christ there is no
promise of life eternal. When the nature of the
punishment of the wicked is properly understood,
it virtually decides its duration to be final, or
everlasting. After death in the mortal state
there is a coming up to judgment. At the judgment bar there is hope of mercy. But when the
sentence of the Judge is once given it is final—
eternal—and without hope of commutation, hence
everlasting.

If the sentence be, "Come, ye blessed of my

Father," then eternal life is the portion; but if it be "Depart ye cursed'" then with weeping, wailing, and gnashing of teeth they "perish," are "destroyed," or "consumed" in the lake of burning, prepared for the devil and his angels. This leads us here to notice:

2. "*Where their worm dieth not, and the fire is not quenched.*" (Mark ix. 45-48.) This certainly implies a fearful doom. But when it is claimed that "worm" means "immortal or never-dying soul," we dispute it. That which is either corrupt or liable to corruption cannot dwell with immortality, nor can such be immortal according to the tenor of scripture. And to speak of immortal and yet corruptible worms, and apply the same to the souls of the damned, is not only an outrage against the truth of heaven's God and against the reason with which He has endowed us, but it is, to say the least, of all mythical traditions the most absurd. Our Lord evidently refers to the valley of Hinnom or *Gehenna* in this figure of speech. This valley lies to the south of Jerusalem, where after the worship of the "fire gods" was introduced by Ahaz, the idolatrous Jews offered their children to Moloch. As Dr. Smith tells us, it afterwards "became the common laystall of the city, where the dead bodies of criminals and the carcasses of animals, and every other kind of filth was cast. . . . From the depth and narrowness of the gorge, and, perhaps, its ever-burning fires, as well as from its being the receptacle of all sorts of putrefying matter,

and all that defiled the holy city, it became in later times the image of the place of everlasting punishment, 'where their worm dieth not and the fire is not quenched.'" (Dict. of the Bible, Vol. I. p. 661.)

Now, in this figure, or type of the fire of the day of wrath, be it observed, that both the *worm* and the *fire* were destroying elements or agencies, and not the carcasses to be destroyed. To invert this meaning is simply to destroy the sense of figurative language, and even of the language itself.

The prophet Isaiah sustains this view when he says: "And they shall go forth and look upon the *carcasses* of men that have transgressed: for their worm shall not die, neither shall their fire be quenched; and they shall be an abhorring to all flesh." (lxvi. 24)

Now, a carcass implies a "dead body," a "corpse," a body fallen into corruption or decay; and to talk of immortal carcasses is ridiculously absurd. The fire that preys upon them cannot be quenched by man. It is the fire of God. "Our God is a *consuming* fire." (Heb. xii. 29.) For, "Then shall that wicked be revealed, whom the Lord *shall consume* with the spirit of his mouth, and *shall destroy* with the brightness of his coming." (II. Thess. ii. 8.) Here there is a clear scriptural statement showing what is the unquenchable fire, which constitutes one of the elements of destruction. What meaneth the "worm that dieth not," the other element of destruction?

Isaiah says: "If ye refuse and rebel ye shall be devoured with the sword." (i. 20.) "For by *fire* and by his *sword* will the Lord plead with all flesh, and the slain of the Lord shall be many." (lxvi. 16.) But what is the sword? Let the scripture reply: "The sword of the Spirit, which is the word of God." (Eph. vi. 17.) This sword proceeds from the mouth of the Judge. "Out of his mouth went a sharp two-edged sword." (Rev. i. 16.) It is wielded as a weapon of judgment, for with it He shall smite the nations when He treads "the wine press of the fierceness and wrath of Almighty God." (Rev. xix. 15.) "And the remnant were slain with the sword of Him that sat ·upon the horse, which sword proceedeth out of his mouth." (21.) "For the word of God is quick and powerful, and sharper than any two-edged sword." (Heb. iv. 12.) And Christ says: "He that rejecteth me and receiveth not my words, hath one that judgeth him: the *word* that I have spoken, the *same* shall judge him in the last day." (John xii. 48.) And thus we perceive that the word of God is indeed as a worm that dieth not, for "Heaven and earth shall pass away, but my word shall not pass away," said Christ.

Therefore, we conclude the word of God is as a savor of "life unto life," or of "death unto death." Hence we can truly infer that the wicked shall perish or be consumed by the exceeding bright glory that shall usher in the great day of God, for no mortal shall behold his glory and live. Even the saints must needs be changed "in a moment, in the twinkling of an eye," from mortal to immortality. And the word of God once despised, his gracious but rejected promises, his merciful offers, his precepts trodden under foot, shall be as gnawing worms upon the consciences of the condemned.

In brief, the Spirit and the word that shall quicken his saints, shall be as the "Spirit of burning" and the sword of the destroying angel to the wicked. The latter shall be consumed by the unquenchable fire; but like Shadrach, Meshach and Abednego, the righteous shall walk in the midst of its flame forever, with the Son of man as their King. They shall inhale it as the fragrant balmy air of the sun-bright land. The same Spirit shall constitute the principle of life in the immortal state.

"Fear not them who kill the body, but are not able to kill the soul: but rather fear Him who is able to destroy both soul and body in hell." (Matt. x. 28.)

This is another text which is misconstrued to support the dogma under consideration. But if viewed aright, it proves the opposite. According to popular belief the soul is immortal, and consequently indestructible. Immortality, being the nature of God, cannot be destroyed. God cannot destroy himself. But if the soul be immortal and indestructible, how comes it that Christ commands us to "Fear Him (i. e. God) who is able to destroy both soul and body in hell?" The soul's being destructible disproves the theory of its im-

mortality. "The soul that sinneth it shall die."
But it is written: "The smoke of their torment
ascendeth up forever and ever: and they have no
rest day nor night, who worship the beast and his
image." (Rev. xiv. 11.) Yes, and we remind our
readers that this is found in a book which confessedly abounds in symbols. It is not considered
a sound rule of interpretation to base a moment-
ous doctrine on symbolic scripture. Yet by comparison with that which is plain, we deem it safe
notwithstanding. The symbolic should always
coincide with the mass of plainly revealed scripture. Revelation should agree with revelation.
Be it observed, however, that it is only the smoke
that ascendeth. The statement does not necessarily imply that their torment continues. "*And
they have no rest day nor night.*" Here we have
a statement which is connected with the other,
and which evidently demonstrates the fact that
time still continues But when eternity dawns
we shall expect to hear the mighty angel's voice
swearing by Him that liveth forever and ever,
that there shall be time no longer. (Rev. x. 6.)
"And there shall be *no night there.*" (xxii. 5.)
It must therefore refer to a judgment scene which
immediately precedes the eternal age. And this
view coincides with the teachings of scripture
throughout.

John the Baptist exclaimed: "He that cometh after me is mightier than I, whose shoes I am
not worthy to bear: He shall baptize you with
the Holy Ghost, and with fire: whose fan is in

his hand, and he will thoroughly purge his floor,
and gather his wheat into the garner; but He will
burn up the chaff with unquenchable fire."
(Matt. iii. 11, 12.) Here the wicked are again
represented as "chaff." The figure is scriptural.
But if the wicked be as "chaff," and if "burned
up," what is left? The fire is "unquenchable;"
it cannot be hindered in its work of consummation. But neither scripture nor nature will bear
out the figure of inconsumable chaff. And now
what more shall we say? We could easily multiply scriptural evidence, but we deem we have
given enough to sustain the boundless mercy of
our God, who retaineth not his anger forever, but
who will even have mercy on the devil himself in
so far as to put an end to his existence, as shown
in II. Thess. ii. 8, for undoubtedly the devil is the
head of the man of sin, even as Christ is head of
the Church. In order to sustain the mythical
dogma of eternal torment, the Bible must needs
be put aside, the dictionaries and lexicons must
be changed so as to give different meanings to
such words as "Destroy," "Consume," "Cut off,"
"Stubble," "Chaff," "Destruction," etc. It is
a sin to underrate God's mercy, but it is a greater
sin to overrate his judgments so far as to teach
that He will send millions of poor vile sinners to
a place of eternal conscious torment.

God is compassionate, his mercy endureth forever. Then He shall not permit poor helpless beings to suffer eternally. God is just. Therefore,
He cannot allow doomed beings of his own creation

to endure *eternal* pangs of woe for an offense which only covered the brief space of a human life. Be it remembered, the brevity of a mortal life, as compared with eternity, is simply inconceivable. The longest period of human life is but as an invisible speck upon the vast belt of ETERNITY. The great Creator cannot, neither will He, stoop to anything incompatible with his attributes. It matters not if the whole world believe in the eternal conscious punishment of the wicked, let God be true even though all men be liars. He will not violate his own word, and that word clearly teaches the ultimate destruction of the wicked. According to God's attributes of mercy and justice, He will reward right and virtue, and punish wrong and vice. In the present this cannot be fully done; because the extent of good and evil wrought by word, and deed, and example, cannot be summed up in the period of any single life. For example, a man's works, whether good or bad, continue to influence society long after he, himself, is deceased. Though dead, yet he speaketh and acteth by the footprints he has left upon the "sands of time." Therefore, a day of judgment is called for in order that mercy and justice may be duly meted out to every man according as his work shall be. This must stand as good reasoning. But reason is compelled to stand still when it is claimed that the justice of God demands the meting out of *eternal* suffering and torment as the expiation of *finite* sins. The attribute of justice implies full retribution for good or evil done, and nothing more or less. To add to or detract from this rule, we must needs lose sight of justice. Here is where the grace and mercy of God step in and mediate in behalf of poor frail humanity. It must be conceded that greater good shall be conferred upon the righteous than what their works merit. This good comes therefore by the grace and mercy of a righteous God. Let this be granted, then grace and mercy, in order to poise on the balance of justice, must needs interpose in behalf of the wicked by lessening, not adding to, their punishment. This accords with the scripture: "For He will finish the *account* (marg.) and cut it short in righteousness: because a short work will the Lord make upon the earth." We therefore conclude that eternal punishment, destruction, or death shall be the portion, or destiny, of the wicked. They shall be as though they had not been. (Ps. xxxvii. 10, 35, 36.) But the righteous shall go into life eternal, and shall rejoice in the sunshine of heaven's glory forever.

CHAPTER XVI.

THE TWO COVENANTS AND THE TWO MINISTRATIONS MADE ONE IN CHRIST.

" If that first covenant had been faultless, then should no place have been sought for the second."—Heb. viii. 7.

The two grand and concomitant gifts God offers to man are eternal life and an everlasting inheritance or home. In order to these ends the plan of salvation was laid. These also constitute the fruition of hope. The promises made unto the fathers, the Mosaical law, and the gospel of grace are but the means for the working out of these ends.

The promise of the home was given before the way of life was open. (Gen. xiii. 14-17.) This is according to the order of God. Eden was prepared before Adam was placed therein. God's people must needs believe. Without faith it is impossible to please Him. Faith lays hold of

15

things future and eternal. Abraham believed God, hence he is called "the father of the faithful." With Abraham the first covenant of promise was made, and this covenant was ratified by Christ, when the second or new covenant, as it is called, was instituted. In order to an understanding of the second covenant we must needs know something of the first.

That the first covenant had its origin in Abraham is evident from the scriptures. "For to Abraham and his seed were the promises made." And Christ is the promised seed. (Gal. iii. 16.) This COVENANT that was before confirmed of God *concerning the Anointed*, the *law* which was four hundred and thirty years after, cannot disannul that it should make the promise of none effect. "For if the inheritance be of the *law* it is no more of promise; but God gave it to Abraham by promise." (17, 18.) "For the promise that he should be the heir of the world was not to Abraham, or to his seed through the law, but through the righteousness of faith. For if they which are of the law be heirs, faith is made void, and the promise made of none effect; because the law worketh wrath; for where no law is, there is no transgression." (Rom. iv. 13-15.) "Wherefore, then serveth the law? It was added because of transgressions, till the seed should come to whom the promise was made." (Gal. iii. 19.) "But that no man is justified by the law in the sight of God, it is evident; for, the just shall live by faith." Therefore, "Christ hath redeemed us from the curse of the law . . . that the blessing of Abraham might come on the Gentiles through Jesus Christ; that we might receive the promise of the Spirit through faith." (13, 14.) And " Christ is become of no effect unto you, whosoever of you are justified by the law; ye are fallen from grace." " But if ye be led of the Spirit ye are *not under law.*" "For as many as are led by the Spirit of God, they are the sons of God. . . . And if children then heirs; heirs of God and joint-heirs with Christ." (Rom. viii. 14-17.) Therefore, being justified by faith, we have peace with God through our Lord Jesus Christ; by whom also we have access by faith into this grace, wherein we stand, and rejoice in hope of the glory of God." (v. 1, 2.) But since the law was added because of transgression, and since we are redeemed from the *curse* of the law through Christ, therefore it is evident that the law was not the covenant, notwithstanding some hold to this belief. On the other hand it is quite evident from the scriptures that the first covenant was the promise of an inheritance to man, including blessing therewith. " For, when God made promise to Abraham because He could swear by no greater, He sware by himself;" (Heb. vi. 13.) saying, " In blessing I will bless thee, and in multiplying I will multiply thy seed as the stars of the heaven and as the sand which is upon the sea shore; and thy seed (which is Christ) shall possess the gate of his enemies; and in thy seed shall all nations of the earth be blessed, because thou hast obeyed my voice." (Gen. xxii. 17, 18.)

But this covenant was ordained in the hand of a Mediator. "Now a mediator is not a mediator of one, (party) but God is one." (Gal. iii. 19, 20.) Under the first covenant Moses was the mediator, and also the figure of Him that was to come, viz: Christ. But to claim that the first covenant originated with Moses is absurd. As mediator he stood between God and his covenanted people—the seed of Abraham—and handed to them the testament or will of God concerning his chosen people of Israel. This testament or code of laws was merely an *addendum*, "added because of transgression." The law, therefore, is but the *conditions* of the covenant; the promise of an everlasting inheritance is the covenant itself. Israel had to comply with the conditions in order to be partakers of the promises, as exemplified in the words of Isaiah: "If ye be willing and obedient, ye shall eat the good of the land, but if ye refuse and rebel ye shall be devoured with the sword; for the mouth of the Lord hath spoken it." But neither the first covenant nor its conditions were perfect in themselves. "For the law having a shadow of good things to come, and not the very image of the things, can never with those sacrifices which they offered year by year continually make the comers thereunto perfect." Walking in a shadow is not walking in the substance. Hence faith pointed forward to Him that was promised, even the seed

in whom all nations were to be blessed. Paul
says, "Before faith came we were kept under the
law (i. e. those who were under the law, viz: the
Jews), *shut up* unto the faith which should afterwards be revealed," and hence the law was but
as a school-master to the Jewish people, (not to
the Gentiles who were never under it) to lead
them to Christ. When Christ came the *true*
Light shone. "Then said He," when God no
longer had pleasure in the sacrifices and offerings
of the law, "Lo, I come to do thy will, O God.
He taketh away the first that He may establish
the second." (Heb. x. 9.)

What then was taken away? Certainly not
the covenant of promise, for it was confirmed by
Christ. "And if ye be Christ's, then are ye
Abraham's seed, and heirs according to the promise." (Gal. iii. 29.) It was therefore that which
was added for transgression which was taken
away, viz: the law of carnal commandments and
ordinances. "For what the law could not do, in
that it was weak through the flesh, God, sending
his own Son in the likeness of sinful flesh, and
by a sacrifice for sin, condemned sin in the flesh."
(Rom. viii. 3, marg.) For since the law was
added because of transgressions, and since Christ
was "wounded for our transgressions," and
"bruised for our iniquities," therefore through
Christ the requirements of the law were fulfilled,
and consequently annulled, for with his stripes
we are healed, and "There is therefore now no
condemnation to them who are in Christ Jesus,

who walk not after the flesh but after the Spirit.
For the law of the Spirit of life in Christ Jesus
hath made me *free* from the law of sin and
death."

The covenant of promise to Abraham and to
his SEED was, as we have shown, the inheritance.
This was to God's people the "day-star" of hope:
for in that lone night in the times of the patriarchs when death reigned, from Adam to Moses,
it was indeed a cheering light, the promise of an
everlasting home. But this inheritance was
under the curse. It must needs be redeemed.
Furthermore, those to whom it was promised
must needs have an immortal life in the future
in order to enjoy it. Therefore in order to its
redemption and an eternal life for its possessors,
Christ came as the great Redeemer, as the author
and finisher of our faith, who is made our High
Priest, "not after the law of a carnal commandment, but after the power of an ENDLESS LIFE."
Consequently the body of the new or second covenant through Christ is eternal life. For as the
gift of God as promised through Abraham is the
INHERITANCE; so, "the gift of God through Jesus
Christ our Lord," IS ETERNAL LIFE. Through
Christ we also receive the Holy Spirit of promise,
"which is the earnest (or surety from heaven) of
our inheritance until the redemption of the purchased possession."

When the true light (John i. 9) came, shadows
were dispersed. He is the *way*, the *truth* and the
life. Shadows are only cast in the one direction.

When we reach the substance and press right on, we can no longer have the shadows. To walk in the shadows we must recede, and our Lord has commanded us to "remember Lot's wife;" therefore we must neither look backwards nor walk backwards, but look ever unto Jesus, "who for the joy that was set before Him endured the cross, despising the shame, and is set down at the right hand of the throne of God." The cross broke down the middle wall or partition which stood between Jew and Gentile, and those who have heard his voice and walked in his ways "hath He quickened together with Him, having forgiven *them* all trespasses; blotting out the handwriting of ordinances that was against *them*, which was contrary to them, and took it out of the way, nailing it to the cross." (Col. ii. 13, 14.) But Christ is the Mediator of this covenant as well. He is the ONE MEDIATOR between God and man.

Moses was only the *figure* or type of Him that was to come. Moses ascended to Mount Sinai in behalf of Israel. Christ ascended into heaven itself in our behalf. The law as given through Moses, although glorious, "is done away," or fulfilled. (II. Cor. iii. 11.) It is called "the ministration of death," and was written and engraven in stones. (7.) But the ministration unto life—the epistle of Christ or new testament —is "written not with ink, but with the Spirit of the living God; not in tables of stone, but in fleshy tables of the heart." (3.)

The law as a "school-master" only served

till Christ came. Now we have a greater than Moses. Henceforth we hear the voice of the good Shepherd saying: "If ye love me, keep my commandments." But the proof of the law's deficiency is seen in the fact that both preaching and faith were vain had Christ not burst the barriers of the tomb and triumphed over death. (I. Cor. xv. 14.) For sins would have still remained unremitted, and without holiness none shall see the Lord. They also who had fallen asleep in the hope of Christ had perished. (17, 18.) But Christ has arisen and has ascended on high, "Made an high priest forever after the order of Melchisedec;" which fact really blends the two covenants into one, since Christ, by his triumph, has become the author or beginner and finisher of our faith.

There is virtually but one covenant of promise between God and his people. In its nature it is two-fold:

1. The promised INHERITANCE, (Gen. xiii. 14-17, and xvii. 7, 8.

2. The promised BLESSING through the promised seed. (Gen. xxii. 15-18, and Rom. vi. 23.)

This blessing is evidently endless life through Christ. When Christ, the promised SEED came the covenant in all its bearings, past, present and future was ratified in heaven. The proof of its ratification is given us in that Christ triumphed over death, and rose from the tomb to an immortal life.

Had Christ not risen, then all were vain. The

shield of faith would have been shattered forever; and hope, the pilgrim's sweet perennial
flower, would have received a deadly blight, never
more to cheer Zion's wayfarer with its fragrance
and its bloom. Those also who had fallen asleep
in the hope of Christ had perished, the day-star
which had guided them having thus been sunk
in oblivion's dismal waves.

But that Christ rose from the dead is established. The scriptures prove it, and the evidence
of millions during the centuries that have inter-
vened sustain it. It is heaven's grandest truth
to man. Having received the seal of God it is
eternally fixed. When Paul had furnished incontrovertible evidence of this essential truth, he
exclaimed in the triumph of his soul, "But now
is Christ risen from the dead, and become the
first-fruits of them that slept." And hope springs
up into immortal bloom in the fact that "In
Christ shall all be made alive, but every man in
his own order: Christ the first-fruits; afterward
they that are Christ's at his coming." Hence
through the resurrection of Christ the promised
INHERITANCE and the blessing of an ENDLESS LIFE
were united, and being ratified in heaven became
the sure hope of the followers of Jesus. As
Isaiah says: "Thou shalt no more be termed
Forsaken; neither shall thy land any more be
termed desolate; but thou shalt be called Heph-
zi-bah, (i. e. my delight is in her) and thy land
Beulah; (i. e. married) for the Lord delighteth in
thee, and thy land shall be married. For as a

young man marrieth a virgin, so shall thy sons
marry thee: and as the bridegroom rejoiceth over
the bride, so shall thy God rejoice over thee."
(lxii. 4, 5.) When two are married they are
regarded as one. Hence when we are joined to
Christ we have the "earnest" or espousal feast
of both the future *life* and *home*, both of which are
sure if we but endure to the end. At Christ's
coming the life shall be given to the faithful; and
at the marriage of the Lamb they shall be joined
to the everlasting inheritance, or home.

To blend everything into a oneness was Christ's
grand mission. He prayed that his disciples
might be made one even as He and his Father
were one. (John xvii. 11, 20-23.) Through Him
Jew and Gentile were placed on a common basis;
heaven and earth were united; things in heaven
and things in earth are to be gathered into one
through his name. (Eph. i. 10.)

A gentleman who owns a large estate has three
sons. He takes them to an eminence and tells
them, "All this estate will I give to you and your
heirs forever upon my decease." Before the
father's death, however, two of those sons become
dissipated and grieve his heart. He makes a will
or testament, and because of their misdeeds he
adds certain conditions to the promise previously
made. But these conditions are not the covenant of promise between them, neither would the
heirs accept them as the deed to that estate.
They were *only added* because of misdeeds, and
it is evident that such only stands as a hindrance

to possession. Better, had conditions never been required.

In like manner God promised to make Abraham and his seed heirs of the world. The promise was repeated to Isaac and to Jacob. But the law or testament of conditions was not added until long after these faithful patriarchs were laid away in their tombs. The waywardness of Israel in their journeyings towards Canaan provoked God, so that He added the conditions of the law. But the covenant of the inheritance was not of law, but of promise. And according to the scriptures the law did not, neither had it power, to disannul the promise. Conditions may be changed, but the "gifts," the "callings," and the "promises" of God are like himself, immutable. "Heaven and earth shall pass away, but my word shall not pass away," saith the Lord. Conditions may be either expressed or understood. The law of righteousness is really an inherent principle in man. "For when the Gentiles who have not the law, do by nature the things contained in the law, these having not the law, are a law unto themselves; who show the work of the law written in their hearts, their conscience also bearing witness, and their thoughts the meanwhile accusing or else excusing one another." (Rom. ii. 14, 15.) But neither the mediator of the first testament of conditions, nor the testament itself, were perfect, being only typical in their nature. "For if that first testament had been faultless, then should no place have been sought for the second."

But when Christ Jesus came, He became the
one true Mediator between God and man, who
has left us a new testament of conditions, which
like himself is perfect. The former was a yoke
of bondage, the latter is the perfect law of liberty.
Abraham's two sons were an "allegory" of the
two testaments, (Gal. iv. 21-31) for the mother of
the one was a bondmaid, and of the other a free
woman. But Christ burst the bands asunder
when He fulfilled the requirements of the law, in
that He bore the penalty of the transgressions for
which the law had been added, on Calvary's cross.
The law, being fulfilled in Him, is consequently
"done away." (II. Cor. iii. 11.) If done away,
there is no longer a bondwoman. If no bondwoman, there can be no longer two testaments;
for if Christ hath fulfilled the requirements of the
first, only one remains. This is what the scriptures teach; hence the two testaments are made
one through Christ. But if there be no longer
bonds, there is no need of the distinction *free;*
for the middle wall between Jew and Gentile
being broken down, there is but the one way of
salvation for all. This also is according to the
scriptures. For "There is neither Jew nor Greek,
there is neither bond nor free." (Gal. iii. 28.)
All are *one* in Jesus Christ. Hence the mission
of the gospel of Christ to those under law was
"To proclaim liberty to the captives, and the
opening of the prison to them that were bound."

The first testament, or Mosaical law, being fulfilled by the Son of God, and "done away,"

according to the scriptures, it cannot be restored by man. Those, therefore, to-day who claim to observe its precepts are not under the law, as the scriptures term it: they are simply in darkness even until now. "For until this day remaineth the same vail untaken away in the reading of the old testament; which vail is done away in Christ. But even unto this day, when Moses is read, the vail is upon their heart. Nevertheless, when it shall turn to the Lord the vail shall be taken away." (II. Cor. iii. 14, 15.)

Why cling to the old? "For if that which is done away was glorious, much more that which remaineth is glorious." If the night has been long and lonely, are we made sad when the day dawns? When light springs forth we can no longer walk in the darkness, unless we willingly seclude ourselves in some dark room or cave.

The first ministration was glorious in its day. To worship God in the temple was the chief delight of the devout Israelite. The Psalmist exclaims: "One thing have I desired of the Lord, that will I seek after; that I may dwell in the HOUSE of the Lord all the days of my life, to behold the beauty of the Lord and to enquire in his TEMPLE." Or again: "I was glad when they said unto me, let us go into the house of the Lord. . . Whither the tribes go up, the tribes of the Lord, unto the testimony of Israel, to give thanks unto the name of the Lord." But that which made it glorious was the fact that it pointed forward to Christ. Consequently it was but the

"Shadow of good things to come." Its glory was, therefore, lost in the more excellent glory of that which supplanted it, viz: the dispensation, or ministration of grace through Jesus Christ.

The light of a single star is cheering on a dark night to a lone traveler; but its glory is lost when the heavens become clear and spangled with its twinkling companions. When the moon arises the stars seem forgotten, and the traveler in its pale and beauteous light can see more clearly where to plant his feet. But the glory of the sun swallows up the light of both moon and stars.

In like manner, works of the law vanish or are rather lost in the works of grace and righteousness. The law of carnal commandments is lost in LOVE, and the power of an endless life. The shadow is lost in the substance. In Christ we behold as it were our spiritual MOON, which reflected and still reflects the light of heaven's Sun of Righteousness to Zion's pilgrims. But yet we only walk by faith. We only see and know in part. Christ has arisen, and has ascended to the zenith, even the Father's right hand; but when he reaches the western horizon of this dispensation of grace, He will come again, and the full blaze of an eternal weight of glory from heaven's almighty King shall meet our wondering gaze. Or again, when a lesser stream of water flows into a greater, the waters mingle and the former is lost sight of. It is not destroyed, but it is lost in the greater stream. So is it with the law. As a stream leading to Christ it is lost in the great river of salvation opened by Him; fulfilled, not destroyed. In like manner, the grace of God in Christ Jesus, and the gift by grace, together with the commandments of Jesus, are in this dispensation being fulfilled in those who walk therein. But when *fulfilled* in us, death shall be swallowed up of life, and mortal shall put on immortality. As the stream of law was lost in grace, so shall the stream of grace be lost in the eternal river of Glory. But all that is good in either of the dispensations shall endure eternally. The stream of law is lost in the river of salvation, and the latter in turn shall eventually reach the ocean of Divine love, and be therein swallowed up. The Mosaical law says," Thou shalt love the Lord thy God with all thine heart," and " thy neighbor as thyself." " Thou shalt not kill," etc. The law of Christ implies all this.

Love is the fulfilling of the law, and since the love of God is shed abroad in the heart by the Holy Ghost in this dispensation, it must be evident that a command to love Him is no longer necessary to those in Christ. Where holy love dwells, the command, "Thou shalt not kill," is superfluous. Love cannot kill. Love gives its life for others. Christ died for us—not when we were his friends, but while we were yet sinners, aliens and even enemies to God. If any one have not the Spirit of Christ he is none of his. " Hereby perceive we the love, because He laid down his life for us. And we ought to lay down our lives for the brethren." (I. John iii. 16.)

The law says, there is "one Lord," but the Spirit bears witness to that "one Lord." The former is but in letter, the latter is in power; the letter killeth but the Spirit giveth life. Therefore under the ministration of the Spirit we can have individual evidence, for, "He that believeth in the Son of God hath the witness in himself."

The law says "Thou shalt not make unto thee any graven image." The Spirit testifieth of the true God, hence the command is unnecessary. It would be evidently absurd to command a person to acknowledge the light of the sun while basking in its refulgent rays.

To place the first creation ahead of the second is reversing the order of God, for, as it is written, "In Adam all die, but *in* Christ shall all be made alive." The law of Moses was good enough in its day, and those to whom it was sent shall be judged thereby. But Moses, any more than John, was *not that Light*. The latter bore witness of that Light, and the former was a figure or type of that Light. When the true LIGHT came it was man's privilege to walk in that Light, and in Him is no darkness at all.

Now, the Spirit beareth witness of that Light, and if we walk in the Spirit, we are not under law, but under grace, "And of his fullness have all we received and grace for grace." And as love is the fulfilling of the law, so also is it the fulfilling of all righteousness.

CHAPTER XVII.

THE TWO-HORNED BEAST AND THE MYSTICAL NUMBER 666.

"And I beheld another beast coming up out of the earth; and he had two horns like a lamb, and he spake as a dragon. And he exerciseth all the power of the first beast before him, and causeth the earth and them which dwell therein to worship the first beast, whose deadly wound was healed."—Rev. xiii. 11, 12.

On the foregoing passage there has been much vain speculation; but of all that has come before our notice, that from the pen of J. N. Andrews, in a pamphlet published at Battle Creek, Mich., is evidently the most absurd. The scriptures enjoin us to give a reason of the hope that is in us, but after perambulating through the intricate windings and twistings of this work, we fail to find even the least shadow of reason in it.

He attempts to locate the two-horned beast in the United States of America, which is evidently

16

wide off the mark, for it is void of a single connecting link with John's prophecy. On page 91
he drags in the Sabbath of the Mosaical law. He
deems the keeping of a seventh day Sabbath as
an essential element of Christianity. The violation of which Sabbath he claims to be the mark
of the beast. Millions of heaven's truest wor-
shipers have observed the first-day Sabbath. This
includes the martyrs and hosts of noble heroes
of the cross, who have borne the burden and the
heat of the day of salvation, and who shall undoubtedly stand at last in the presence of the
King of kings, and wave their palms of victory.
But granting his theory, all this host must be
branded with the mark of the beast. If the violation of their Sabbath be the mark of the beast,
we fear many of themselves will bear that mark,
for they claim a knowledge of this law, and to
them that know to do good and do it not, it is
the greater sin. By their fruits ye shall know
them. " With what judgment ye judge, ye shall
be judged."

But if the violation of their Sabbath be condemnation and its observance salvation, then the
preaching of this Sabbath becomes their gospel.

However, this was not the gospel Paul preached,
and which the early Church received, by which
also they were saved. For Paul says: " I delivered unto you first of all that which I also received,
how that Christ died for our sins according to
the scriptures, and that He was buried, and that
He rose again the third day according to the

scriptures." This is the substance of the gospel which brings salvation, and this is the gospel wherein we stand. (I. Cor. xv. 1-23.) We desire however, to be distinctly understood, that we have no fault to find with people for worshiping God on the seventh, or any day of the week, but we prefer as a day of rest and worship the Lord's day, or first day of the week, since on that day Christ rose from the dead. To claim that Christians are still under the Mosaical law is decidedly unscriptural.

But we shall not follow the mystic meanderings of Battle Creek Adventism along the stream of error, nor yet grope our way after its votaries through the mists and darkness into which delusive visions have enveloped them. Instead, we shall endeavor to present the truth in its simplicity. Truth is mighty and must prevail.

Nearly all commentators agree that the first beast mentioned in the thirteenth chapter of Revelation designates the great papal power, but in regard to the second, or two-horned beast, there have been many conjectures. _

"*I beheld another beast.*" (verse 11.) The word *theerion*, from which beast is translated, can be truly rendered, wild, evil, or venomous beast.

In regard to the first beast, (verse 1) history comes to our aid. That Justinian granted power to the Pope in 538 A. D., is an historical fact. That this power was to continue unbroken for forty-two months prophetical time, which is generally accepted as an equivalent to 1,260 years of

common time, is given by the Revelator in verse
fifth. Adding 1,260 years to 538, the date when
this power virtually commenced, and it brings us
to 1798 A. D. And in this very year, according
to secular history, the French army entered
Rome and expelled Pius VI. from the Vatican.
Because he would not yield his temporal sover-
eignty he was carried to France, and one year
after he died at Valence. Since then the power
of the Vatican has waned.

In like manner history aids both in locating
and designating the second evil beast. Let us
look at Great Britain in the reign of Henry VIII.
Henry's notoriety as a monster needs no comment here. Were we compelled to choose between him and the Pope contemporary with him,
we would much rather prefer the latter. The
scriptural title, *venomous beast*, was morally applicable to him. Falling in love with one of the
maids of honor he divorced Queen Catherine.
Marrying Anna Boleyn, his next step was to be-
head her, and his second wife, after this, he also
beheaded. Because of a split with Rome, on
account of Clement VII. refusing to sanction his
proceedings against Queen Catherine, a most
dreadful persecution ensued. Men were hanged,
burned and beheaded simply for not acquiescing
in his eccentric beliefs, and two good and brave
men, Sir Thomas Moore and Bishop Fisher, were
executed for denying his royal supremacy. Polit-
ically, no king ever violated the rights of English-
men, or the specifications of Magna Charta, more

flagrantly than he.   We are told, " For law he
entertained no reverence, and on life he placed no
value."   He was absolutely despotic and viciously
cruel.

Horns are the symbols of power.   The Revelator tells us " He had two horns."   Virtually,
Henry was the king of Great Britain and Ireland.
James, one of his immediate successors, claimed
to be king of Great Britain, France and Ireland.
Therefore, Great Britain and Ireland were as two
horns or powers, which the monster Henry controlled.

"*Like a Lamb.*"   Hitherto this kingdom had
lain as a lamb, peacefully nestled and nurtured
by the papal power.   In order to see this you
have but to turn up the pages of any authentic
work on British history.   Especially we notice it
in the reign of Henry IV. and Henry V., when
the poor Wycliffites suffered martyrdom and most
barbarous treatment, just because of the king's
zealous attachment to the established religion,
viz: Roman Catholicism.

But even in the early part of the reign of Henry
VIII. England nestled like a lamb in the papal
arms.   The continent was ringing with the notes
of reformation under the intrepid Luther.   From
Henry's pen soon appeared a book against the
reformer.   A copy of this work, splendidly bound,
was presented to the Pope.   The Pope, well
pleased with the gift, conferred the title of *Fidei
Defensor* on the royal author.

But now behold Henry—two-horned evil beast
—cast off his lamb-like attributes, and rising up
in the majesty of a despot, he claims all the power, all prerogatives of the first beast, when in 1534
he is recognized by parliament as the only supreme head on earth of the Church of England;
and thus literally fulfilling the words: "And He
exerciseth all the power of the first beast before
Him, and causeth the earth and them that dwell
therein to worship the first beast, whose deadly
wound was healed." (Rev. xiii. 12.) In this
manner the trammels of popery were shaken off
only to be placed on the shoulders of another
being more vile.

"*He spake as a dragon*," or devil, which is as literally true of Henry VIII. as that the sun shines.
That he exercised all the power of the first beast
before him, is clearly evinced from the pages of
history.

The first of the six articles of the "*Bloody Statute*" instituted by him ran thus:

"The Eucharist is really the present natural
body and blood of Christ under the forms, but
without the substance, of bread and wine, which
are transmuted by the act of consecration."

Poor, but brave Lambert, a school-master who
could not believe this, was compelled to confront
the king and bishops at Westminster Hall, in
November, 1538. Lambert would not bend from
his belief. "Fellow, wilt thou live or die?"
exclaimed Henry. "My soul I commit to God,"

said the school-master, "and my body to your grace's clemency." "Then must thou die," and die he did in the red flame at Smithfield. (Collier's British Empire, p. 232.)

But still more cruel was the fate of Annie Ascue, a lady of Lincolnshire. First disowned by her husband for her adherence to what she felt to be truth, and then arrested in London, she was finally tried at Guildhall. When on trial, she said: "That which you call your God is a piece of bread, for proof thereof, let it lie in a box three months and it will be mouldy. I am persuaded it cannot be God." Sentence of death followed at once, and she, with three others, were burned in front of St. Bartholomew's Church on the 16th of July, 1546. The fagot blazed in Scotland as well.

And as to the image erected, (verse 15) the matter is plain, for when the split from Rome took place, there must needs be a substitute formed, and the following will speak for itself:

CONSTITUTIONAL.

THE FIRST BEAST.	THE IMAGE.
The Romish Church.	The Anglican Church.
The Pope as supreme head.	Henry VIII. as supreme head.
Absolute power.	The same.
Cruel enactments against all opposers.	Cruel enactments against papists or any other who dared oppose.
The yoke of Cardinalship.	The yoke of prelacy.

DOCTRINAL.

A Triune God as the foundation of their faith, and consequently a pre-existing Christ co-equal and co-eternal with the Father.	The same.
A never-dying soul, which can exist as a being independent of the body after death.	The same.
A heaven in the skies where man flees at death.	The same.
A hell of unending torments for damned souls.	The same.

SUNDRY.

Robes or surplices, miters, scepters, crucifixes, etc.	Similar.

And thus we might go on showing that the image is an almost exact likeness of the original, but a word to the wise is sufficient. It makes our soul shudder as we consider the origin of this image. The starting point was an unjust demand for a divorce. History tells us: "This step led to the great and glorious reformation," as well, we add, to the erecting of this image.

But what honest mind does not revolt against such a monster as Henry VIII. as the basis of a church of God, also claiming to be its supreme earthly head? Those who would not bow to his mandates could not hold office under the crown, or otherwise were martyred, thus fulfilling the words of scripture, "that no man might buy or sell, save he that had the mark." (v. 17.) O, Blackness of Darkness, thy sandy, foundation shall soon crumble before the storm of God's impending wrath, and thy supporters shall cry, alas, alas!

That the formation of the Anglican church at that particular period of history was virtually intended as a deadly blow aimed at the papal hierarchy, history clearly demonstrates. The abolition in 1533 of *annates* or first-fruits which had formerly supported the Papal power, " the forbidding of appeals to Rome, and the appointment of prelates by any but the king," (1533) together with the demolition of the monasteries that followed, indubitably proves this point. The beautiful stained glass windows were splintered, and the lovely bells which had filled the air at morn and eventide with silvery strains were either sold or melted down. The choice pictures which had adorned the walls were destroyed in the flames, and the piles of magnificent architecture and sculptured work which had for centuries adorned the land were either leveled, unroofed, or turned into stables. Iconoclasm held full sway.

But in 1539 Henry threw himself back into the hands of the Roman Catholic party, and immediately were issued those " Six Articles," whose awful results gave them the title of "The Bloody Statute." With this and other twistings, amendments, double dealing, etc., the "deadly wound" lately aimed at Popery was healed, and people were henceforth made to worship the first beast. For, notwithstanding all the waverings to and fro, the first beast still remained, and so did the image. In the reign of Queen Elizabeth the acts of *Supremacy* and *Uniformity* were ratified. The former of these required all who held office to declare on oath that the Queen was the only supreme governor in the realm, both in *temporal* and *spiritual* things. (Rev. xiii. 17.) The latter insisted that all must use King Edward's book of common prayer, and heavy penalties were attached to the violation of the same, and as Collier informs us, " The Anglican church assumed almost its present shape in 1562, when the Forty-two Articles were reduced to Thirty-nine." As to the earth and them who dwell therein being caused to worship the first beast, it becomes evident, when we consider that they who worship any *image* or *likeness* are but acknowledging or worshiping the thing which that image represents; for an image or likeness of any thing is no more the thing itself than a shadow is the substance from which it is cast. It was no longer Roman Catholicism, it was the creed of the Anglican church—another form, but the leading tenets of faith continued the same, as shown in our formula.

Instead of the Pope as head, there was the vile Henry. Nor can we see that it was bettered much by the accession of Queen Elizabeth. A queen whose hand could sign the death warrant of Queen Mary of Scotland was truly unfit for the head of a church of the living God. Nor can we see it in the order of heaven that women should ever be head of God's church. And when we consider in connection therewith that the whole thing was established by blood—the blood of innocents—it proves it to be the very inverse of the church of Christ, which was established not by the destroying of the lives of others, but by the laying down of the life of Him who came mankind to save, and whose governing power was LOVE. They could now pay tithes at home instead of to Rome. They could hence worship a triune God of their own. Their ideas of immortality, heaven, and hell, although an exact likeness of the dogmas of Rome, yet they were embodied in a new regime. Offshoots from this image sprung up in many quarters, assuming new names, and thus Babylon of the latter days began to wax and grow great, and soon she could say in her heart, "I sit a queen—and shall see no sorrow." Yet as a millstone cast into the sea is she to be thrown down, and found no more at all. The apostle enjoined, "Beware of dogs, beware of evil workers, beware of the concision," but all such crept in, nay, came in as a flood, and people, even the masses, allowed themselves to be swept down the stream. And darkness as a consequence has prevailed. But the clouds are fast breaking up, and the glorious light of truth is pouring through the rifts. Although the beast is worshiped, and multitudes bow down at the shrine of the image, the days of both are numbered. The arm of Jehovah is stretched forth, and the great tribulation of the latter days is upon us. The Spirit of Jehovah is moving upon the face of the waters, (peoples, nations, etc.) and "Come out of her, my people," is the sound proclaimed by the messengers of the Most High.   Let us now consider the number of this beast:

"Here is wisdom.   Let him that hath understanding, count the number of the beast; for it is the number of a man; and his number is 666."— Rev. xiii. 18.

This number 666 has been the cause of much speculation and earnest study as well.   By the many it has been considered as a sort of scriptural enigma.   Unlike other prophetical numbers we are explicitly told " It is the number of a *man*." Therefore it must apply in some way to an individual or person.   In order to find just such a person, we must again appeal to history.   Let it be granted that our location and demonstration of the image as given and as applied to the reign of Henry VIII. be correct, then the number 666 must also apply to the same period.

In order to the formation of any body there must needs be a *foundation*, *a body* and a *head*.   When the new church was formed in Henry's reign, we find that for its foundation the *three creeds*, Apostolic, Athanasian, and Nicene, ranked equal to the Bible in authority.   Instead of the seven sacraments of the Romish Church, only *three*, Baptism, the Supper, and Penance, held their ground. Here then we have for each of the lower extremities of the image the number *three*, which, when put together, make *six*.   That these *three* creeds and *three* sacraments, as imposed, were indeed the foundation or fundamental portion of this new departure in matters of faith, none can deny.

As to the body of the image, history clearly tells us that when devastation had swept through the land, and when the monasteries of the Roman Church were demolished, only *six bishoprics*— .Westminster, Oxford, Peterborough, Bristol, Chester, and Gloucester—grew out of their ruins.

Here is another *six* which evidently makes up the body of this new structure. For the body of any church is composed of its members or supporters, and since these six bishoprics contained at least the majority of the supporters of this new church, therefore they constituted its body. As to the *head*, it is the head which governs the body and dictates and forms the laws for its guidance. In 1539 Henry, as the supreme head—although he professedly threw himself back into the hands of the Roman Catholic party—had issued *The Bloody Statute*, which contained just *Six Articles*. Here is another six emanating from the head of the body or church.

This with the others make three 6's, which are the number of a man, and which also have a striking connection with the constitution of the Anglican church. But the reign of Henry is full of 6's. For example, take the year 1539, the same in which the *Bloody Statute* was passed, and its sum is 18, which in turn is the sum of three 6's. Henry had also six wives. We however adhere to that which we have first given, as being the only figures which truly apply to the scriptural 666.

To recapitulate: The *SIX* Articles of the
Bloody Statute emanating from the acknowledged
supreme head on earth of the church is strikingly significant to say the least; and when we
take into consideration the amount of innocent
blood shed just because of a denial of its first article, we cannot fail to see its aptitude of application
to one who may well and truly be designated an
evil beast as well as a man.   The main body to be
ruled over, or rather the body which accepted these
dogmas, and acted the part of tyrannical lords
over God's heritage, is open to the vision of all in
the *SIX Bishoprics* already named.   These resting on the two-fold base of *three* creeds and *three*
sacraments make up the complete foundation in
the third *SIX*.

Prophecy is but a future history foretold.
When the thing comes to pass, we have only to
compare the one with the other, in order to
arrive at the truth.   We have demonstrated that
history (we have quoted mostly from Collier's
British Empire) coincides with John's prophecy,
and he that runneth may read.

We deem that we have clearly pointed out the
image and the number 666.   Then what follows?
Simply that the whole has been constructed and
constituted contrary to the teachings of Christ.
If contrary to the teachings of Christ, it is also
contrary to Christ himself, because if we reject
his teachings we reject also himself.   If we love
Him, we must heed his sayings.

But to be contrary to Christ is an equivalent

for Anti-Christ. Both in their teachings and in their practices they have shown themselves to be contrary to Christ. They teach there are three Gods. Christ says there is but ONE LORD. They claim the three are equal. Christ says: "My Father is greater than I." They tell their disciples they will go to heaven at death and be with Jesus. Jesus told his disciples, "Where I go ye cannot come." And further, for He says: "No man hath ascended up to heaven." They say this earth is not their home. Christ says: "Blessed are the meek, for *they shall inherit the earth*." He further enjoins his disciples to pray, "Thy kingdom *come*, thy will be done in *earth*, as it is in heaven." They compelled man on the penalty of suffering torture and death to accept their dogmas, and with fire and sword hundreds of innocents were cut down. Christ said: "If I be lifted up, I will draw all men unto me." He came not to destroy, but to save; and love divine is his compelling force. He taught the very opposite of slaughter. Not as wolves to cut down the sheep did He send his disciples forth, but as sheep in the midst of wolves. Christianity suffers; but this church has imposed the horrors of shackles, the stake, the block and axe, the lonely cell, the inquisition, and sanctioned the deeds of a bloody Claverhouse and Jeffries. Instead of shackles, Christ burst the bands asunder, and instituted the glorious liberty of the sons of God. The deeds of this so-called church of God have been simply diabolical. The innocent blood shed cries out to heaven, "How long, O Lord, holy and true, dost thou not judge and avenge our blood on them that dwell on the earth." The response is given: "Behold, I come quickly." The time is at hand. The monster Antichrist shall soon appear to every eye in all his hideousness. Let us illustrate: On the shores of the dark waters of Perdition, where the waves of centuries have been washing up the shifting sands, three ominous pillars rise. The names inscribed thereon by an unseen hand are:

DOGMA.   FABLE.   MYTH.

Between the first and second columns stands the beast "Having seven heads and ten horns." (Rev. xiii. 1.) Between the second and third is to be seen the image of the beast. The foundation and the sands of the foundation are red with the blood of innocents. On the right hand we behold a field of carnage where all the chilling horrors of the Inquisition are being carried out. On the left, headed by Henry VIII., we see another horrifying scene, in which the notorious Jeffries, Claverhouse, etc., perform their ignominious part. Over the whole scene hangs a dark cloud, and written thereon in characters of blood is the one word:

MYSTERY.

God moves upon the face of the deep. The waves lash the shore. The sands are silently washing away. The structure totters on its base. The heavens grow dark. (Matt. xxiv. 29.) A fiery chariot appears, bearing back to earth the

precursor of the Messiah. (Mal. iv. 5.) He
sounds his trump: "Hear, O people, the Lord
our God is ONE LORD." Perdition's billows roll
in great commotion. The sands ebb outward.
And suddenly with mighty crash the triune pillars fall into the waters dark and deep, and the
multitudes of her supporters, "standing afar off,"
cry: "Alas, alas, that great city Babylon, that
mighty city! for in one hour is thy judgment
come." Then shall the eyes of all people be
opened, and they shall know who is God, and
that besides Him there is no other. Then shall
they know Him whom God hath appointed Judge
of quick and dead, even the Lord Christ. O
Babylon, Babylon, thou mighty city exalted to
the heaven, even now the handwriting is upon
thy walls, "Weighed in the balances and found
wanting." O reader, flee into the arms of thy
Saviour. Seek the true refuge ere the storm
of wrath descends. And ye who are yet within
the walls of the doomed city, hark, 'tis the voice
of heaven calling, "Come out of her, my people,
that ye be not partakers of her sins, and that ye
receive not of her plagues, for her sins have
reached unto heaven."

17

CHAPTER XVIII.

THE NEW BIRTH.

"Verily, verily, I say unto thee, except any one (Diaglott version) be born of water and of the Spirit, he cannot enter into the kingdom of God."—John iii. 5.

This statement of our blessed Master is plain and decisive. It is also vitally important. Compliance or non-compliance with its conditions will respectively either admit into or exclude from the kingdom of God. But the expression "Kingdom of God" is variously used in the scriptures. If it be taken in its widest sense in this instance, few indeed shall be saved. It is severally used as follows:

1. It is used in a spiritual sense, as for example, "The kingdom of God is not meat and drink; but righteousness, and peace, and joy in the Holy Ghost." (Rom. xiv. 17.)

2. It is used in a wide or universal sense, as in the parable of the "mustard seed;" (Luke xiii. 18, 19,) or as in the words of Christ: "Verily I

say unto you, I will drink no more of the fruit of
the vine, until that day that I drink it new in the
kingdom of God." (Mark xiv. 25.)

3. It is used in a restricted or representative
sense. An earthly kingdom is represented by its
rulers, its parliament, and its ambassadors. In
like manner the members of the Christ body—
Christ himself and his true Church—are the rep-
resentatives of the kingdom of God on earth in
the present; and in the future they shall be its
rulers, as kings and priests unto God. This we
have clearly shown in a previous chapter on "predestination." Christ evidently uses the term in
this restricted sense in the passage, "But if I
cast out devils by the Spirit of God, then the
kingdom of God is come unto you." (Matt. xii.
28.) For Christ stood before them as the noble
representative and foundation of that kingdom
upon earth. God bore witness thereto in that
his mighty power was demonstrated through
Christ. When the Pharisees asked "When the
kingdom of God should come," Christ replied:
"The kingdom of God cometh not with outward
show: (marg.) neither shall they say, Lo here! or,
lo there! for, behold, the kingdom of God is
among (marg.) you." (Luke xvii. 20, 21.) The
text gives "*within*" instead of "*among you.*" But
when we consider the parties addressed, (Pharisees) and especially that they "demanded" of
Christ an answer, the inaptitude of the former
rendering becomes quite apparent. Christ by his
Spirit may be said to dwell in, or within, his true

followers; but it is grossly incompatible with both
scripture and reason to claim that the kingdom
of God was established in pharisaical hearts. In
another instance Christ addresses this same class:
"Woe unto you, scribes and Pharisees, hypocrites! for you are like unto whited sepulchres,
which indeed appear beautiful outward, but are
within full of dead *men's* bones, and of all uncleanness. Even so ye also outwardly appear righteous unto men, but within ye are full of hypocrisy and iniquity." (Matt. xxiii. 27, 28.) This
sustains the point adduced. That the kingdom
of God was *among* them is only another example
of the restricted use of this term. The Ambassador of heaven stood before them, and in Him was
vested the power of the kingdom. In the text
under consideration, we believe the term, "Kingdom of God" is used in this limited sense. One
thing is apparent, that Christ's particular mission
at that time was to select representative men—
men who would sit with Him at last in his throne
—a bride that would say unto all nations "Come."
These were called to be overcomers. They must
needs tread the narrow way. To become one of
this class the conditions of the text must needs
be carried out. But to apply the general tenor
of this text to all people would compel us to trample under foot some of the sweetest and most
merciful sayings of Christ. For example: "Whosoever shall give to drink unto one of these little ones (the representative members of the kingdom of God) a cup of cold water only in the name

of a disciple, verily I say unto you, he shall in no wise lose his reward." (Matt. x. 42.) Again, no one will for a moment doubt but that John the Baptist will be in God's Kingdom. Christ says concerning him: "Among those that are born of women there is not a greater prophet than John the Baptist: but *he that is least in the kingdom of God* is greater than he." (Luke vii. 28.) Now it is evident that the term "Kingdom of God," as used here, can be construed in no other sense than a limited one. Therefore we conclude that the strict portions of God's word apply only to those who are called with the high and holy calling of God in Christ Jesus; and that all others outside of this class shall be judged at last according to the deeds done in the body.

"*Born of water and of the Spirit.*" An evangelist of the M. E. Church called on us lately, and during the conversation that ensued he claimed to be already born of God and of the Spirit. We, of course, endeavored to show him the absurdity of such a claim. The adversative positions being defined, the conversation ran thus:

"Well, my friend, you claim to have been born of God—born of the Spirit; do I understand you aright?"

"You do," he replied; "and I further hold that every Christian can claim the same."

"Then am I to understand that it is an immortal being whom I address?—for if your claim be true, according to the unerring word of God, you can be no less."

"How do you make that out? What do you
mean?" he inquired, somewhat embarrassed.

"The words of Jesus are my guide, and I simply mean that since you claim to have been already 'born of the Spirit,' you must therefore be
a spirit, or immortal; for 'that which is born of
the Spirit *is spirit*,' is what Jesus told Nicode-
mus." (6.)

Then followed a brief discussion, the substance
of which is contained in the exposition of the
above text, as follows:

Born of water, or "born out of water," as it
can be truly rendered, evidently refers to baptism.

"But," objects one, "baptism is a symbol of
death, not of birth." We admit this, but. "That
which thou sowest is not quickened, except it
die," and in order to our being "born out of
water," we must first die (symbolically) in the
water. "Therefore we are buried with Him
(Christ) by baptism into *death*." (Rom. vi. 4.)
But as new creatures in Christ we "are risen
with Him through the faith of the operation of
God who hath raised Him (i. e. Christ) from the
dead." (Col. ii. 12.) Planted in the likeness of
Christ's death through faith, we reckon ourselves
"to be dead indeed unto sin, but alive unto God
through Jesus Christ our Lord." (Rom. vi. 11.)
"Knowing this, that our old man (the Adamic
nature) is crucified with Him, that the body of
sin might be destroyed, that henceforth we should
not serve sin." (verse 6.) Our sinful nature is
buried, as it were, beneath the waters of baptism,

and we put on the new nature of Christ. " For as many of you as have been baptized into Christ have put on Christ." (Gal. iii. 27.) Therefore a new creature is by faith "born out of water," but this only implies a change of nature in the mortal state. Henceforth heavenly aspirations take the place of earthly. As "babes in Christ" we are begotten of God to a higher state of being, viz: immortality.

Born of the Spirit. As water baptism precedes the water birth, so baptism of the Spirit precedes the Spirit birth; for "if anyone have not the Spirit of Christ he is none of his." (Rom. viii. 9.) And hence we perceive the significance of the question, as given by Paul, " Have ye received the Holy Ghost since ye believed?" As water baptism implies death to the " old man," or Adamic nature, so through the baptism and aid of the Spirit we *put to death* (literal rendering) the deeds of the body in order to life eternal. (Rom. viii. 13.) Through the Spirit we are begotten of God. The seed of immortality is planted in us which is —the first-fruits of the Spirit—the seal of God, the earnest of our inheritance. But in the resurrection every *seed* shall receive his own body. (I. Cor. xv. 38.) This mortal shall then put on immortality. "It is sown in corruption, it is raised in incorruption; it is sown in weakness, it is raised in power; it is sown a natural body, it is raised a spiritual body." The mortal state is but a period of probation through which we must pass acceptably to God in order to attain to that which is immortal and eternal. "But he that is begotten of God keepeth himself, and that wicked one toucheth him not." (I. John v. 18.) Hence power is given with which to overcome in all things. But "whosoever is born of God sinneth not," for those who shall inherit that land shall be all righteous. (Is. lx. 21.) Sin shall be no more. But to claim that we can be born of the Spirit while yet in the mortal state is neither sustained by reason, common sense, nor scripture; it is simply absurd. We, however, through faith and obedience to God, are through the Spirit begotten, as it were, in the great womb of nature to an immortal life; but that life is hid with Christ in God until He who is our life shall appear. When the last trump shall sound, if the Spirit of God has been yours as the seed or germ of a new being, "He that raised up Christ from the dead shall also quicken your mortal bodies by his Spirit that dwelleth in you." (Rom. viii. 11.) "For we know that every creature (marg.) groaneth and travaileth in pain together until now. And not only they but ourselves also, who have the first-fruits of the Spirit, even we ourselves, groan within ourselves waiting for the adoption, to wit, the redemption of our body." (22, 23.) This text alone clearly shows that Paul considered the present but a period of travail and pain in which the being groaned and longed for the day of redemption when, "born of the Spirit," it should enter into life eternal. We therefore conclude

that according to the scriptures the order of God
is as follows:

1. Baptism of water.	Born out of water.
Adamic nature dies.	New creature in Christ form-ed.
Buried with Him by baptism into death.	Risen with Him, alive unto God and godliness.
2. Baptism of Spirit.	Born of Spirit.
Put to death the deeds of the body.	"To him that overcometh will I grant to sit with me in my throne."
Begotten of God.	Born of God.
Sown in weakness.	Raised in power.

The connecting link between mortality and immortality shall be the baptism of fire. As to the
rite of baptism, acording to the construction of
the language of the commission as given by
Christ, it implies three separate actions into three
given names. (Matt. xxviii. 19.)   There are also
three distinct administrations of baptism, viz:
Baptism of *water*, administered by man as
the servant of God, and baptism of the *Holy
Ghost* and of *fire*, administered by Christ. (Luke
iii. 16.)   In order to the second we must needs
pass through the first, (Acts ii. 38, 39) and in
order to the last, we must needs pass through the
first and second.   Those who fail to pass through
the baptism of fire shall rise from the dead to be
judged by Christ and his saints.   The class that
shall pass through the fire of that day unscathed
shall be changed in a moment, in the twinkling of
an eye, and shall be caught up to meet the Lord
in the air.

  " Every man's work shall be made manifest;

for the day shall declare it, because it shall be revealed by *fire*, and the *fire* shall try every man's work of what sort it is." (I. Cor. iii. 13.) For "the heavens and the earth, which are now, by the same word are kept in store, reserved unto *fire* against the day of judgment and perdition of ungodly men." (II. Pet. iii. 7.) "When the Lord Jesus shall be revealed from heaven with the angels of his power, (marg.) in flaming *fire* yielding vengeance on them that know not God, and that obey not the gospel of our Lord Jesus Christ, . . . when He shall come to be glorified in his saints." (II. Thess. i. 7-10.) These passages define clearly when the baptism of fire shall take place.

Blessed REGENERATION, all hail! "Ye must be born again." Who does not long for the heavenly birth? Dear reader, are you living for it? "He that believeth and is baptized shall be saved." "For the promise (of the Holy Ghost) is unto you, and to your children, and to all that are afar off, even as many as the Lord our God shall call." This is a legacy of inestimable value. Lay hold of it by faith, having first obeyed from the heart the form of doctrine delivered unto us, (Matt. xxviii. 19) for once we are made the recipients of the unspeakable gift, it is the surety from heaven to us of that transcendent glory which shall be revealed in us as we pass through the *baptism of fire* into the immortal and incorruptible state, at the coming of the Messiah.

CHAPTER XIX.

INFIDELITY VS. TRUE FAITH.

(A LECTURE.)

True liberty is worthy of defense. There is something inspiring in the word. It is an element of truth. It is heaven begotten. Its dimensions are illimitable—wide as the universe. It is the atmosphere of heaven. "Where the Spirit of the Lord is there is liberty." The Rock of Ages is its foundation. The heavens are its canopy. When we inhale its balmy air we become elevated in the moral and the intellectual scale; and we aspire to the enviable position of sons of God.

He who stands guard on the battlements of Truth is a defender of liberty. But he whose aim is ever directed against Truth is a slave of the devil. "Ye shall know them by their fruits." The contention, however, between truth and error, between right and wrong, and between faith and unbelief is a contention of principle against principle, and not of being against fellow-being.

> The blow of *right*
> Is of power the might.

And the sword of truth ever falls with crashing effect upon the tottering fabric of error. Every defender of liberty should make true his shafts. Every assertion made, every principle set forth should poise upon the balances of truth. Ingersoll is looked upon, by many, as one of the ablest champions of liberty's army. But many of his assertions are most extravagant, and utterly false. In one of his lectures he says:

"The Bible has built every inquisition, made every religious martyr, driven every stake, set every fagot, lighted every torch. It has made every thumb-screw, every rack, dislocated every joint."

To charge the Bible with misdeeds of wicked and cruel monsters is manifestly wrong. That the Bible has been misused is an historical fact. But simple justice demands that that misuse should be laid to the charge of the misuser, and not to the thing misused. And it is nothing less than an infamous libel to charge the Bible with the bloody deeds of a Nero, a Jeffries, or a Claverhouse. See that poor, honest, innocent man, John Brown, of Priesthill, (Ayrshire, Scotland) as he is about to be shot down by the blood-thirsty Claverhouse. His only crime was that he endeavored to worship the God of his fathers under the banner of true liberty. His home was isolated and lay

among the heath-clad hills. His wife and children stand beside him as he kneels upon the heath
before the door of his cot. He breathes a fervent
prayer to God—a prayer that might have melted
the heart of a savage. But pleadings of wife and
children are in vain. The cruel hand of that mur-
derous monster is raised. He fires, and the brains
of one of earth's noblemen are scattered on the
heath to be gathered up by the hands of a loving
and heart-broken wife. Charge the Bible with
this dastardly, inhuman, and devilish act! Charge
the Bible with a thousand of such deeds! Yes,
you may, but the imputation must be weighed
upon the balances of humanity and justice. "*Set
every fagot!*" Behold that martyr in the midst
of the flame. The flesh is crisping upon his bones.
He has braved the battle and the breeze in defence
of religion and liberty, and now he suffers at the
hands of cruel men. The Bible is his solace, and
the foundation of his faith. The gross misuse of
that Bible only belongs to his murderers. In the
midst of his intense sufferings he chants a hymn
of praise to God. The Spirit of the Bible bears
him through the fiery ordeal. He dies in peaceful hope. Now in the light of common sense and
reason, who would dare charge the Bible with his
death? You might just as reasonably charge
Christ with his own crucifixion, or Garfield with
his own assassination. This modern exponent of
infidelity tells us further, that

"The Bible has covered the earth with blood,
the human face with tears; has crushed honesty;

has offered a premium for rascality, stupidity, and hypocrisy."

We have already dispensed with the first charge made here. As to the second, we admit it, only in a different sense to that inferred by Ingersoll. The Bible has covered the human face with tears, and its spirit has filled the human heart with sorrow. But these tears are shed for the wayward and the erring ones of our race. True humanity weeps over fallen humanity, and with an outstretched arm endeavors to lift a sinking brother. This is the Spirit of Christianity. The psalmist says, "Rivers of waters run down mine eyes, because they keep not thy law." Jesus wept. His heart was also exceeding sorrowful, even unto death, for poor sinful mortals.

> O blessed Spirit of God's holy Son!
> That teacheth man to lift the fallen one—
> That weepeth o'er the erring, helps the poor—
> That turneth not the wand'rer from the door—
> That comforteth the lonely and the sad,
> But in the midst of sorrow maketh glad.

When men—fellow-beings—walk in sin's dark ways—when we behold with open eyes those whom we have learned to love, or at least to respect, treading a downward path which leads to infamy, hopelessness and death—when we hear the name of Him, who sticketh closer than a brother, blasphemed—when we see right and truth, and liberty trampled in the dust—even when a feeble child of faith has its hope shattered by the poisonous shaft of infidelity—in every circumstance which calls for true humanity to weep, Christianity steps in with condolence most sweet, and mingles with our tears. The noblest hearts of earth are those who can weep for others' woes.

"*It has crushed honesty.*" The tenor of script-ure throughout maintains honesty. Will pre-cepts that enjoin good crush good? No more will that which maintains honesty crush honesty. The absurdity of this charge is evident. The Bi-ble enjoins man to "provide things honest in the sight of all men," and "whatsoever things are honest" to think on these things. The church was also encouraged to learn or "profess honest trades for necessary uses;" (Tit. iii. 14, *marg.*) and to "walk honestly toward them that are without;" having a "good conscience, in all things willing to live honestly;" "that we may lead a quiet and peaceable life in all godliness and hon-esty;" "having our conversation honest;" for "a double minded man is unstable in all his ways." The man who despises these injunctions of the Bible has little honesty to be crushed. Nor does it require far-seeing to perceive that the charge we have been animadverting upon is in itself dis-honest.

"*It has offered a premium for rascality, stupid-ity and hypocrisy.*" What premium? Let the Bible make its own reply. "Upon the wicked he shall rain snares, fire and brimstone, and an horrible tempest; this shall be the portion of their cup." (Ps. xi. 6.) In regard to the eternal city we read, "There shall in no wise enter into it any thing that defileth, neither whatsoever worketh abomination or maketh a lie." "Fret not thyself because of evildoers, neither be thou envious against the workers of iniquity, for they shall soon be cut down like the grass, and wither as the green herb." As to hypocrisy, Christ scathed it. "Woe unto you scribes and Pharisees, hypocrites! because ye build the tombs of the prophets, and garnish the sepulchres of the righteous." "Woe unto you scribes and Pharisees, hypocrites! for ye are as graves which appear not, and the men that walk over them are not aware of them." "Ye serpents, ye generation of vipers, how can ye escape the damnation of hell?" Job says: "The hypocrite's hope shall perish." Rather a direful premium think you not? And methinks the author of the foregoing charge would shrink from the acceptance of such a reward himself, hardened though he be. In the language of Christianity we call such "premiums" by their correct name, viz: punishment. The wages of sin is death. We again quote:

"The Bible has opposed every man of science. . . . It has been a perpetual obstruction upon the highway of progress."

If liberty was enchained, if science was retarded in the dark past, and history informs us that this was indeed the case, so also was the Bible held in the chains of the power of darkness. But light burst in that dark lone night, when in the fifteenth and sixteenth centuries, the Bible and science contemporaneously began to diffuse their precious light. Since that time they have run together. True science and the Bible must ever coincide with each other. It is only by the misapprehensions or the misapplications of the principles of either or both that they are made to apparently differ or disagree. It is an indubitable fact that the rapid advance of modern science is inseparably intertwined with the diffusion of gospel light. The Bible and science are twin brothers. God is the author of both; and when each understands the other their mutual agreement is inevitable. Men may and do differ, but the principles of truth and the principles of science can never disagree. Like the sun's rays, the principles of truth and science blend together and yield a common flood of light. Theories may prove false but science is not science except it be true.

"Voltaire believed himself to triumph against faith, when in the name of the then prevalent theory, which regarded the sun as the sole source of light, he taxed the Bible with absurdity. 'The Bible teaches,' said he, 'that the light was created before the sun: this is absurd, as it has been demonstrated that the sun produces light.' Voltaire confounded in his science, theory and fact. If he had remembered that theory is infallible, he would have respected what he too lightly ridiculed."—*Didon's Science without God, p. 40.*

"*Obstruction upon the highway of progress.*" Who has carried knowledge to every land? Who built our schools, our colleges, our charitable institutions? Was it infidelity? By what means are such works and such institutions supported

18

to-day? Certainly not by infidelity. Was it infidelity that so nobly pushed its way to heathen
lands, denying itself of comforts, companions and
ofttimes the endearments of home, and braving
danger and death as well, all in order to dissem-
inate light and knowledge to the poor benighted
races of the earth? No; this is the work of the
Bible. And in those dark lands schools have
been set up and knowledge has increased. Wonderful "obstruction" indeed! Heaven has touched
it with a skillful hand and given it a glorious re-
versible motion. Notwithstanding all the attacks
made upon it the Bible still goes on its mission
to every part of the world. That this good work
is being multiplied is evident from the following
words which were spoken at the recent annual
meeting of the British and Foreign Bible Society:

"Still the Book goes on its way, carrying its
blessing wherever it goes, and showing no signs
of being effete. The Bible Society, like an inex-
haustible fountain, sends forth east, west, north
and south, at the rate of some 9,400 copies every
working day. Last year it issued 92,500 copies
in excess of the year before. Since the commencement of its work it has sent into circula-
tion nearly ninety-four millions of copies and upwards of three hundred versions." Contrasted
with this record, how vain are the words of Ingersoll: 'I am opposed to the Bible, and am going
to do what I can against it.'"

We deem the following one of the most puerile
hits ever made by this opponent of Christianity:

"All the clergymen of this world can never get

one drop of rain out of the sky; all the clergymen of the civilized world could not save one
human life if they tried it."

We might retort, granting they cannot, can
infidelity? But what right has Mr. Ingersoll to
make this assertion? Does he know all things?
Is he a god? He admits that everything is governed by fixed. law. The human race forms a
part of that everything. Christianity has much
to do with humanity, and in turn :

> "Prayer is the Christian's vital breath,
> The Christian's native air."

Therefore prayer must be a constituent of that
everything which is governed by law. This granted, then lives may have been prolonged, and rain
may have fallen only in answer to the fulfillment
of this law of prayer. None of nature's laws are
meaningless. When they are violated something
has to suffer. Were the law of evaporation to
cease suddenly in the performance of its wondrous part in the economy of nature, the result
would soon be disastrous beyond conception.
The earth would speedily become a barren waste,
and the animal and vegetable kingdoms would
soon be extinct.

Prayer is the evaporation of the mighty stream
of Christianity. It ascends upward as sweet incense, and returneth in showers of blessing. Let
prayer cease, and let all mankind instead curse
and blaspheme the name of God, and who dare
contemplate the result! It would be a miserable
world to live in, provided the Creator permitted

it to last. Even infidels would be afraid to trust each other. And we hesitate not in asserting that the world would wish the rejected element restored again. It would eventually become so unbearable that infidelity would betake itself to its closet and attempt a prayer for Christianity's return. In the present state of things infidelity stands in the shadow of the Christian's hope— Ingersoll stood there at his brother's grave—but take that away and infidelity would be left hopelessly, dismally, awfully *alone*.

To return: "Men ought always to pray and not to faint." When man fails to cry to God, his nature must needs groan in order to supply the deficiency of unfulfilled law. Paul recognized this law in the words, "We know that the whole creation groaneth and travaileth in pain together until now. And not only they, but ourselves also, who have the first-fruits of the Spirit, even we ourselves groan within ourselves, waiting for the adoption, to wit: the redemption of our body." (Rom. viii. 22, 23.) The existence of law is recognized by perception. Where we perceive the effect we look for a cause. Where there is cause there is an agent behind it. Christianity is an acknowledged cause which has produced marvelous effects. It has revolutionized the world. Therefore it should not be despised. Prayer is one of the motive powers of Christianity. In like manner, therefore, prayer should not be despised. Christians pray because they believe there are intelligences in the heavens. Infidelity inquires, what reason have Christians for this belief? We deem they have good reason, as we will presently show:

1. To deny, or to have genuine doubts concerning the existence of a Supreme Being is simply equivalent to a denial of our own senses.

A complicated machine stands before us. Came it here by chance, without inventor, machinist, or maker? Did the city of New York spring up spontaneously, or by chance, without designers, mechanics, or builders, or capitalists? It would be much easier to believe that such were possible than that the vast system of Nature, with all its suns, and stars, and planets, and moons, etc., together with all the laws which govern their motions, the beings who inhabit them, the matter which grows upon them, the wonders contained in them, the beauties which adorn them, and the power which sustains them all in space so rare, that all these marvels should spring into position and existence without a designer—without a Creator—without an overseer—without a life-giver, in brief, without an original. After all, it takes more faith to be an infidel than it does to be a Christian.

2. (*a.*) Matter exists in Nature in two states, *organized* and *unorganized*—" organized " when it is collected into forms adapted to the support of life. (*b.*) Bodies of matter in Nature may exist in two different states, viz: *solid* and *fluid.* Fluids exist in two forms, viz: *liquids*, and *gases* or *vapors*.

But matter cannot determine its own quantity or quality. Let us inquire. Earth, what are thy dimensions; tell me what thou seest in thy flight through space? Tree, why dost thou shoot upward toward the heavens? Stone, of what art thou composed? Air, what are thy constituents? Lightning, what art thou? There is no intelligence within to make reply. On this point the Bishop of Carlisle says:

"Design or no design, purpose or no purpose, a mass of matter cannot determine its own quantity; the amount of energy which exists unchanged and unchangeable in a material system cannot determine its own amount; the straight line in which the center of the system moves and the uniform velocity with which it moves cannot determine themselves; yet all these things have been determined somehow. Therefore they must have been determined by an agent which is outside the material system, or, in other words, which is not itself material. There may have been, so far as my argument is concerned, no good purpose, nor any purpose at all, in the determination, but it is absolutely impossible, so far as I can perceive, to avoid the conclusion that a determining cause exists. I am disposed to call this result *a demonstration from natural premises of the existence of the Supernatural.*"—*Nineteenth Century.*

Neither is matter capable of forming the laws by which it is governed. That matter is governed by fixed laws has already been demonstrated by science. Take for example, the law of gravitation, contrasted with which all the forces of earth are but a mere speck. What discovered this law? We reply, the very genius of intelligence. But here then is a law of inconceivable magnitude and power, existent in nature, which governs matter, and which cannot be determined by matter, whence its origin? Since it requires the very genius of earthly intelligence to determine and demonstrate this law it must be evident that an intelligence, infinitely superior to any earthly intelligence, must have established the law in the universe. We deem it therefore a just conclusion, since a law of supernatural magnitude does exist in nature, which in itself gives evidence of supernatural intelligence, and which can only be demonstrated and understood by the more enlightened of earthly intelligences, it follows, that there must necessarily exist a heavenly intelligence possessing both volition and omnipotence. The laws of nature and their originator are both alike unseen. Is it rational to accept the former and deny the latter? "Here is a book which I really admire," says one. "From its perusal my mind has been greatly benefited. But it has no author.. The demonstrations of science given in it are most lucid, and it really contains unmistakable evidences of astute wisdom. How it came here I know not, but I cannot and will not believe it has an author." We would brand this as the very effervescence of folly. But what are all the books of earth compared or rather contrasted with the vast book of Nature! They are only as infinitesimal motes occupying a portion of nature's page so small that the finite eye could not perceive them from a common centre any more than it could behold inhabitants upon the most distant star. Then who will tell me that this vast book of nature, with all its magnificent and multitudinous displays of heavenly wisdom, has no author? Reason must needs be sadly debased when it would even intimate such a belief. Belief did we say? It is rather a denial of everything which we call real. Alas, after all, how little we know. As another has tersely written:

"Although with great daring man strives · to penetrate into the girdle of mystery which meets us at every point, it may be said that baffled and disappointed he only discerns more plainly his own ignorance. In every branch of science the wisest philosophers confess that they have attained but to the very infancy of knowledge, that with all their earnest researches they are, as Newton, but children gathering shells on the shore, with the profound and illimitable sea undiscovered by their side. One would think this humbling fact would lead men to acknowledge the supremacy of God, but alas, too often they seem only to be hardening their hearts and becoming less able to respect and love the great Creator, by whose will and power all consist."

3. *Intelligence must have a source.* Man possesses intelligence and volition in certain degrees. As a mortal creature he has a material brain. Intelligence acts within this brain and thoughts flow as a result. But when he dies, as the Psalmist says, "in that very day his thoughts perish." But intelligence as the great molder of the hu-

man mind continues its noble work; i. e., in a general, not in an individual sense. Whence this intelligence? Is its source of earth, or of heaven? Age after age mortals have sailed out upon the sea of universal knowledge, but no one has yet discovered *Satisfying Point.*

> Be satisfied, not in this state shall we,
> Where little more than echo fills the soul;
> As wistfully we gaze o'er boundless sea,
> We long to reach the satisfying goal.

Just here is where the Bible steps in with becoming grace and tells poor hungering, thirsting, fainting, despairing mortals to look upward. But in times of peril or distress of affliction or death man intuitively looks heavenward.

4. Intelligence dwells within material beings, and as a power it acts upon matter, but it does not necessarily form a constituent of matter. As the law of gravitation is to the matter upon which it acts, so is intelligence to the matter upon which it exerts an influence. Both are controlling forces in the economy of nature. As "the mind is the standard of the man," so we deem intelligence the grand standard of the universe. Hence Solomon enjoins: " Get wisdom, and with all thy getting, get understanding."

Science tells us of various kinds of attraction which exert their respective influences upon matter. Newton's law is thus expressed: "Any two bodies exert upon each other a mutual attraction, which varies directly as the product of their masses, and inversely as the square of their dis-

tance apart." If their masses be equal, their action or velocity or power will be equal. If one be
infinitely great in comparison to the other, its action or motion will be infinitely small in comparison to that of the other; and the more nearly
they approach each other the more rapid their
motion becomes. (*Peck's Nat. Phil.*) According
to cohesive attraction particles of the same matter unite and are held together. Capillary attraction is the force by which fluids rise above their
level in confined situations. The lightning in
one thunder cloud is attracted by the lightning
of another, although considerable space may in-
tervene. And thus we find that in nature, like
matter, like fluids, like gases, like creatures, like
beings, like affections, and like minds have an affinity for each other. And in this same manner,
get past it who will, intelligence is attracted heavenward. A cohesive attraction, we might say,
draws the mind upward; and as if by the law of
capillary attraction, intelligence, in this confined
mortal situation, rises above its level, and catch-
ing, as it were, the flame of heavenly intelligence,
enlightens the world. Inherently we are taught
that heaven is the grand source of all intelligence.
By looking upward we find a mutual attraction—
unseen but not unfelt. The law of gravitation is
not seen, yet the motions of natural bodies bear
witness to its truth. In like manner this heavenly attraction is not seen only in the motions of
the Christian world. Where is the mortal who
at some period or other of his life has not felt the

power of this attraction of heaven? And through this affinity, called in the Bible, " communion of the Holy Ghost," we are taught there is a God who is infinitely greater than the intelligences of earth. By applying Newton's law, only in a spiritual sense, we argue: Since God, as he is manifested in nature, is infinite in wisdom and omnipotent; and since according as revealed to us by the affinity of intelligence He is high over all, which manifestations are in harmony with both science and reason; it therefore follows, that man is infinitely ignorant and impotent in comparison, all of which accords with the scriptures: " There is one God and Father of all, who is above all, and through all;" and " one day is with the Lord as a thousand years," and *vice versa.* Again, thus "saith the Lord. For as the heavens are higher than the earth, so are my ways higher than your ways, and my thoughts than your thoughts." Through this affinity, intelligence also feels and acknowledges its dependence on this higher power, which it calls God. As the sun attracts the earth and keeps it in its orbit, so God attracts his children and keeps them in the path of righteousness. Christ acknowledged this in the words, " No man can come to me, except the Father who hath sent me draw him." (John vi. 44.)

5. When man is in distress or danger, or in the toils of death he involuntarily calls to heaven for mercy or for help. The vilest sinners look upward then; and in such extremities even infidels have been known to cry for mercy, and for

an extended lease of life that they might undo the evil done in their lives.

The dissatisfied soul looks upward, and hope is begotten within, that points forward through time to an eternal shore. This heavenly affinity tells of a sun-bright land—a sweet home—beyond the tossing billows of life's dark sea, where companionships shall be eternal, for death shall be no more. The Psalmist exclaimed, while anticipating this glad time, "I shall be satisfied, when I awake, with thy (God's) likeness." And the poet sweetly expresses it:

"Thither my weak and weary feet are tending;
Saviour and Lord, with thy frail child abide;
Guide me towards home, where, all my wanderings ended,
I then shall see Thee and 'be satisfied!'"

6. Volition and intelligence in man is evidently the stamp of a divine creation. From previous demonstrations, we deem this deduction allowable and just. Man depends on a higher power than matter—a power which permeates material beings, and which pervades and controls the universe. As Didon truly says:

"What, indeed, remains to man when he is limited to matter, and what is he worth when he no longer believes himself the son of God? He turns to animalism. And then you see him absorbed in the endeavor to bring himself to the level of the mammalia of which he is the companion, and among whom he seeks for ancestors."—*Science Without God, p. 17.*

When volition and intelligence act in unison within a being, progression is the certain result.

By adding continuous application, the being is ever ascending to a higher plane. This evidently proves volition and intelligence to be of heavenly origin. And since intelligent beings cannot in the present mortal state scale "perfection's sacred height," it is most reasonable to hope for a higher state of being in the great hereafter. Men do not spend their labors wittingly in vain. A company spend tens of thousands of dollars in sinking a mine. Just when they have all their machinery set up, when the vein has been reached, and when ample remuneration for toil and means expended lies before them, the head of the company steps up and gives orders to cave in the mine, and destroy the machinery. "What folly, what madness," you exclaim. And it would be nothing less. But let us apply the figure to that wondrous mine of wealth, viz: the intelligent mind. Just as it is attaining to working condition, when the machinery (the brain)is set to scan the heavens and the earth, when the giddy heights of knowledge and of wisdom are being scaled, the messenger of death comes along and caves it in. Shall that mine of wealth be lost—forever lost? No. The treasure is reserved in heaven, only to be restored again when Christ shall come and raise the slumberers from the tomb. To suppose even for a moment that all the labor of intelligence will be lost, insinuates against the Author of all good—heaven's wondrous Artisan.

7. Infidelity says: "Let science advance." Christianity gives the wheels of science a hun-

dred revolutions for infidelity's one. But if beyond this life there is no hope, tell me where is the benefit to be derived? Improve talents, cultivate the mental capacities, tire out the body, weary the brain, spend every energy, climb hills of fame; and worry and fret, and sigh and grieve, meet reverses of fortune, or pile up wealth, and beautify homes, train up children, educate the young, etc., all to end in *Death!* This would indeed fill up the picture of life as given in the words of Shakespeare:

> "Life's but a walking shadow,
> A poor player
> That struts and frets his hour upon the stage,
> And then is heard no more."

Even the very cemeteries, following in this dismal line, would have a dreariness unknown to Christian regions of the dead. No inscriptions of hope are seen; only one inscription of gloom, and that answers for all—"*Farewell, my friends, farewell forever!*"

8. Mathematical science considers magnitude and the proportions of magnitude. The learned Dr. Chalmers once acknowledged that in the ignorance and pride of his early ministry he had forgotten two magnitudes. "I thought not," said he, "of the littleness of time; I recklessly thought not of the greatness of eternity." How true! But let us closely examine these two magnitudes, for we claim that human beings have to do with both of them.

(a.) *The brevity of time.*

(b.) *The illimitableness of eternity.*

It will be perceived that the latter is infinitely the greater of the two. The longest limit of a human life is but an invisible mote on the vast belt called eternity. Go visit each sun and moon and star in the wide universe, and spend a million years on each; go around them all again; yea, visit each a million times, and go over the ground again, and undiminished, *eternity* still rolls on, and on, and ever on. Infidelity deals only with the former—the brevity of time. This mere speck of time it spends in crying out against that which it does not understand. For the Bible is a problem that contains certain data which when wrought out proves its authenticity. Like any other book of science it has its peculiar rules. One rule applies to both science and the Bible, viz: To study simple elements first, and when these are mastered, proceed with the more difficult portions. But is it wise to spend a brief lifetime vainly endeavoring to stem salvation's tide? Viewing it even from the bridge of doubt, would it not be wise to err on the safe side, and make at least some preparation for the great unseen? The Bible demonstrates the greatest of all magnitudes which relate to man, viz: *eternal life.*

Christianity takes in all of these: 1. The brevity of time. 2. The illimitableness of eternity. 3. The great problem of eternal life for man. It must be acknowledged to consider these in all their bearings is wise. And view it as you will, Christians have the best of it. For what are all the magnitudes of science to us if the great problem of future life remains unsolved?

9. According to the laws of nature, retarding or opposing forces exist. Such are also necessary. The motions of the planets are governed by the law of gravitation. Without the opposing or retarding force of gravitation where would this our planet flee? Infinite space alone could answer where. The lightning's vivid gleam and the thunder's crashing peal terrifies ofttimes the weak hearted or timid amongst mankind. But this is one of nature's best purifiers. When the thunder storm is over we breathe a purer air. What wise man therefore would curse the lightnings?

In the spiritual world retarding forces are also necessary. Hence infidelity we deem is a necessary evil. The electric flash of Ingeroll's eyes may gleam, and the thunders of his voice may peal forth amid the crowds of earthly intelligences that gather around him; but truth will only come out of the conflict the more refined and beautiful. The spiritual atmosphere will be clarified, and Christians will ultimately breathe a sweeter, a purer, and a freer air. But alas for infidelity!—like the lightnings it sinks into mother earth and is seen no more. After all, this is only according to its own creed.

10. When atheism shuts out God, Nature is denied as well; and reason and perception are trampled under foot. For God is made manifest through his works. Perception beholds Him in

the grand economy of Nature. And reason perceives the hand of intelligence and wisdom behind Nature's vast curtains and marvelous designs.

The God of infidelity is cruel. He attempts the destruction of the beauteous day-star of hope, which has cheered millions of our fellow-beings in their pilgrimage through the lone night of weeping and sorrow. And instead of replacing it with a brighter star, which would be nothing more than we might expect from a god, he only leaves the blackness of darkness behind. But he also despises the finer feelings of humanity. He scoffs at a tender mother as she teaches her child to pray to "Our Father who art in heaven." And he discards the sweetest light that ever shone on earth—the gospel of salvation. When the dark shadows of death fall upon our homes, the words of a Voltaire, a Paine, or an Ingersoll are but a miserable solace. We are aware that extravagant things are committed in the name of religion, as well as among other classes. But we give the following item of news from the Boston *Globe*, as it breathes the dire hope of atheism. We will only give a couple of extracts from the article; and for the sake of existing friends we will suppress the names:

"An atheist, who lived near Wilkesbarre, Penn., committed suicide recently. He placed a revolver in his mouth and fired three shots. The first tore away his lip, the second came out of his forehead above the eye, and the third went through the head, coming out directly on the top, and scattering his brains on the floor."

And in a letter he left for a friend, he says:

"I die in my atheistical faith as fearlessly as the heathen dieth in his faith of his existence. I believe not in conscious existence, nor in sensitiveness after death. It is the end, the final end of man, as well as the common animals. Ye will judge this, and blame it; nevertheless it is truthful. I considered and concluded that to commit suicide would be the best thing that I could possibly do."

Now, if the creed of atheism be correct, that man will have nothing to answer for. But why is it, we inquire, that intelligence shudderingly revolts against such deeds as this? What sane mind would exclaim: "It is well." If there be no God, if there be no hereafter, then it is well thus to end a miserable existence. Man does not hesitate to put an end to the existence of an animal agonizing under some incurable malady, and he deems the act humane. And again I ask, why does intelligence declaim against such a deed and stamp it as a diabolical act? Because a still, small voice within, which tells us of a God and a hereafter, whispers it is wrong. Here Christianity and intelligence agree. And common law maintains the right, and brands such acts as grossly reprehensible. The analogies of Nature condemn it. We do not see a planet suddenly leave its orbit and cast itself upon the sun. Were such to happen, then science would exclaim that Nature's law had been broken. As it is in Nature, so is it with man as a constituent of Nature.

"There's a divinity that shapes our ends,
Rough hew them how we will."

But when man deviates from the path of life, as ordained of God, and ends his existence, he cannot be considered sane. And he will certainly be held responsible for his acts before a future bar of judgment.

11. Nature's laws cannot be violated with impunity. Science sustains us here. With this all must agree. But what does this lead to? When man commits an act like the one we have cited, he is beyond retributive justice for the present. There are thousands of cases daily where the laws of Nature have been violated, and that with impunity so far as their having retributive justice meted out to them here. And where does this lead? There is but one inevitable conclusion, viz: The law of compensation being granted, a day of judgment in the future is demanded. This is what the Bible teaches, and intelligence is compelled to coincide therewith, as it is both reasonable and right.

12. No book has been so maltreated as the Bible. Yet it has triumphed in every conflict, and to-day it stands before the world as the Book of all books. In sunshine or in storm, in peace or in war, in the dark ages of the past or in the blaze of enlightenment that has burst upon the world during the present century, in health or in affliction, in prosperity or in adversity, in joy or in sorrow, in the quiet reposes of faith or in the fierce conflicts with error, in restful hope

or in trials and temptations, in life or in the lone valley of death, the Bible has proved itself the one only reliable book. It offers refuge from the storms and tempests of a world deluged in sin and wickedness. It offers pardon to those whose sins oppress them. It is filled with cheering and precious promises, which bear us onward and upward. Its light dispels the darkness of superstition and of infidelity, for as the earth would be dark without the sun, so would the great family of mankind be dark indeed without a God. Its precepts are excellent and form the basis of all common law. It gives peace to the perplexed, and yields comfort to the mourner, such as cannot elsewhere be found. It gives joy to the disconsolate, and offers support to the weak. It is a stay for the tempest-tost. It protects, and is as a shadow from the heat of life's continuous conflict with error. It is as a voice to still the winds and waves of opposition that beat against our bark. As an anchor of the soul it chains us to the unseen shore. As the breath of heaven it sheds upon our hearts the holy love of God. It is as a balm for every wound, and a help in every time of trouble. It reproves the erring, rebukes evil, warns the wicked, and sanctifies the faithful. It lifts man upward, and points him to God as "Our Father in the heavens." It leads to Christ as to an elder brother. It tells where floweth a river whose streams make glad the city of God. It speaks of a better land where Christ shall rule in righteousness, and where saints immortalized shall dwell together in endless felicity. A blessed heritage indeed! As to its work it aids the poor, clothes the naked, blesses our homes, helps to rule our households, and governs our lives. It ministers to the afflicted and the distressed. It bursts the bands of sin. It liberates the captives. In fine, it mingles with everything good, and true, and noble, and virtuous, and holy and right.

> "My Book! my Book! my grand old Book!
>   Heaven speed thee on thy way!
> From pole to pole, as ages roll,
>   The harbinger of day:
> Till Christ, the Light, shall banish night
>   From this terrestrial ball,
> And earth shall see her jubilee,
>   And God be all in all!"

13. Objections raised against the Bible should be carefully and thoughtfully weighed.

Joshua's inspiration is disputed on the ground that he commanded the sun and moon to stand still. Had he said, earth cease revolving, it would have been in harmony with science. Professor Garrison, in a lecture recently delivered in Chicago, expressed himself on this subject, as follows:

"Solomon said: 'The sun ariseth and setteth and hasteneth back to the place where he arose.' Now I submit that no formula of words could have been employed so as to more positively establish the ignorance of Solomon. We say the sun rises and sets, yet we all know the sun moves not. We are told that Joshua commanded the sun to stand still; but since that is proven false we are told that it was the earth that stood still. Now, we know that is utterly impossible, for, at the rapid rate the earth moves, to stop suddenly would hurl every movable object on its surface to eternal space."—*Inter-Ocean.*

This is the common breath of infidelity. It is one of the strings of the infidel's harp that has been stretched a good many times in the endeavor to add a few fresh notes, at least, to an old worn out tune. This time Solomon is brought in.

Where is the Queen of Sheba, that she may be convinced of her mistake? Must the proverbs be cast to the winds, for by a single unscientific utterance the wisdom of Solomon is demolished, and his ignorance established, yea " positively established." Thus saith the wisdom of the nineteenth century A. D. In every contention of truth let us be honest, let us be just: certain idioms of speech have been allowable in all ages. It must also be acknowledged that in those days of old they had not the educational facilities of our day. To condemn the ancients, therefore for doing what we still do with all our superior advantages would evidently be unjust. People should speak according to their knowledge. Professor Garrison condemns Solomon for using an idiom of speech which has been common in all ages, as he himself admits in the words, " We say the sun rises and sets, yet we all know the sun moves not." Shall we therefore conclude that the ignorance of all is established because this idiomatic phrase is generally used? Certainly

if we condemn Solomon's knowledge for using it
the same judgment falls back upon the boasted
intelligence of to-day. That the phrase is idiomatic cannot be gainsaid. Let us quote from a
few authors:

"The setting sun."—*Rogers.*

"Tis morning; and th' sun with ruddy orb ascending, fires
the horizon."—*Cowper.*

"As the gates I entered with sunrise."—*Milton.*

"When the sun rose on Anglo Saxon England."—*Collier.*

"A stream of sunset fell through the stained window."—
Hemans.

"But soon the sun with milder rays descends to the cool
ocean, where his journey ends."—*Pope.*

"When the broad sun sinks down on Ettrick's western
fell."—*Scott.*

"Beside that milestone where the level sun, nigh unto setting, shed his last low rays."—*Whittier.*

"The sun was just rising as we crossed the Guadalquiver
and drew near the city. . . . The dew still glistened on
every leaf and spray; for the burning sun had not yet climbed
the tall hedge-row of wild figs and aloes which skirts the
roadside."—*Longfellow.*

Now according to Mr. G's mode of reasoning
the ignorance of all these authors is established.
Solomon's statement will compare with any of
them. If the extravagant use of this idiom be al-
lotted to any we should deem Longfellow the
rightful winner, for he tells us, "The burning sun
had not yet climbed the tall hedge-row of wild
figs and aloes." And we must have a new set of
almanac compilers who will not make such a display of ignorance as to place at the top of every

monthly column "sun rises" and "sun sets.'
Granted that this is a sanctioned idiom; then the
phrase "sun stand still" must also be accepted;
for the same principle of language is implied in both
phrases. As the sun is said to rise (apparently)
so if its apparent motion were to cease it might
be said to stand still. What is this but a strife
of words when done? Let us examine Mr. G's
next assertion. He says: "Now we *know* that
(the earth ceasing to revolve) is utterly impossible, for, at the rapid rate the earth moves, to
stop suddenly would hurl every movable object
on its surface to eternal space." Most positive
assertion, indeed! Mr. G. evidently confounds
theory with fact. But theory should be well tested and proven to be demonstrable before positive
declarations or assertions are deduced therefrom.
The motions of the earth are certainly wonderful—about 19 miles per second in its orbit, and on
its axis over 1,000 miles per hour. But how can
any one demonstrate that every object on the
earth's surface would be hurled to eternal space
providing its rotary motion were to cease? A rule
or theory must work two ways. Fact demonstrates to us, that the earth flees onward and also
rotates without a single apparent effect being produced upon any of the beings on its surface.
Even the atmosphere, rare though it be, passes
along unruffled. If the stopping of the earth
would be attended with such disastrous effects,
surely its rapid motion should be at least perceptible.

Man's power has already been shown to be infinitely small in comparison with God's. Yet man can drive a locomotive through the atmosphere at the rate of sixty miles per hour, and in a very brief space of time, by the use of steam brakes, and by reversing the machinery, he can be flying at the same rate in an opposite direction. I have perceived, while in my berth on board an ocean steamship, by the sound of the machinery alone, that the engine was stopped and then reversed, but I could not realize from perception that we were moving in an opposite direction to what we had been a few minutes previous. But the ship called the earth moves more silently through space than any ship of man's invention can move in water; and the retarding forces which the earth meets in her journey through space must be very slight indeed, else such a rare body as the atmosphere would most certainly be ruffled. Then, since the captain of an earthly ship can reverse the motion of his vessel without disastrous consequences, although the retarding forces are quite perceptible, think you it is impossible for the great, the mighty Controller of the universe simply to stop the rotary machinery, as it were, of the earth without reversing its motion at all, and that without even being perceived? We are told in the good old Book that the sun did stand still (i. e. apparently) so that the day was lengthened out, and we accept it as fact until science can propound a theory vastly superior to anything it has yet

given us proving to the contrary. As to the
mighty revolutions and wondrous motions of the
heavenly bodies, which are really inconceivable
to the finite mind, can science demonstrate what
is the silent power by which they are controlled?
No more than it can demonstrate what is the
principle called life. There is a limit beyond
which mortal cannot penetrate. It is, therefore,
vain for man to dictate to the Creator, for " None
can stay his hand, or say unto him, what doest
Thou." The words of Cowper come in here with
befitting grace:

> "Knowledge is proud that he has learned so much,
> Wisdom is humble that he knows no more."

As to the mistakes of Moses: If poor blind
infidelity could only get the beam out of its own
eye, it might then judge righteously concerning
the writings of the servant of the most high God.
Fact tells us that the law of Moses has influenced
the world, and that for its good, some 4,400 years.
When the great day of reckoning comes methinks
that will yield an eternal weight of interest to the
despised Moses. But in that great day undoubtedly Ingersoll's mistakes will be showed up to his
grief. Every man shall receive according as his
work shall be in that day. But I never had profound respect for a man who would flagrantly
tear up the sod and kick among the dust of the
silent and sacred dead. The motto of intelligence
is "Peace to their ashes." If we live up to all
the good of their lives, the apparent evil will be
obscured—lost in the tide of a holy love which

binds true humanity together. Ingersoll ends his lecture, "Mistakes of Moses," with the following words:

"I cannot better close this lecture than by quoting four lines from Robert Burns:

'To make a happy fireside clime
      To weans and wife—
That's the true pathos and sublime
      Of human life.'"

But why does he stop here? Since he quotes Burns, let us hear Burns further concerning his opinion as to what makes the fireside clime happy:

"The cheerful supper done, wi' serious face,
   They round the ingle (*fireside*) form a circle wide:
The sire turns o'er, with patriarchal grace,
   The big ha' Bible, ance his father's pride;
   His bonnet, reverently, is laid aside,
His lyart haffets (*gray cheeks*) wearing thin and bare;
   Those strains that once did sweet in Zion glide,
He wales (*selects*) a portion with judicious care;
And let us worship God, he says, with solemn air.

                    * *
                     *

Then kneeling down to HEAVEN'S ETERNAL KING,
   The saint, the father, and the husband prays:
Hope 'springs exulting on triumphant wing,'
   That thus they all shall meet in future days:
   There ever bask in uncreated rays,
No more to sigh or shed the bitter tear,
   Together hymning their Creator's praise,
In such society, yet still more dear;
While circling time moves round in an eternal sphere."

Compared with which, how drear the fireside of an infidel's home!

14. *The mistakes of infidelity.* The counsels
of the Bible, together with its precepts, are excellent. To cast such away is surely a gross mistake. To throw away the wheat with the chaff,
for traditions of men are not always in accord
with the Bible; to discountenance the mass of
good done by Christianity, and to set up instead
the cruelties and atrocious murders perpetrated
by the monsters of past ages, attributing the
same to the Bible; to deny the source from which
flows all good; to vituperate the words or actions
of the dead; to wound the tender emotions of fellow-beings by pouring invectives against that for
which they have a reverence; to speak satirically
of the God of our fathers; to laugh to scorn a
tender mother's prayers; to break the cup of consolation held in the hand of a bereaved companion; to make man believe there is no future hope
by casting the black mantle of atheism and doubt
over his eyes; these are but a few of the many
mistakes made by cold, bleak, barren, hopeless,
lifeless, comfortless and wretched infidelity. But
the greatest mistake of all is the despising of a
judgment to come. Behold that vast audience
applauding the oratorical displays and witticisms
of their champion leader of so-called liberty. Invective after invective are being poured out
against God and his word. When lo! a sound—
an awful sound—is heard. 'Tis the voice of the
archangel and the trump of doom. The scene is
changed. The handwriting of God is imprinted
on every conscience.

WEIGHED IN THE BALANCES AND FOUND WANTING!

The boasted triumph ends in gloom. Rocks, mountains, "fall on us, and hide us from the face of Him that sitteth on the throne, and from the wrath of the Lamb: For the great day of his wrath is come, and who shall be able to stand!" As a miserable wreck the ship of infidelity sinks upon the dark waters of perdition. The despairing shrieks of the doomed passengers and crew make one last long wail, and then sink to rise no more for ever! Infidelity, farewell!

15. The religion of Christ is nothing less than wisdom's purest essence. To depart from evil and do good is wise. To cast off pride and walk in the vale of humility; to love instead of hate our fellow beings; to aid instead of oppressing mankind; to shun iniquity and cultivate virtue is wise. To acknowledge the Creator is wise. If we appreciate the works of an author we will gladly acknowledge the author himself. Who does not look with pleasure and admiration upon the pages of Nature's vast book? Admiring the works, reflects glory upon the author. This leads to adoration of the great Original, which is certainly nothing less than wisdom aspiring heavenward. To advance every good work; to stretch forth our hand to fallen humanity; to help bear the heavy burdens of our fellow travelers in the journey of life, is both laudable and wise. To accept light in exchange for darkness, peace for trouble and sorrow, rest for anxious care, joy for mourning, and the garment of praise for the spirit

of heaviness, is both wise and satisfying. To receive faith in exchange for painful doubt, and a comforting hope for dark presentiments, is both wise and profitable; for such adds length and blessing to our days in the life that now is, and fits us for the life which is to come. But all these things are implied in the religion of Christ, and nothing less will meet its requirements. Therefore the religion of Christ is the very embodiment of wisdom. Happy is the man that findeth this wisdom.

Finally, no book but the Bible has the power to lift fallen mortals. Its work proves it to be inspired. It invites the weary and heavy laden to come, nor does it fail to give them the promised rest. It points the sinner to the Lamb of God for expiation, and he receives the evidence of its preciousness, the evidence of his pardon, when the peace that passeth knowledge flows into his soul. It is beyond the power of infidelity to supplant such words as these: "Peace I leave with you, my peace I give unto you; not as the world giveth, give I unto you. Let not your heart be troubled, neither let it be afraid." There is a power in the words. They go to the heart. They are the words of God as spoken through his Son. There is a heavenly pathos in the passage which flows in gentle sweetness into our souls. Bring all the bright sayings of infidel heroes and pile them in a heap before me. I will place this one passage before them, and its excellence, its glory will outshine them all: "And I heard a

great voice out of heaven saying, Behold, the
tabernacle of God is with men, and He will dwell
with them, and they shall be his people, and God
himself shall be with them, and be their God.
And God shall wipe away all tears from their eyes;
and there shall be no more death, neither sorrow
nor crying, neither shall there be any more pain:
for the former things are passed away." Blessed
Bible! precious treasure! my guide, my staff, my
changeless friend, my lamp to cheer earth's
gloomy night, and tell me of a morn of joy, I shall
defend thee still.

"My sword! my sword! my two-edged sword! by thy uner-
    ring might,
I deal my foe the deadly blow in faith's unequal fight;
Thy tempered blade, that lent me aid in every conflict past,
Shall make me more than conqueror, through Him who loved,
    at last."

CHAPTER XX.

.

THE COMING OF THE MESSIAH—HIS RIGHTFUL THRONE.

"I will come again, and receive you unto myself; that where I am, there ye may be also."—John xiv. **3.**

"And the Lord God shall give unto Him the throne of his father David; and he shall reign over the house of Jacob forever; and of his kingdom there shall be no end."—Luke i. **32, 33.**

There are those who endeavor to explain away, or at least to mystify, those portions of scripture referring to the second coming of the Messiah. The day of "gloominess"—the great "time of trouble"—the "signs in heaven," etc., are all declared to be in the past. These, it is claimed, were fulfilled at the destruction of Jerusalem. Others there are who declare that all scripture relative to the second coming can only be understood in a spiritual sense; and they vainly endeavor to show that Christ has already come the second time. But a true knowledge of the word of God dissipates all such theories. If the scriptures in one instance will admit of plain, repeated and forcible statements being spiritualized, so that they are made to represent the very opposite of what they clearly teach, how shall we ever arrive at a knowledge of the truth? For, applying the same rule to all points of doctrine, there can be no certain knowledge as to what is true, or what is false; and even the knowledge we glean of God himself would be uncertain and unsatisfying. But thanks be to God, it is our privilege to know Him in whom we have believed, and also to understand his word. If we walk out upon God's highway of truth, we will find it indeed a pathway of light which "shineth more and more unto the perfect day."

But the coming of the Lord is so intimately connected with the day of judgment, the day of wrath, and the time of trouble, when all the inhabitants of the earth shall mourn, that undoubtedly there are many who would prefer a belief which attempts to obliterate the dark side of the picture, and tries to make believe that the doctrine of the resurrection—the foundation of true hope—is done away by the transmigration of the soul at death. It is blessed to know that a thousand such theories cannot destroy a single iota of that word which can never fail. Neither one jot nor tittle of God's word shall pass away unfulfilled. But why should any object to the dark side of the picture? "The morning cometh, and also the night." Were it not for darkness light

20

would be undervalued. The clouds once broken
only tend to intensify the brilliancy of the sunshine. Only for affliction and death we would not
sufficiently appreciate health and life. Without
contrast no picture is true to Nature, and Nature's pictures are but typical of the end of all
things natural. Therefore, Nature's night of
gloom surely cometh, but just as certainly cometh the rising of the eternal sun which shall usher
in the day of glory. According to the scriptures
there is a storm coming—a fearful storm for those
out of Christ. "For the stars of heaven and the
constellations thereof shall not give their light:
the sun shall be darkened in his going forth, and
the moon shall not cause her light to shine. And
I will punish the world for their evil; and the
wicked for their iniquity; and I will cause the
arrogancy of the proud to cease, and will lay low
the haughtiness of the terrible." (Is. xiii. 10, 11.)
"In that day a man shall cast his idols of silver,
and his idols of gold, which they made each
one for himself to worship, to the moles and to
the bats; to go into the clefts of the rocks . .
for fear of the LORD, and for the glory of his majesty, when He ariseth to shake terribly the
earth." (ii. 20, 21.) "Alas for the day! for the
day of the Lord is at hand, and as a destruction
from the Almighty shall it come." (Joel i. 15.)
"For the day of the Lord is great, and very terrible, and who can abide it?" (ii. 11.) "And
the heavens departed as a scroll when it is rolled
together. . . . And the kings of the earth,

and the great men, and the rich men, and the chief captains, and the mighty men, and every bondman, and every free man, hid themselves in the dens and in the rocks of the mountains; and said to the mountains and rocks, Fall on us, and hide us from the face of Him that sitteth on the throne, and from the wrath of the Lamb; for the great day of his wrath is come; and who shall be able to stand?" (Rev. vi. 14-17.)

"And then shall appear the sign of the Son of man in heaven: and then shall all the tribes of the earth mourn, and they shall see the Son of man coming in the clouds of heaven with power and great glory." (Matt. xxiv. 30.) "For the Lord himself shall descend from heaven with a shout, with the voice of the archangel, and with the trump of God." These are but a few of the storm-signals which God has hung out upon the farthermost shore of the sea of Time.

But there is a silver lining to those clouds of the day of wrath. Faith beholds in the sweet promises of God, a bright glory beyond.

1. *He will come again.* "Thine eyes shall see the King in his beauty," said the prophet Isaiah. Daniel saw "one like the Son of man *who* came with the clouds of heaven," "and there was given Him dominion, and glory, and a kingdom." We have already quoted some of Christ's own words concerning his coming. At his ascension while his disciples stood gazing heavenward, "behold, two men stood by them in white apparel; who also said, Ye men of Galilee why stand ye

gazing up into heaven? this same Jesus, who is taken up from you into heaven, shall so come in like manner as ye have seen Him go into heaven." (Acts i. 10, 11.)   Paul says, "unto them that look for Him shall He appear the second time without sin unto salvation."   "For yet a little while, and He that shall come will come, and will not tarry."   And the clear note of Revelation is, "Behold I come quickly."   This promise is the bright and morning star of redemption.   Were it removed from the spiritual heavens the night would be indeed dismal and lone.   It shines however all through the sacred pages.   The promise is sure.   "He that shall come, will come."   The last note of prophesy in the word of God gives forth no uncertain sound, "Surely I come quickly."

2.   *But why should He return?*   Because this earth is his rightful dominion, as we have shown in previous chapters.   To Abraham and his SEED were his promises made.   Christ is that seed. "And the Lord shall be king over all the earth: in that day shall there be one Lord, and his name one."

3.   *He shall sit on David's throne.*   God promised it to David.   "And when the days be fulfilled and thou shalt sleep with thy fathers, I will set up thy seed after thee. . . .   He shall build an house for my name, and I will stablish the throne of his kingdom forever." (II. Sam. vii. 12, 13.)   "The Lord hath sworn in truth unto David; He will not turn from it; Of the fruit of thy body will I set upon thy throne." (Ps. cxxxii. 11.)   This

was confirmed by the prophets. " The word of the Lord came to Jeremiah, saying, Thus saith the Lord; If ye can break my covenant of the day, and of the night, and that there should not be day and night in their season; then may also my covenant be broken with David my servant, that he should not have a son to reign upon his throne." (xxxiii. 19-21.) The words of Ezekiel to Zedekiah imply the same thing: " And thou profane wicked prince of Israel, whose day is come, when iniquity shall have an end. Thus saith the Lord God: Remove the diadem, and take off the crown; this shall not be the same: exalt him that is low, and abase him that is high. I will overturn, overturn, overturn it: and it shall be no more until he come whose right it is; and I will give it him." (xxi. 25-27.) And David's throne has been " overturned" ever since and shall not be restored until He come whose right it is. To these testimonies we add the plain and positive words of Gabriel. When speaking of Jesus to Mary he said: " He shall be great, and shall be called the Son of the Highest; and the Lord God shall give unto Him the throne of his father David: And he shall reign over the house of Jacob forever; and of his kingdom there shall be no end." Now this messenger informs us that he is Gabriel that stands in the presence of God. (Luke i. 19.) His authority therefore being established, his words must be duly weighed. This truth is still further demonstrated in that Christ rose from the dead. (Acts. ii. 29-35.) The truth there-

fore is established beyond controversy by the
word of God that Christ shall eternally reign on
David's throne. But modern perversions of the
scripture endeavor to spiritualize these plain statements so as to carry David's throne up to a kingdom somewhere in the skies. Allow me here to
define modern spiritualizing as the art of explain-
ing away truth. David's throne was on the holy
hill of Zion. (Ps. ii. 6.) "For the Lord hath
chosen Zion; he hath desired it for his habitation. (cxxxii. 13.) He calls it "the mountain of
his holiness. Beautiful for situation, the joy of
the whole earth, is Mount Zion, on the sides of
the north, the city of the great King." (xlviii.
1, 2.) David never had a throne in the heavens,
"For David is not ascended into the heavens."
(Acts. ii. 34.) Christ has ascended into the heavens, but not to sit upon his own throne. He is
set with the Father in his throne. As David himself says, " The Lord said unto my Lord, Sit thou
on my right hand, until I make thy foes thy footstool." But when the seventh angel sounds the
kingdoms of this world become the kingdoms of
our Lord and of his Christ. "And the Lord shall
be king over all the earth." " And we shall reign
on the earth." "For if ye be Christ's, then are ye
Abraham's seed, and heirs according to the promise." "Joint heirs with Christ," who has said,
" To him that overcometh will I grant to sit with
me in my throne, even as I also overcame and
am set down with my Father in his throne."
There is no ambiguity in these scriptures. The

doctrine is plain. The truth is evident. Isaiah puts on, as it were, the finishing touch in the words, "Then the moon shall be confounded, and the sun ashamed, when the Lord of hosts shall reign in Mount Zion, and in Jerusalem, and before his ancients gloriously." (xxiv. 23.)

That Christ shall reign on David's veritable throne is established:

(*a.*) By God's oath and by the word of prophecy.

(*b.*) By Gabriel's announcement to the mother of Jesus.

(*c.*) By the resurrection of Christ from the dead, as given by the Holy Ghost through Peter.

(*d.*) By Christ's own words in the parable, "A certain nobleman went into a far country to receive for himself a kingdom, and to return."

God's oath cannot be broken. Gabriel was not sent from heaven to mislead the mother of Jesus, nor to tell her an untruth. Nor was Peter mistaken when he names the resurrection of Christ as the seal or surety from heaven that the promise to David was ratified in heaven. Therefore, we have good reason to hope for the fulfillment of the promise. And for this we have been taught by Christ himself to pray. This leads me to notice:

4. *A wonderful petition:* "Thy kingdom come, Thy will be done on earth as it is in heaven." (Matt. vi. 10.)

The doctrine upon which we have been writing is evidently implied in this petition. God's kingdom is holy, and its inhabitants are immortal and incorrupt. The curse still rests upon the earth, and its inhabitants are mortal and corrupt. But we are taught to look for a new earth, (i. e. renewed) wherein dwelleth righteousness. A new earth does not imply another earth any more than a new creature implies a different being. When the earth is renewed there shall be no more curse. The whole earth shall then be filled with the glory of the Lord, (see Is. vi. 3) and the saints shall possess the kingdom. "Neither can they die any more: for they are equal unto the angels." (Luke xx. 36.) This wonderful petition shall then have been answered, and the will of God shall at that time be done on the earth as it is in heaven. "The earth is the Lord's, and the fulness thereof." It is now isolated, but when Christ comes it shall be attached to the great universal kingdom of Jehovah. Christ shall take possession of his rightful throne, and shall rule the earth in righteousness. As an isolated province, we desire annexation to the great and holy kingdom of God, hence we pray: "Thy kingdom come." It is a mistaken idea that we shall go to God's kingdom. The tabernacle of God is to be with men, (Rev. xxi. 3) and not *vice versa*.

Granted that the kingdom has now come, as many profess to believe, then the will of God must consequently now be performed on earth as it is in heaven. But this will not coincide with the present state or order of things, therefore the kingdom is yet to come. Christ reigns at God's right hand "Till he hath put all enemies under his feet. The last enemy that shall be destroyed is death." Hence He cannot receive his own kingdom until death is destroyed. "Thy kingdom come," we have said, is a wonderful petition. Why? Because it implies wonderful changes and events, viz: the renewing of the earth—the coming of the Messiah—the resurrection of the dead—the eternal judgment—the immortality of the saints—the destruction of the wicked—the establishing of Christ on the throne of his father David, where he shall reign as our Immanuel—the earth becoming a tributary province of the universal kingdom of God—the opening of the heavens—in brief, all things created or made new—Paradise restored.

5. *Why should we offer this petition?* Because: As disciples, we long to see our Redeemer, and his response is, "Surely I come quickly." We are tired of the unrighteous rule of nations. We desire to see sin removed, and death vanquished. As weary pilgrims, we sigh for the rest that remaineth for the people of God. We have jewels laid away in the silent grave, and we long to clasp them again to our bosom. This is the night of weeping, we desire the bright morning, where joy shall be unmingled with sorrow. Where

> "Everlasting spring abides,
> And never fading flowers."

We long to reach our abiding place—our sweet Edenic home. We desire to see that glorious being whom we now address as "Our Father who art in heaven," that we may, with the voice im-

mortal, say "Hallowed be Thy name." Because
of these, and many other equally bright reasons,
we pray, as Christ has enjoined, "Thy kingdom
come."

6. *The kingdom of heaven is at hand.* Eighteen centuries ago the apostle could exclaim:
"The night is far spent, the day is at hand." But
that same apostle also said: "Let no man deceive you by any means: for that day shall not
come, except there come a falling away first, and
that man of sin be revealed, the son of perdition."
(II. Thess. ii. 3.) Solemn truth! The falling
away has come, and the man of sin is ripening
for the great day of revelation, when the Lord
Jesus shall descend in flaming fire. "And then
shall that wicked be revealed." The day is near.
Faith is now almost lost in sight. A few reasons
we will here subjoin:

(*a.*) "There shall come in the last days scoffers,
walking after their own lusts, and saying: Where
is the promise of his coming? for since the fathers fell asleep, all things continue as they were
from the beginning of the creation." (II. Pet.
iii. 3, 4.) This has been repeatedly fulfilled in our
own ears. Therefore the "last days" must be
upon us.

(*b.*) "In the last days perilous times shall
come. For men shall be lovers of their own
selves, covetous, boasters, proud, blasphemers,
disobedient to parents, unthankful, unholy, without natural affection, truce breakers, false accus-
ers, incontinent, fierce, despisers of those that

are good, traitors, heady, high-minded," etc. (II. Tim. iii. 1-4.) That these characteristics most strikingly apply to this day and generation cannot be gainsaid. Again this proves that the last days are here.

(c.) "And there shall be signs in the sun, and in the moon, and in the stars; and upon the earth distress of nations, with perplexity; the sea and the waves roaring; men's hearts failing them for fear, and for looking after those things which are coming on the earth: for the powers of heaven shall be shaken." (Luke xxi. 25, 26.) Astronomers have been making dire predictions, and it cannot be disputed that upon the earth there is distress of nations with perplexity. Shipwrecks and storms at sea; tornadoes, cyclones, floods, fires, and calamities on land, are indeed filling the hearts of many with fear so that they are failing them. A New York paper recounts "The Disasters of a Month" in a two-column article. A Boston paper goes over the same ground under the heading, "The Terrible Year," and western papers follow in the same track, and use the ominous caption, "The Black Year." The second of these goes on to say:

"Was there ever such a year for strange, terrible, and grotesquely horrible accidents, casualties, and crime? It seems as if some malignant influence has been cast over the world. Nature seems to be unhinged, and the times out of joint."

What follows? Christ says: "And then shall they see the Son of man coming in a cloud with power and great glory." (27.) Even when these things begin to come to pass we are to lift up our heads, for our redemption draweth nigh.

(*d.*) When we view the parable of the Ten Virgins, and compare it with the movements of the Church during the last forty years, we can form but one conclusion, viz: that the virgins have gone forth to meet the Bridegroom, and that we are now in the tarrying time.

(*e.*) The most potent reason we can give that Christ's coming is at the very door, is the fact that the Spirit of God is abroad in the earth preparing a Bride for his reception. (Rev. xix. 7.) When John appeared as the voice of one crying in the wilderness, "Prepare ye the way of the Lord," it was not long till Christ made his appearance. Again, in these latter days the voice is heard crying, prepare for the coming of the Messiah. Nor will it be long until the glory bursts forth upon our wondering vision. "Behold I come as a thief. Blessed is he that watcheth and keepeth his garments." (Rev. xvi. 15.)

Do we love Christ? Then we will desire to see Him. This doctrine incites us to action. It also encourages us onward in the Christian race. O precious morn, all hail! And blessed Father yet we cry: "Thy kingdom come, Thy will be done on earth as it is in heaven." Then shall we see our precious Lord face to face. There we shall enter our hallowed home—the Paradise of God.

"Instead of the thorn shall come up the fir-tree, and instead of the brier shall come up the myrtle tree;" "and the desert shall rejoice and blossom

as the rose." And saints immortal shall behold
with unbeclouded vision "the glory of the Lord
and the excellency of our God;" "for they shall see
eye to eye when the Lord shall bring again Zion."
"And the ransomed of the Lord shall return,
and come to Zion with songs and everlasting joy
upon their heads: they shall obtain joy and gladness, and sorrow and sighing shall flee away."
All the ends of the earth shall see the salvation
of our God. Then shall the redeemed host strike
their golden harps and sing the song of Moses the
servant of God, and the song of the Lamb, saying, "Great and marvelous are thy works, Lord
God Almighty; just and true are thy ways thou
King of saints. Who shall not fear thee, O Lord,
and glorify thy name? for thou only art holy."
(Rev. xv. 3, 4.) Then also shall the seraphim cry
one to another, "Holy, holy, holy, is the Lord of
hosts: the whole earth is full of his glory." (Is.
vi. 3.) The earth restored to pristine bloom and
loveliness, and filled with the glory of the Lord—
how sweet to contemplate the scene! Those
Eden fields and groves clad with everlasting ver-
dure—those fruits so delicious, and flowers of
beauty rare—the vine-clad hills, and rills pellucid
—the lovely songsters that flit through the balmy
air from grove to grove, and send forth their innocent chant of praise to the all-glorious Creator—
how grand! Yet these are but faint anticipations
of what shall be in that sweet time of REGENERA-
TION, when the weary shall find that rest which
remains for the people of God—

"Their toils and trials o'er."

"And God shall wipe away all tears from their eyes." Sweet land of eternal sunshine, all hail! Precious Redeemer, welcome to thy throne!

Dear reader, prepare to meet thy God, for the kingdom of heaven is at hand. The midnight hour is near. Behold the Bridegroom cometh! "Even so, come, Lord Jesus." Amen.

> The clock of heaven strikes a certain sound!
> Say, fellow-traveler, whither art thou bound?
> If yet unsaved, O, to yon shelter flee.
> Hark! 'tis the Saviour calls, "Come unto me."
> O, make thy peace with God, while He is near,
> *Now* is God's time, *to-day*, if ye but hear.
> Once in the ark, time's tide may swiftly run,
> For then thy prayer shall be, "Thy Kingdom come."
> And welcome then we cry, the sun-bright shore,
> Where angels shall proclaim, "Time is no more:"
> Where saints shall dwell with Christ, forever blest,
> And weary pilgrims have unending rest.

The End

❊INDEX❊

www.ingramcontent.com/pod-product-compliance
Lightning Source LLC
Chambersburg PA
CBHW021219270326
41929CB00010B/1193